The
Covered Bridges
of
Ohio
An Atlas and History

by

Miriam Wood

Covered Bridges of Ohio
an Atlas and History

Copyright © 1993 by Miriam F. Wood

(A Chronological record of Historical events and other information on Ohio's wooden truss bridges.)
1. Wooden Truss Bridges found in Ohio - History.
2. Builders of Ohio's Wooden Truss Bridges - History.
3. Past and Present Preservation Efforts.
Selected Bibliography
Over 100 References
Includes Index; over 1200 entries

Library of Congress Catalog Card Number 93- 60766

Printed in the United States of America by The Old Trail Printing Company, Columbus, Ohio.

Dedicated to the hundreds of "Bridgers" of Ohio and elsewhere in America who not only enjoy the charm and elegance of historic bridges, but who also have taken an active part in the preservation of these wonderful bits of Americana of yesteryear

Acknowledgements

The author recognizes and expresses deep appreciation to the many people who have helped her with this research for over 30 years. A special recognition must go to John Diehl of Cincinnati, Chairman of the Ohio Covered Bridge Committee who has been my friend and mentor in the field of covered bridge technology for many years. Also deserving of special recognition are the many fellow bridge enthusiasts who have shared their research and pictures with me for a long, long time: Richard S Allen, Louis S "Stock" Bower, Henry Davidson, Bill Helsel, Jim Gnagy, Hallie Jones, Anita Knight, Mary Lane, Jean LaGue, Brian McKee, Terry Miller, Bob McManness, Eldon Neff, Myrtle Patterson, Charles Pratt, David Simmons and Rich Wade.

It is with special gratitude that I honor here the memory of the late Seth S Schlotterbeck and the late Raymond E Wilson, two gentlemen who were very knowledgeable about wooden truss technology and who were so generous in sharing that knowledge with me.

I am also indebted to Jim Hern for his great help and technical assistance in guiding this book from rough manuscript to camera-ready computer copy as well as for his assistance in the finishing stages of this project.

The greatest thanks of all must go to my husband, Richard A Wood, "Dick", for the superb artwork done for this book, his endless patience throughout this huge undertaking, and the many hours he spent editing the manuscript. I also acknowledge with gratitude the artwork done by my son, Howard P Wood, "Howie".

Research for this book was done using the resources of many libraries, museums and court houses and newspapers: the Archives/Library of the Ohio Historical Society; The State Library of Ohio; The Ohioana Library; the Ohio Historic Bridge Association; The Public Library of Columbus and Franklin County; Smith Library of Regional History (Oxford, Ohio); Ross County Historical Society/John Grabb; Garst Museum/Toni T Seiler (Darke County); Jackson County Commissioners; Athens County Recorders Office/ Helen Thompson; United States Military Academy Library/ Marie T Cappes, Librarian; Ohio Department of Transportation, Bureau of Bridges and Bureau of Environmental Services; Roscoe Village Foundation; Lancaster (Ohio) Eagle-Gazette; Germantown (Ohio) Press; and the National Archives, Suitland, Maryland.

Cover design by Jim Hern

Figure Credits

The author acknowledges with gratitude the following people who have given me permission to use the following pictures listed by figure number:

Carl T Akerman, 125.

Grace Allison, 194.

Tom Brown, 172.

Nancy Bucey, 282.

Verla B Clapp, 224.

Mr & Mrs Leon Darr, 179, 198b.

Henry Davidson, 51.

John A Diehl, 2, 71, 106, 123, 124, 146, 175, 186, 198a, 208, 219, 222, 238, 257, 258, 271, 293.

Preston Fettrow, Sr. 227.

Germantown Press, 74.

James Gnagy, 33.

William Helsel, 85, 163, 296.

James Henry, 120, 121.

James Hern, sketch 145.

Ron Hilbert, 279.

Hocking County Historical Society, 139.

Ethel Johnson, 170.

Hallie Jones, 12, 200.

Joanne J Kelly, 142.

Ruth Kennedy, 13, 283

Anita Knight, 148, 150, 154, 161, 233.

Jean LaGue, 135.

Brian McKee, 127, 188, 216b.

Robert McManness, 216a.

David Miars, 274.

Terry E Miller, 181, 182, 183.

Kathern Oberle, 5.

Ohio Historic Bridge Association, 7, 39, 45, 111, 119, 196, 197, 250, 272 (originals by the late C L Tenney), 96 (Coleman Collection), 107, 155, 218, 286 (from various donors).

Richard Palsgrove, 230

Ross Co.Historical Soc., 15, 17, 42, 43, 83, 115, 116, 134.

Steve Shonk, 278

David Simmons, 40, 252.

Smith Libr.of Regional Hist., 261 (original by Frank McCord).

Phil Stoodt, 104, 211, 212.

United States Military Academy Library, 23.

Polly D Waggle, 68.

Tom Walczak, 253.

Mr & Mrs Lester Wallis, 249.

Mrs Russel Williams, 285.

Howard P Wood, sketches 21, 164.

Miriam Wood Collection, 29, 59, 60, 62, 63, 86, 102, 174, 178, 201, 234, 235, 236, 276, 288, 294 (originals by Eldon Neff); 255, 267, 269, 289 (originals from George Gould); 88, 93, 130, 156, 159, 214, 256, 287 (originals from Ohio Department of Transportation); 8, 54, 58, 126, 242, 244, 246 (originals from late Seth S Schlotterbeck); 25, 40 (originals from late Charles Goslin); 143, (orignal from late Lora Ridenour); 27, (original from late Wm.Brandt Henry); 90 (original from late Wm.Green); 209 (original from late Gaylord Sprang); 113 (original from late L W Goodwin); all others from Wood Collection.

All other sketches and truss drawings by Richard A Wood.

Unnumbered pictures: Slate Mills Bridge from the Ross County Historical Society Pg. xiv ; Fobes Road Bridge from the OHBA Coleman Collection Pg 124; Spring Street Bridge from Grace Allison Pg 124; Broadway Bridge from the Darke County Historical Society, courtesy of Toni T Seiler Pg 148; Covington Bridge from R L Palsgrove Pg.148; Miriam Wood Collection, originally from ODOT: Sloane Bridge Pg 147, Ray Bridge Pg 176 and Harrisburg Bridge Pg 178. Doyle Road Bridge interior Pg 124, Hogan's Bridge Pg 179, Jaynes Bridge Pg 66, and Crownover Mill Bridge Pg 66, Miriam Wood collection.

All unnumbered illustrations carry the
number of the page where they are
mentioned in parenthesis ( ) on the
pages where they are shown.

Front Cover: John Bright #2 Bridge, Ohio University Campus, Lancaster

Back Cover: Bergstresser Bridge, Canal Winchester

Contents

The Covered Bridges of Ohio
An Atlas and History
by Miriam F. Wood

In the fall of the year 1809 on the deck of a boat headed downstream on the Ohio River, Zadok Cramer, skilled navigator on the Allegheny, Monongehela, and Ohio Rivers, stood watching for landmarks. As the boat passed the mouth of Little Beaver Creek on the Ohio-Pennsylvania border, Mr. Cramer trained his spyglass up the creek to the mills of his friend, John Bever. There he saw something he had not expected which he later described in his book, The Navigator, published in 1814.

> "At the upper grist mill near the mouth of the creek, is a handsome arched bridge, substantially made and well-covered-in, adding great facility to emigrants and travelers passing into the State of Ohio from this quarter."[1]

Thus is described what was probably the first covered bridge in Ohio. The bridge at John Bever's mill is also described by Fortescue Cumings in his Sketches of a Tour to the Western Country, published in 1810.[2]

The Old Slate Mills Bridge over the North Fork of Paint Creek
west of Chillicothe in Ross County

Chapter I
A Background - Ohio Covered Bridge Beginnings

The Ohio Country was part of the vast and unsettled Northwest territories of the new United States. It was Indian country and many tribes made their homes in this area. Among the better known tribes were the Shawnee, Miami, Delaware, and Wyandots. Numerous military expeditions in the 18th century waged war against the native Americans who fought back savagely and courageously to defend their homeland against the encroaching white man. It was a losing battle and Indian villages in the eastern, southern and central parts of the Ohio territory were gradually eliminated as white settlers moved in. The Greenville Treaty of 1795 limited Indian occupation of Ohio to the northwest and north central areas. By 1830, most of the Indians in the Ohio territory were on reservations and generally they were no longer a threat to Ohio's early settlers.

The first permanent settlement in Ohio was made at Fort Harmer at the mouth of the Muskingum River in 1788, seven years before the Greenville Treaty. This settlement became the City of Marietta, named for Queen Marie Antoinette of France, to honor the French for their aid to us during the Revolutionary War. From 1788 on, settlers poured into Ohio via the great Ohio River and up its major tributaries, the Muskingum, Hocking, Scioto and Miami Rivers. They also came into Ohio overland from Appalachian foothill trails and stream valleys. Some came into Ohio from Lake Erie and thence southward on the Cuyahoga, Grand and Sandusky Rivers. Ohio was a land rich in natural resources and beauty, a wilderness from which these pioneers could carve out homes, farms and businesses.

The settlement and economic development of the Buckeye State was hampered at first by a lack of good roads. The hardy pioneers had to utilize the waterways and Indian trails early on, but eventually, crude roads were hacked out of the wilderness. For example, Zane's Trace connected Wheeling, West Virginia (then Fort Henry) to Maysville (then Limestone)

Kentucky. McArthur's College-Township Road ran from Athens to Oxford; and Wayne's Road ran northward out of Cincinnati. Generally, these trails were established prior to 1800.

In 1796, Congress commissioned Colonel Ebenezer Zane to lay out a trace following old Indian trails from Fort Henry (Wheeling) to Limestone (Maysville). He was to establish ferries at three major river crossings: Muskingum, Hocking and Scioto Rivers. For this work, Zane received 640 acres at each crossing. The town of Zanesville, Ohio, site of one of Zane's crossings, was named for the Colonel. Zane finished his Trace in 1797. The new "road" was nothing more than a rough trail through the woods, but it was of the utmost importance to the early Ohio and Kentucky settlers. One early traveler described Zane's Trace as "rough fare".

Early Ohio historian Caleb Atwater declared that he would rather find his way through the forest with a compass than to travel our early roads. He also noted that in 1803 when Ohio was admitted to the Union there was not a bridge in the state.[3] The crude Indian trails that formed our first roads were in deplorable condition and the frequent rains and snows of this area only made matters worse. Travelers were mired axle-deep in mud during the wet season and lost in clouds of dust in the dry weather. There were often delays at major stream crossings even where ferries were in operation. Many frugal travelers preferred to take a chance on fording streams to avoid paying out such high ferry tolls as 7 cents per person or 60 cents for a loaded wagon. With the roadways in such terrible shape it is small wonder that travelers in early Ohio preferred to make their journeys by water if at all possible. The improvement of existing roads and establishment of new roads was an early concern of Ohio's counties and the early commissioners journals are full of petitions asking for roads and permanent bridges.

The College-Township Road, parts of which are today's US Route 50 across southern Ohio, was laid out in 1799 by Duncan McArthur, land speculator, soldier and later, governor of Ohio. The road was designed to connect two widely-separated townships of land which had been reserved by Congress in 1787 in support of higher education.[4] At the starting point of the road was a plot of land consisting of two townships within the Ohio Company Purchase. At the other end of the road the plot of land reserved for educational purposes lay just west of the Symmes Purchase. Thus, this road extended west from Athens in Athens County through the towns of McArthur, Chillicothe, Greenfield, and eventually on to Oxford in Butler County.

The first two land grant colleges in the nation were formed from these two land reserves: Ohio University at Athens in 1804 and Miami University at Oxford in 1809. Many covered bridges played their part in facilitating travel on this important road. Some were small bridges and little-known while others were large well-built structures, some of which survived into the 1930s. The largest of these bridges was the Kilgore Ford Bridge over the Scioto River just east of Chillicothe. Other notable covered bridges also served the College-Township Road over the Hocking River at Athens, and in Vinton County, where the road crossed Raccoon and Salt Creeks.

Figure 1 shows the location of some of Ohio's earliest roads from pre-1800 to 1820. The route

Figure 1. Ohio's Early Roads, pre-1800-1840

of the National Road through Ohio (1830s-1840s) also is shown by the dashed line.

The first National Congress to meet after the young nation achieved its independence was concerned amongst other things with the problems of transportation. They discussed ways of meeting the need for good roads. But it wasn't until the Jefferson Administration in 1806 that Congress passed the National Road Act providing for a national road to open east-west travel starting from Cumberland, Maryland. This Road has been known by various names: the Cumberland Pike or simply the Pike; the National Road; and US Route 40. The eastern section of this great Road opened for travel in 1818. It was constructed into Ohio in the 1820s and 1830s, essentially following Zane's Trace to Zanesville in Muskingum County and then westward over other primitive trails to Columbus and then west to Richmond, Indiana.

The National Road crossed the West Channel of the Ohio River from Wheeling Island into Ohio at Bridgeport on a two-lane covered bridge that was the only covered bridge ever to span any portion of this great waterway on Ohio's border, Figure 2. Construction of the Bridgeport Bridge began in 1836. But the contractor, William Lebarron, abandoned the work which was then taken over by the Zane Brothers and completed in 1838. The bridge later became the property of the Wheeling and Belmont Bridge Company. It served until 1903.

Those familiar with the Ohio River at Bridgeport will ask just how the East Channel of the Ohio River was crossed in the 1830s. The answer is that the river was forded from Wheeling to Wheeling Island until 1849 when the present metal suspension bridge was built. This bridge is still in daily use.

The Bridgeport Bridge was the only covered bridge on the National Road in Belmont County. However, Belmont County and its neighbors to the west, Guernsey and Muskingum Counties, all had fine stone bridges on the Old Pike. These were sturdy structures built of sandstone by the early contractors. Some of these were "S" bridges, so called because the bridge was built at right angles to the stream, resulting in an "S" shape bridge. While

Figure 2. Bridgeport Covered Bridge 1836-1903

Figure 3. Wills Creek Bridge at Cambridge 1828-1913

such a zigzag route was not a problem for horse-drawn vehicles, they proved to be a real hazard to early motorists and were bypassed or eliminated altogether in the 20th century. Over a dozen of the old stone bridges still stand on bypassed sections of the Old Road.[5]

Guernsey County had one covered bridge on the National Road: a two-lane structure over Wills Creek on the west edge of Cambridge, Figure 3. The bridge plan was drawn up by master bridge designer Lewis Wernwag and built by Shannon and Kincaid in 1828. The great flood of 1913 damaged this bridge so badly that it was condemned and removed shortly thereafter.

The Old Pike crossed Salt Creek in Muskingum County on a two-lane covered bridge whose builder and building date are not known. In the 1920s, the Ohio Highway Department strengthened the old structure by placing segmented wooden arches under the floor, Figure 4. This repair allowed the bridge to serve another 10 years or so.

Perhaps the most famous of all the covered bridges on the National Road was the old "Y" Bridge at Zanesville over the Licking and Muskingum Rivers. The unique "Y" Bridge was a privately-owned toll bridge which will be discussed at length in a later chapter.

Through Licking County, the National Road was carried by covered bridges over Bell Run, the South Fork of the Licking River, and later in time, the Reservoir Feeder. In Franklin County, there were several covered bridges on the National Road. In the eastern half of the county there were covered bridges over Blacklick, Big Walnut and Alum Creeks. Figure 5 shows the Walnut Creek Bridge being dismantled in 1903.

The covered bridge over the Scioto River in downtown Columbus was a 340 foot, two-lane Town lattice truss structure with sidewalks on each side, Figure 6. The bridge was built in 1832 by Captain Brewerton of the Army Corps of Engineers. In 1881, the Franklin County Commissioners appointed a committee to study this bridge and see if it was still safe to carry traffic. In their report, this committee stated that while the bridge was still safe and adequate for the traffic it carried, it was no longer suitable for its location. In other words, a more modern structure was called for and the fol-

Figure 4. Salt Creek Bridge on the Old Pike

Figure 5. Walnut Creek Bridge at Hibernia 1869-1903

lowing year, 1882, the old covered bridge was demolished.

West of Columbus, another large covered bridge serving the National Road spanned Big Darby Creek on the Franklin-Madison County

Figure 6. Scioto River Bridge at Columbus   1832-1883

4

line. It was destroyed by a flood in 1881. There was only one other covered bridge on the Old Pike in Madison County and that spanned Little Darby Creek at West Jefferson.

Further west in Clark County, there were several covered bridges on the National Road. Two of Clark County's National Road covered bridges were located at mile 45 and 46 west of Columbus. They spanned Buck Creek and the Mad River. Figure 7 shows the Mad River bridge as it was being dismantled in the early 1930s.

Figure 7. Mad River Bridge on the National Road, c.1932

The 1839 contract drawn up for the construction of the latter two bridges between the Army Engineers responsible for building the National Road and Mr. David Sniveley, the contractor, gives a Nineteenth Century flavor to this account of the building of the Old Road through Ohio. The agreement stated in part...

"The said David Sniveley of the first part, for and in consideration of the payments hereinafter mentioned, does hereby covenant and agree, to build and complete on the 45th and 46th miles west of Columbus on the Cumberland Road in Ohio, in a faithful and workmanlike manner and according to the plans and specifications furnished by the aforesaid superintendant of said Road, the wooden superstructure of two bridges, the first over the Mad River of 150 foot span, between the abutments, and 180 foot of truss frames to be constructed on the lattice principle, and of the best yellow poplar and oak, free from sap, knots, shakes and other defects.

The superstructures are to be weatherboarded with yellow poplar and shingled with white pine and the truss frames and all parts exposed to the weather, to receive two coats of white lead paint. The dimensions, mode of framing, and finish to be according to the plans furnished by the second party under directions of the superintendant of the Road, his assistants and agents. It is further stipulated that the said David Sniveley shall complete the bridges aforesaid in the manner herein understood and agreed upon, on or before the first day of November, 1839, and that he shall fell all timber which may be required in the construction before the first of November next ensuing."

This agreement was signed on November 26, 1838 between Sniveley and Captain George Dutton of the Army Corps of Engineers.[6]

Two more covered bridges were built for the National Road west of Clark County in 1841. One was at Tadmore Station on the Miami-Montgomery County line over both the Great Miami River and the Miami and Erie Canal. The other covered bridge west of Clark County spanned the Stillwater River at Englewood in Montgomery County. There were no covered bridges on the Old Road in Preble County, although this western Ohio county was building covered bridges in this time period and even earlier. By the early 1840s, the National Road was completed though Ohio and points west. Ohio's transportation system was growing rapidly and bridge building, of course, kept pace.

Some of the roadways in early Ohio were known as turnpikes. A turnpike was a privately owned and operated road that turned travelers through tollgates so that they could not avoid paying a fee. Tolls paid for the roads and bridges, and in addition, made a good profit for the owners. Most of Ohio's early covered bridges were built to serve these privately-built roads and many of them were two-lane structures.

It was 1829 when the Camden-Eaton Turnpike Company was building their road in Preble County in western Ohio. They approached Orlistus Roberts, prominent landowner along

Seven Mile Creek south of Eaton to see if he would build a bridge for them on their right-of-way near his farm. Roberts agreed and that same year he began construction of the two lane bridge that we still know as the Roberts Bridge, Figure 8. The story goes that Roberts became ill and died before he could complete the bridge and that the work was finished by

Figure 8. Roberts Covered Bridge, built 1829 as it looked in 1888 when it was only 59 years old.

his 17-year-old apprentice, James Lyman Campbell. Later, Campbell married Roberts widow and today, the graves of all three of these Preble County pioneers can be seen on the old Roberts farm.

The Camden-Eaton Pike became US Route 127, the main road between Toledo and Cincinnati. In the late 1920s, the State rerouted US 127, leaving the Roberts Bridge to serve a lonely stretch of county road. In August 1986, arsonists set fire to this historic structure. Although its trusses were badly charred, the sturdy Burr arches prevented it from collapsing. The bridge remained on its original site while plans were made for its future. Finally, it was decided to move the remnants of the old bridge into the county seat of Eaton which was done in late 1990. The bridge was rebuilt during the spring and summer of 1991 and rededicated on its new site over Seven Mile Creek on September 15, 1991, Figure 9.

By the late 1800s, many of Ohio's turnpikes and their bridges had been turned over to county ownership and still later most of them became Federal or State Highways. There were still many covered bridges on Ohio's state highway system in the 1920s and 1930s and it wasn't until after World War II when men and materials became available, that the majority of them were replaced. By the 1950s, most covered bridges on Ohio's state routes were gone. Brown County's Eagle Creek Bridge on SR 763 is the sole survivor and there are plans to by-pass it soon.

The early Ohio roads simply were not sufficient to meet the needs of the farmers to get their produce to market or for merchants to

Figure 9. Roberts Bridge on Dedication Day, September 15, 1991, at its new location in Eaton

ship their wares to the shops. An example of this problem was found in Vinton County where there was a good supply of high-grade clay. A pottery industry was started there, but it died out because of competition from the pottery industries of eastern Ohio with their access to the National Road.[7] The pikes were of vital importance to those within their reach, but for many Ohio counties, access to markets was virtually closed off since they were too far from major transportation routes.

Governor Ethan Allen Brown, in his inaugral address in 1818, proclaimed the need for a better and cheaper transportation system for Ohio's products so that they could be sold more competitively in the markets. Brown was a strong proponent of a canal system. He was later to be called the "Father of Ohio Canals". In due course, in February 1820, the Ohio Legislature passed an Act providing for three canal commissioners responsible for getting this project underway. Problems and pitfalls dogged the Legislature and Commissioners for many months. It wasn't until July 4, 1825 that the first spadeful of dirt was turned at Licking Summit near Newark in Licking County to begin the Ohio and Erie Canal. The honor of turning this first spadeful of dirt went to DeWitt Clinton, at that time Governor of New York and father of the Erie Canal. On July 21st of that same year a similar ceremony was held

Figure 10. Ohio's Canal System

at Middletown in Butler County to begin the Miami and Erie Canal.[8] When completed, circa 1848, there were over 800 miles of canal in Ohio, Figure 10.

Many wooden bridges spanned the Ohio canals, carrying both public highways and private farm roads. The last such canal covered bridge standing on its original site was the Barger Farm Bridge near Waverly in Pike County, Figure 11. This bridge was a fully-

Figure 11. Barger Farm Canal Bridge, Pike County

covered, 47 foot long single kingpost structure with a trapdoor in the floor to facilitate loading the canal boats waiting below. Abandoned and not maintained for many years, this unusual bridge collapsed into the old canal bed in the 1970s where its rotting timbers remain today.

On the fairgrounds at Lancaster in Fairfield County is a little covered bridge built in 1899 to span the canal at Basil (now within the town of Baltimore: Basil was once a separate town just to the west of Baltimore). The little Basil canal bridge was the fourth covered bridge to span the canal at this site. After the 1913 flood, the canal was filled in and the bridge was moved north of town to Roley Road to span Paw Paw Creek. In 1974, its useful life over, the little bridge was dismantled and taken to the county fairgrounds where it stands today just inside the main entrance. Figure 12 shows the Basil canal bridge circa 1900 with the old Leonard Bridge over Walnut Creek in the background.

The most interesting of the canal bridges were the covered aquaducts: Ohio had two large ones. The Ohio and Erie canal crossed the

Figure 12. Basil Canal Bridge, Leonard Bridge in background over Walnut Creek

Scioto River at Circleville in Pickaway County on what was probably the best known of these two covered canal aquaducts, Figure 13. This sturdy landmark was built in 1838 by John Hough and stood until 1915 when it was destroyed by fire. The Miami and Erie Canal had a massive covered aquaduct over the Great Miami River near Vandalia in Montgomery County. It was built in 1859 by D.H. Morrison and stood until the early 1900s, Figure 14. In addition to these massive covered aquaducts, there were numerous smaller timber truss aquaducts which were uncovered

(and therefore needing frequent repairs) that were built to serve the needs of Ohio's canals, Figure 15.

The great importance of the canals and the faith put in them to improve Ohio's economic status can be summed up in a toast given by a dignitary at a luncheon after construction began on that section of the Ohio and Erie Canal known as the Columbus Side Cut, April 30, 1827:

"The Ohio Canal—the Great Artery which will carry vitality to the extensive cities of the Union." [9]

As we know, this rosy future for the canals in Ohio never fully materialized due to the appearance and rapid development of the railroads in the state.

The railroads first came on the scene in Ohio almost simultaneously with Ohio canal development in the 1830s. By the 1850s, the railroads were going full-steam, often in direct competition with canal traffic. The canals were in trouble. In 1856, the earnings from the canals in Ohio fell below operating costs. The state leased the canals to private interests in the 1860s, but they proved so unprofitable that the leasees turned them back to the state in 1877 and the system was almost derelict. There were attempts to renovate the canals around the turn of the century, but it was a futile effort.

Figure 13. Circleville Aquaduct over Scioto River, 1838-1915

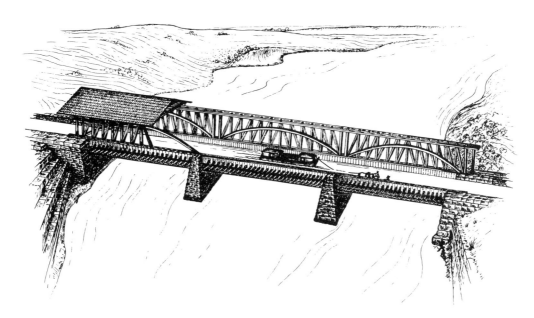

Figure 14. Artist's conception of a cutaway view of the Miami River Aquaduct on Miami and Erie Canal

Canal traffic continued in some areas in a small way, but they could not compete with the railroads; their day was done.[10]

As the canals went out of operation, the bridges which spanned them on public roads were frequently sold to the highest bidder. The price was usually quite reasonable, but there was a catch: the buyer had to agree to remove the bridge, fill in the canal and build up a roadway at the former bridge site. The canal aquaducts were usually left in place and they eventually fell into ruin and collapsed. One such stone aquaduct which did not collapse now carries a county road over Raccoon Creek in Licking County.

The first railroad lines were built in Ohio in

the 1830s and by 1852, there were 890 miles of railroad in operation in the state. This figure climbed rapidly to 3,324 miles of track in use by 1869. Principle routes are shown in Figure 16.

In 1869, an important change was accomplished in railroad management inasmuch as short lines were consolidated into through lines connecting Chicago with East Coast cities. The consolidation of some of the smaller Ohio rail lines improved operations and with this improved efficiency rail lines and their bridges were better maintained.[11]

Hundreds of wooden truss bridges were built to carry the rapidly expanding rail lines. In their haste to lay track and build bridges,

Figure 15. Uncovered canal aquaduct over Paint Creek south of Chillicothe

Figure 17. Railroad Bridge over Scioto River east of Chillicothe. Kilgore's Ford Bridge in background.

railroad companies would throw up a wooden truss bridge and leave it uncovered, sometimes intending to come back later to roof and side it. But many were never covered. Figure 17 shows the uncovered Howe truss bridge of the Marietta and Cincinnati Railroad over the Scioto River east of Chillicothe at Kilgore's Ford. (In the background can be seen the Kilgore's Ford Bridge.)

Inspectors rode the rails and inspected each line yearly. Their reports, 1869 to 1888, are now the best source of information on early railroad bridges in Ohio. By 1880, there were 846 wooden bridges in use on Ohio's railroads, the oldest, per the record, was built in 1853 on the Baltimore and Ohio Railroad's Central Division line.[12] Figure 18 shows the fully-covered Tunnel Hill Bridge on the Baltimore and Ohio Railroad at Cambridge, circa 1870s. The Cincinnati and Muskingum Valley Railroad had 38 wooden truss bridges in use in 1886. That same year, the Columbus and Hocking Valley Railroad had a total of 64 wooden truss bridges in use.

The young Buckeye State was developing a fine transportation system with a great network of roads, canals and railroads. The need for many substantial bridges was great. In Ohio, the era of the covered bridge was in full sway.

Figure 16. Ohio's Railway System, late 1800s

Figure 18. Tunnel Hill Railroad Bridge west of Cambridge over Wills Creek

10

CHAPTER II

BRIDGES, BUILDERS AND BARGAINS

Ohio has always been acknowledged as a paradise for the dedicated "bridger" and even more so for those who want to study the various truss types of wooden bridges since examples of many types still stand in the Buckeye State. This chapter describes several of the commonly-built truss designs and presents brief sketches of some of the men who built them. Data on prices for building these structures also are given.

WHAT IS A TRUSS?

It is important to give the reader some background information here on bridge trusses. Just what is a bridge truss? A truss is that arrangement of timber beams and braces, usually triangular in layout, that forms a rigid framework to support its own weight plus the weight of floor, roof, sides and of course, any load traveling across the bridge. In Figure 19a, a sketch is shown of the basic triangular arrangement of timbers known as a kingpost truss (KP) and five variations of that design, Figure 19b-f. The kingpost is the center vertical truss member and is in tension while the truss diagonals or braces are in compression. For longer spans, the multiple kingpost (MKP) was developed which consists of a series of vertical posts and braces. One truss section consisting of a vertical and diagonal member is called a panel. Note that the panels are joined top and bottom by horizontal beams known as chords which run the length of the framework. Floor beams and flooring are laid down on, or suspended from, the lower chord. Roof beams and roofing are joined to the upper chord. Thus described, the structure is known as a through truss bridge.

A direct outgrowth of the kingpost truss was the queenpost (QP) as shown in Figure 19b. A true queenpost always has a separate upper chord (horizontal beam) between the two truss verticals of the center panel. Longer spans

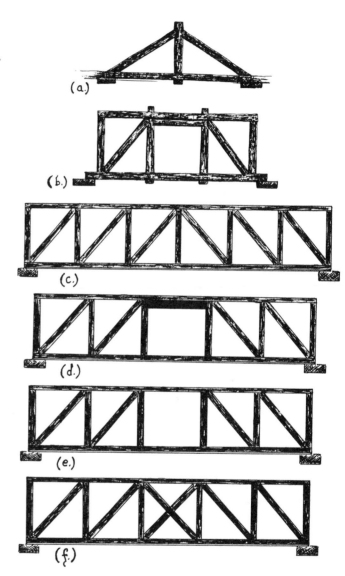

Figure 19 a-f. The Kingpost Truss and Variations
a. Kingpost, b. Queenpost, c. MKP, d. MKP/QP
Combination, e. MKP with open center panel,
f. MKP with X brace in center panel

with a center QP truss are augmented by the typical vertical post and diagonal brace panels of the MKP truss, Figure 19d.

Ohio's smaller streams and canals were frequently spanned by a single kingpost truss. Often, these short spans were only half height and were referred to as low, half or pony trusses to distinguish them from the full height wooden bridges that were roofed and sided. Many of these pony trusses had the sides well covered to protect the trusses from moisture. A pony kingpost truss under construction is shown in Figure 20. If the roadway ran between the trusses, the bridge was always called a through truss. If the trusses were below the roadway, the bridge was known as a deck truss, Figure 21. Deck trusses were more commonly used for railroad bridges than for highway bridges.

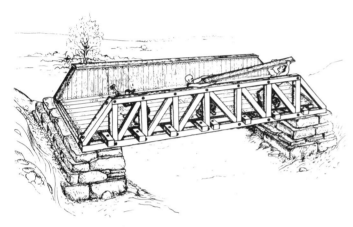

Figure 20. A covered Pony MKP under construction in the late 1870s

*Figure 21. Deck Howe Truss...
the favored truss of the railroads*

Ohio has had many multiple kingpost truss bridges built with an open center panel which at first glance appears to be a queenpost but unless that extra top chord is present, the bridge is not a queenpost truss. Still another variation of the basic multiple kingpost truss was built with an X brace in the center panel. All of these variations of the kingpost truss are

shown in Figure 19. The nomenclature used to describe the trusses shown in Figure 19 is a matter of semantics and not everyone will agree with it. However, these names will be used thoughout this book.

We know that the wooden truss bridge dates back to antiquity, but it wasn't until the 1500s that Italian architect, Andrea Palladio published wood bridge truss designs. Figure 22 shows the Palladio designs: a basic multiple kingpost, a queenpost-like truss, and two arch trusses.[13]

Many people believe that the covered bridge is a peculiarly American phenomenon, but it was actually under Swiss and German leadership that the wooden bridge truss was widely developed and used.[14] This development was

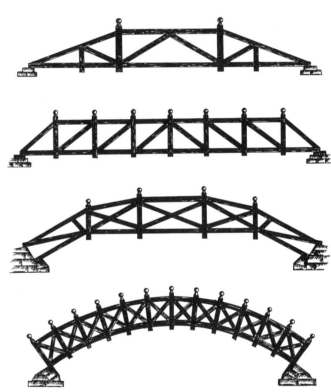

Figure 22. Palladio Designs, 1500s

an almost exclusive province of the carpenter-technicians who had an intuitive grasp of the strengths and limitations of wood and a "feel" for the best way to build large, strong structures. They eventually added arches to the basic triangular trusswork of their wooden bridges and then covered them with roof and siding.

Why cover a wooden bridge? Moisture from rain and snow working down into the joints where one timber joins another, will eventually cause rotting and weakening of these vital truss joints, leading to warping, sagging and failure of the structure. The early bridge builders found that a well-maintained and covered wood truss bridge gave many more years of service than the relatively short life of an uncovered wood truss. So, the roof was not to protect the floor (the cheapest part to replace) or to provide shade on a hot summer day (a great side benefit) or to give lovers a place to stop and exchange a kiss or two (another bonus), it was a vital part of the bridge to protect the timbers and assure a long life for the trusses.

A variety of truss designs and the people knowledgeable about constructing them was exported to the Western Hemisphere from the Old World. Some of this expertise found its way west of the Alleghenies and into Ohio with our early pioneers. Later, as we will describe, adaptations of designs and new inventions relating to wooden trusses were accredited to Ohio bridge builders.

Figure 23. Catherinus Buckingham

CATHERINUS BUCKINGHAM AND THE MULTIPLE KINGPOST TRUSS

By far the most common of all wooden truss designs used in Ohio was the basic multiple kingpost truss. It was never patented and therefore, no royalties could be charged for its use. This design eventually became known in Ohio as a Buckingham truss after Catherinus Buckingham, West Point graduate and Adjutant General of Ohio, Figure 23. His father, Ebenezer Buckingham, was one of the owners of the Muskingum and Licking Bridge Company in Zanesville. This company owned and maintained the Y Bridge over the confluence of the Licking and Muskingum Rivers at

Figure 24. The Y Bridge at Zanesville, 1832-1900

Zanesville. In 1832, the second Y Bridge was in bad shape and Ebenezer Buckingham asked his son to design a new bridge.[15]

The bridge plans designed by Catherinus Buckingham were for a two-lane multiple kingpost truss with double truss timbers for maximum strength, Figure 24. The new bridge was completed in December, 1832 and was so greatly admired that the truss became known as a Buckingham in honor of its builder.[16] Many Ohio bridge contractors built their reputations using the Buckingham truss. A roll-call of the names of some of these men would read: John and Simon Shrake of Licking County; G.J. and J.B. Haggerty, also of Licking County; Jordon Hall Banks and Jacob Morgan of Tuscarawas County; William A. Dean of Perry County; E.B. Henderson of Washington County; Jacob R. Brandt and James W. Buchanan of Fairfield County; Thomas and George Fisher of Muskingum County and many, many others. While the multiple kingpost truss was frequently called a Buckingham, that did not mean that other builders using this design always used double truss timbers. Generally speaking, most Ohio multiple kingpost truss bridges were built with single truss timbers. A brief sketch of the lives and work of some of the better-known builders of the Buckingham truss is in order here.

THE JACOB R. BRANDT STORY

Jacob Rugh Brandt was born in 1836 in Greenfield Township, Fairfield County, Ohio, a son of Adam and Elizabeth Rugh Brandt. Jacob grew up to be a farmer, skilled mechanic, draftsman and builder of churches, schools and bridges. Family stories say that Jacob learned his bridge building trade from Jonathon Coulson, pioneer Fairfield County bridge builder. A member of the Brandt family, uncle or cousin to Jacob, was named Jonathon Coulson Brandt, which hints of a close family relationship with Jonathon Coulson. The names of both Coulson and Brandt appear over the portal of the Rushville Bridge, Figure 25, that spanned Rush Creek between Rushville and West Rushville on the old Zane Trace. Coulson built this bridge in 1845 and Brandt rebuilt it in 1891.[17]

Figure 25. The Rushville Bridge

Jacob R. Brandt won his first bridge contract in 1858 at age 22. He worked in Fairfield County drawing up plans for bridges for the county commissioners and building smaller bridges. He designed plans for wooden and combination truss bridges as well as houses and churches.

It was in 1864 that Brandt got the contract for his first large bridge, the 97 foot McLeery Bridge in Fairfield County near Baltimore. The bridge cost $12.50 per linear foot. A portion of it is still in existance on the farm of James Walter south of Baltimore, Ohio. In 1866, the contract for a bridge over Walnut Creek near Loucks Mill went to Brandt for $18.45 per linear foot. This bridge was a 130 foot multiple kingpost with arches, Figure 26. It was closed to traffic in the late 1970s and in 1983, was

Figure 26. Brandt's Loucks Bridge

dismantled and moved to Texas. As far as is known now, it was never rebuilt and its fate is unknown.

It seems that in the late 1800s in Fairfield county, one bridge builder would be awarded most of the contracts and so it was about 1870 that William Black gained prominence in the county and Brandt is seldom mentioned for a period of time. We know that he worked in other Ohio counties, building bridges, and that he continued to build other structures in Fairfield County.

In 1888, Brandt's Fairfield County bridge career was rejuvenated when he got the contract for the 109 foot Peter Ety Bridge over Walnut Creek at $11.00 per linear foot. His last contract for a new "house" bridge came in December 1900 when he got the job of building a new covered bridge at Rock Mill for $575.

At some point in his long career, Jacob Brandt got the nickname "Blue Jeans" because of his preference for wearing clothing made of this sturdy fabric. Family stories say that he was a very meticulous person who was known to keep a change of work clothes handy so he could change if he got dirty. Brandt was just as committed to perfection in his work and carpenters who worked for him knew they had to do the job right or be prepared to do it over again.

William Brandt Henry, grandson of "Blue Jeans", told of how his grandfather would cut the trusses for a bridge. The Brandt home on present US 22 west of Lancaster, had a driveway the length of a football field and on each side was a space about 12 feet wide. It was along this driveway that "Blue Jeans" laid out, cut and fit the truss timbers before taking them to the bridge site.[18] After an outstanding career that spanned 43 years, Jacob R. Brandt died in 1911. Figure 27 is a picture of Jacob R. Brandt in his later years.

JAMES WILSON BUCHANAN

James Wilson Buchanan was one of the carpenters who learned the bridge building trade from "Blue Jeans" Brandt. Like Brandt, Buchanan was also a native of Greenfield Township, Fairfield County, born there in 1846 to Stephen P. and Emily Crane Buchanan. Young

Figure 27. Jacob R. Brandt, 1836-1911

James Buchanan marched off to the Civil War in 1864 at age 17 with the 17th Ohio Volunteer Infantry from Lancaster, Ohio. He was with Sherman's forces in Georgia.[19] It was after the war that he began to work with Brandt before contracting on his own. Buchanan lost out on two of his early bids to William Black. Buchanan worked at repairing and rebuilding bridges in Fairfield County during this time period and finally got his first contract by underbidding the popular August Borneman. Contracts for full-size wood truss bridges began going to Buchanan in 1888. A trademark of a Buchanan-built bridge was its noticeable camber. Camber in a bridge is a slight upward curve (or in some cases, not so slight) of the framework, Figure 28.

The largest covered bridge built by Buchanan was the State Dam Bridge over Walnut Creek, a 157 foot multiple kingpost with arches that was built in 1894 for $2,200., or about $14. per linear foot, Figure 29. Buchanan continued to build "house" bridges in Fairfield County until 1916. In addition to the wooden truss bridges, Buchanan also built combination and metal truss structures. Like Brandt, Buchanan built

15

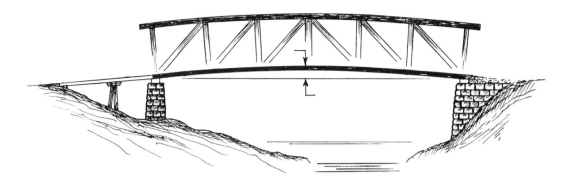

Figure 28. Sketch shows what is meant by camber in a bridge. Note the curvature of both the upper and lower chords.

Figure 29. The State Dam Bridge

houses and barns and, during the winter months, he taught school. In his later years, James Buchanan was postmaster at Basil, Ohio and served on the Board of Education. He died in 1924.

WILLIAM A. DEAN

William A. Dean of Clayton Township, Perry County, was born in Ohio in 1838, son of James Dean of Dean Hill Farm in Hopewell Township, Perry County. Dean's bridge building career was spent in his home county where, from 1874 to 1886, he built 23 Buckingham truss bridges of both the full and pony height sizes. He was also active in bridge repair work in Perry County during this time. Like Buchanan, Dean built camber into his bridges. A study of the Parks Bridge, a six panel, 68 foot

Buckingham truss built in 1882 by Dean to span a branch of Jonathon Creek in Hopewell Township, shows the complexity of sculpted timbers for even this most simple truss design, Figure 30. William Dean was obviously a master at cutting, notching and fitting the truss timbers. Two of his bridges still stand and carry daily traffic: the Parks Bridge and the Jacks Hollow Bridge, Figure 31, built in 1879 to span Kents Run in the extreme northeastern section of Perry County.

EBENEZER B. HENDERSON

While Brandt, Buchanan and Dean spent most or all of their bridge building careers in their home counties, there was another well-known Ohio builder of covered bridges who traveled all over the eastern and southeastern sections of Ohio building Buckingham trusses and putting up sturdy masonry to support those bridges: Ebenezer B. Henderson. Ohio-born in 1835, he lived in Beverly in Washington County where he had his home and shop on Fifth Street. Henderson was one of the most prolific builders of the Buckingham truss in Ohio. From 1872 to 1896, he built 28 bridges in Washington County, and all but one were Buckingham trusses. His Watertown Bridge over Wolf Creek was a Warren truss. During this period of intense building activity in Washington County, Henderson was also working in Coshocton, Guernsey, Jackson and Muskingum Counties and we know that he also bid unsuccessfully on bridges in Hocking and Pickaway Counties. Like most of the other bridge builders, E.B. Henderson also built houses and barns.

Henderson started out in 1872 building a 54 foot multiple kingpost truss near Vincent in

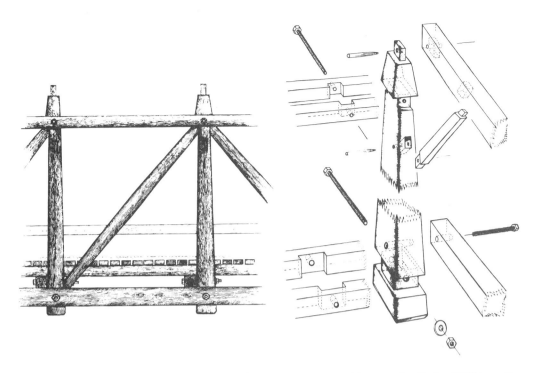

Figure 30. Complexity of Sculpted Timbers in Kingpost Trusses built by William Dean

Figure 31. Jack's Hollow Bridge

covered bridges over the Little Muskingum River in Washington County and his longest bridge was the Stillwell Bridge over the Muskingum River in Muskingum County. According to his obituary, Ebenezer B. Henderson who died in 1903, was once an "erector" for the King Bridge Company. He is buried at Beverly in Washington County. His well-built covered bridges and the fine masonry work of the Hills Bridge stand as monuments to this outstanding technician.

Washington County for $8.25 per linear foot. He also did the masonry for this little bridge. In 1878, he bid unsuccessfully on the Hills Bridge at $9. per linear foot and lost out to the Hocking Valley Bridge Works who built a Howe truss for $13.25 per linear foot. Henderson did get the contract for the foundations of the Hills Bridge. Three Henderson-built covered bridges still stand in Washington County today: Shinn, Figure 32, built in 1886; Bell, built 1888; and Henry, built 1894. Henderson built some large

Figure 32. The Shinn Bridge

17

THE SHRAKES OF LICKING COUNTY

The name Shrake is found often in the bridge building records of eastern and southern Ohio. This family built the Buckingham truss and also laid up bridge foundations. John Shrake was the senior bridge builder in this family and his name is found in county records as far north as Marion County, as far west as Madison County, and as far south as Washington County on the Ohio River. John Shrake was active in his trade from the 1850s through the early 1870s. It was in the early 1870s that the name Simon Shrake began to appear with great frequency in the Licking County Commissioners Journals. He built the wood truss bridges of both the full-size and pony truss variety. Simon sometimes worked in partnership with John who was probably an uncle. The bridge building career of Simon Shrake went into the 1880s. There were two other Shrakes, F.T. and P.Q. who were also builders of wood truss bridges in the 1870s and 1880s.

John Shrake was one of the few "outsiders" to build bridges in Fairfield County in the 1800s. In 1871, he built the Waterloo/Shade Bridge over Walnut Creek (now relocated to the Pierson Farm). Earlier, in 1863, John Shrake built the Helmick Bridge in Coshocton County, Figure 33. It is believed that these are the last Shrake-built covered bridges still standing.

Figure 33. John Shrake's Helmick Bridge built in 1863

QUEENPOST TRUSS BRIDGES IN OHIO

Ohio had relatively few true queenpost truss bridges. But, at least six were built in Vinton County, four of them by George Washington Pilcher, Civil War Veteran, preacher and prominent stone mason.[20] Pilcher's Mt. Olive Road Bridge over the Middle Fork of Salt Creek north of Allensville is an excellent example of an Ohio queenpost truss, Figure 34.

Figure 34. The Mount Olive Road Bridge

Two other good examples of the queenpost truss are the Jediah Hill Bridge in Hamilton County built in 1850 by Jediah Hill and the Hartman Bridge in Lockville Park in Fairfield County, built in 1888 by William Funk. The Hartman Bridge was built to span Pleasant Run east of Lancaster and in the late 1960s, it was dismantled and moved to Lockville Park where it was rebuilt over the old Ohio and Erie Canal. Figure 35 shows the bridge during reconstruction and the distinctive queenpost configuration of the center panel can be clearly seen.

When Fairfield County's Hizey Bridge was being dismantled a few years ago prior to moving it to the property of Jim Visintine, the discovery was made that instead of an open center panel multiple kingpost truss, there was a queenpost truss. This had been hidden under the arch installed after damage to the bridge was sustained in the 1913 flood. James

Figure 35. Queenpost truss Hartman Bridge

Buchanan was hired by Fairfield County to repair this bridge that he had built just 23 years earlier. It cost $250. to install the arches.

In the above sections on multiple kingpost/ Buckingham and queenpost truss bridges we have occasionally mentioned price per linear foot. Price was usually the determining factor in the choice of bridge truss designs and since the kingposts and queenpost designs were not patented, these were most popular in Ohio.

Pony truss bridges of the Buckingham or queenpost styles generally cost from $4.50 to $6.00 per linear foot. A full-size Buckingham truss cost in the $7.00 to $9.00 per linear foot range for a 35 foot to 90 foot bridge. A longer bridge, such as Henderson's Stillwell Bridge over the Muskingum River cost at least $12.00 per linear foot. Top price we have seen for a Buckingham truss was $14. per linear foot in 1878 when the Smith Bridge Company built the Graham's Crossing Bridge over Captina Creek in Belmont County.

In the early days, Muskingum County built a multiple kingpost truss for only $5.55 per linear foot, but it was to be left uncovered until a later date--doubtless because the county couldn't afford to finish the bridge at that time.

The Salt Creek Bridge in Muskingum County was built in 1876 and not roofed until 1879, probably for the same reason.

In 1888, William Funk was paid $7.50 per linear foot for the Hartman Bridge which the Fairfield County Commissioners referred to as a "covered Buckingham". Obviously, to them, this was simply a variation of the Buckingham truss, although, in fact, this bridge has a queenpost style truss.

THE BURR ARCH TRUSS

Theodore Burr was born in Connecticut in 1771 and became a well-known East Coast bridge builder. He began building bridges in New York State around 1800 and for several years experimented with various truss designs. In 1804, Burr received a patent on a new idea in wooden bridge trusses which featured massive arches with their ends bedded into the face of the abutments. The arches were fastened to multiple kingpost trusses.[21] In 1817, Mr. Burr was granted another bridge patent that was similar to his 1804 patent but in which the kingposts are slightly flared in relation to the center vertical kingpost as shown in Figure 36.

In the Burr arch or Burr kingpost truss plan the arches are always fitted into the face of the abutments below the bridge seat. In most cases where a multiple kingpost truss bridge has arches, we have found that these arches rest on the lower chord and were a later addition to strengthen a failing structure. However, these added arches were not always tied to the lower chords. Sometimes, they were secured to the face of the abutments as was the case with Brown County's New Hope Road Bridge.

We do not know just how many true Burr arch trusses were built in Ohio, but present research accounts for over 30 of this type. A prime example is the Roberts Bridge, Figure 10. Figure 37 shows an interior view of this bridge.

Prices for the Burr truss tended to be high. There was the cost of the arch and many Burr trusses were built with double truss timbers. This redundancy made for a very strong bridge. Perhaps the highest price paid in Ohio for a Burr truss was in 1867 when the Pickaway

19

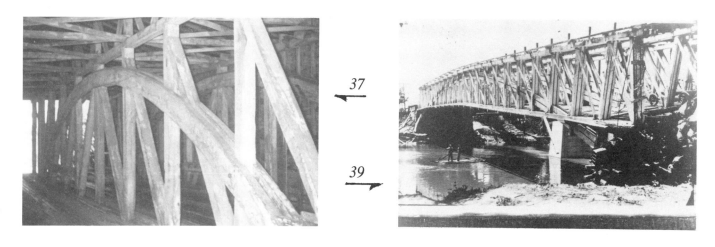

Figure 36. The Burr Truss Design, patented 1804

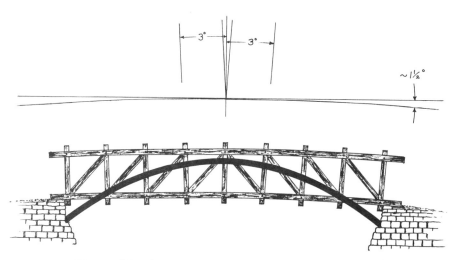

37 ←

39 →

Figure 37. The interior of the Roberts Bridge; Ohio's Last Burr Truss

Figure 39. The Unhoused Trusses of the Seymour Bridge, circa 1930

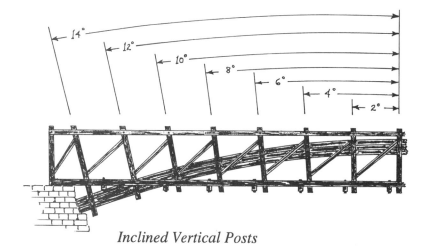

Inclined Vertical Posts

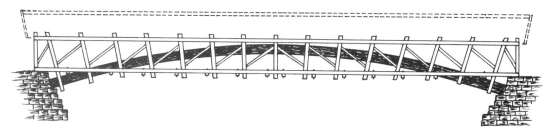

Figure 38. Lewis Wernwag's truss design patented in 1829

County officials paid $25.00 per linear foot for the Lindsey Ford Bridge over the Scioto River. The Commissioners specified an "improved double Burr with independent arches". Of course, this was a multi-span bridge. In 1868, Union County paid $16.40 for a one-span Burr truss of 126 feet over Mill Creek.

THE WERNWAG TRUSS--- LEWIS WERNWAG

Another of the early American bridge builders whose influence, like that of Theodore Burr, extended into Ohio, was Lewis Wernwag. Wernwag was born in Germany in 1770 and came to America as a young man, perhaps to escape enforced military service. A graduate of the University of Berlin, Lewis Wernwag was a skilled and gifted mechanic who quickly gained acclaim for his sturdy, well-built bridges.[22] Wernwag's career lasted 27 years, from 1810 to 1838, during which time he built bridges in Maryland, Virginia, Delaware, Pennsylvania, Kentucky and possibly Ohio. His most outstanding bridge is generally considered to be the "Colossus" built in 1812 to span the Schuylkill River at Fairmont, Pennsylvania.

In December 1829, while a resident of Jefferson County, Virginia, Wernwag received a patent for an arched wooden bridge truss. Like Burr's truss, the arches were fitted into the face of the abutments below the bridge seat. The kingposts of the Wernwag truss are quite definitely flared like the Burr truss, but there were other differences as shown in Figure 38. Ohio had a number of Wernwag truss bridges, all of which are gone now except the Bebb Park Bridge in Butler County. It is interesting to note that only in Butler County was the name Wernwag mentioned in county records in connection with a bridge truss.

It is said that Wernwag designed the two-lane, single span, 211 foot Wernwag truss known as the Seymour Bridge, which carried old US 50 over Paint Creek in Ross County. The bridge was built in 1840 by J.W. Slee whose name remains today on the parapet stone left at the entrance to the present bridge. Figure 39 shows the Seymour Bridge unhoused prior to removal in 1934 due to abutment failure.

One other Ohio covered bridge that we know was designed by Lewis Wernwag was the old National Road Bridge over Wills Creek at Cambridge. This bridge was built in 1828 by Shannon and Kincaid. While no one knows for certain, this may have been a lattice truss, while others feel that it was the usual Wernwag with heavy arches and flared kingposts.[23] These arches can be seen in an old side view of the bridge, Figure 3. Greene County, Ohio had two Wernwag trusses: Jacoby Road over the Little Miami River, built in 1869, and the Henville Road Bridge over Caesars Creek built in 1872. Both bridges were built by Henry E. Hebble. The Jacoby Road Bridge cost over $15. per linear foot and the Henville Road Bridge cost $12.50 per linear foot.

THE BRIDGE BUILDING BOWER FAMILY

One of the builders who learned his craft from Lewis Wernwag and later came to Ohio, was Jacob N. Bower. Bower was born in Maryland in 1819 and served his apprenticeship under several bridge builders, including Lewis Wernwag. Bower worked his way west from Maryland, pausing long enough to build bridges in Pennsylvania, Ohio, West Virginia and Kentucky. Eventually, he settled in Brown County, Ohio where he continued in the bridge building trade. His sons, Isaac, Ben, Devault and Louis (orignally spelled Lewis for Lewis Wernwag) worked with him. Family tradition says that they built bridges in Brown and surrounding counties. One of the sons, Devault, was killed in an accident while working on a covered bridge in Ohio. Jacob Bower died in 1906 and is buried at Ripley, Ohio.[24]

Figure 40. The New Hope Bridge

The Bower Family moved on to Fleming County, Kentucky at the urging of county officials there who had heard of their bridge building skills. It was here, in 1905, that Louis S. "Stock" Bower was born, a third generation Bower bridge builder and the last of the Bower family bridge builders. His father, Louis S. Bower, Sr., son of Jacob, built his last covered bridge in 1910 in Kentucky and thereafter devoted his skills to bridge repairs. He rebuilt the Bethel-New Hope Road Bridge in Brown County in 1932 and years later, in 1977, son Stock Bower again rebuilt this fine old structure, Figure 40.

The elder Louis S. Bower died in an auto accident in Ohio in 1936 enroute home from a meeting with Monroe County officials about the repair of the Foraker Bridge. When these people heard nothing further from Mr. Bower, they called his home and were distressed to learn of his death. They asked to speak to the younger Bower who was surprised that they had heard of him. Stock traveled to Monroe County and rebuilt the Foraker Bridge and thus began his career as head of the Bower Bridge Company.[25] This company was active for many years in the repair and rebuilding of covered bridges in Ohio, Kentucky and West Virginia.

THE TIED ARCH---OHIO'S FIRST COMBINATION TRUSS

Another type of truss used in Ohio's wooden bridges to a limited extent was the tied arch, Figure 41. Always rare in Ohio, this truss design was not built here after the mid-1800s. The existance of four of these bridges has been documented, three of them in Ross County. In the tied arch design, the arch is used in place of a triangular truss with the ends of the arches securely tied to the lower chords. The load is carried by metal suspension rods that are anchored into the arch as well as the lower chord.[26]

In the case of the best-known and most elaborate of Ohio's tied arch bridges, these arches were stiffened by kingpost trusses within the radius of the arches. Figure 42 shows this bridge over the Scioto River at Chillicothe after it was unhoused in preparation for demolition. This bridge, known as the Bridge Street Bridge, was built by private investors in 1817 and eventually became a part of the Zanesville to Maysville Turnpike. There was a long trestle approach on the north end of the bridge. The bridge itself had two tied arch spans totaling 300 feet that reached to the high bank on the south side of the river at Chillicothe.

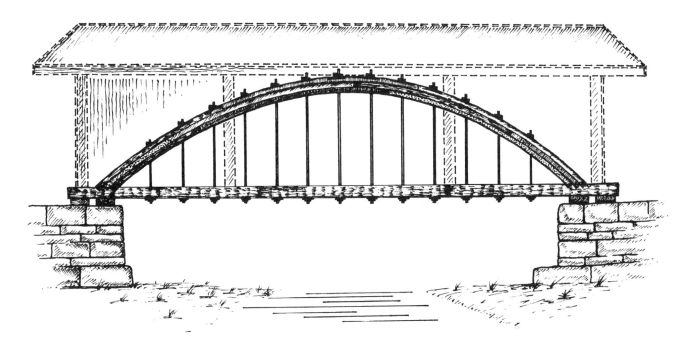

Figure 41. The Tied Arch Design was rare in Ohio, but we did build a few in the early 1800s

Figure 42. End View of The Old Bridge Street Bridge at Chillicothe During Demolition in 1886

The bridge was a two-lane structure and therefore had three arched trusses, one on each side as well as a center truss. Each lane was 12 foot four inches wide. Each arch was made of ten layers of 3" x 10.5" oak planks, in long lengths, breaking joints; each arch layer was spiked to the one below at intervals of two feet with 7" spikes; and the ten thicknesses were bolted together every five foot with 1" x 1" square wrought iron bolts.

In 1844, the trestle approach was replaced by a third covered span, featuring a multiple kingpost truss with arches. A side view of this bridge, Figure 43, shows the humpback appearance of the two tied arch spans. It looked this way because there were no horizontal upper chords as in a more conventional truss arrangement. When the old bridge was to be torn down in 1886, the timbers resisted every effort to pull them apart, so those in charge piled brushwood through the structure and set it on fire as a "sure fire" way to get the job done.[27]

Figure 43. Side view of Bridge Street Bridge, circa 1880, showing Uneven Roof Line Where Two Tied Arch Trusses Met at the MKP Truss of the Third Span

Ross County had a five span tied arch bridge over the north fork of Paint Creek at Slate Mills, west of Chillicothe. It was built c. 1840 and removed in the early 1900s. A third and smaller tied arch bridge carried the Gallipolis Pike over Salt Creek east of Richmondale. The fourth known tied arch bridge was at Pine Grove in Hocking County over Clear Creek near present-day US 33. The Pine Grove Bridge was abandoned by 1900 and in very poor condition.

A word is in order to clarify the term combination truss as used here in this study of Ohio's wooden truss bridges. A combination truss is one where both wood and metal truss members were used. The tied arch truss is an example of an early combination truss though a relatively small amount of metal was used. The same can be said about the Howe, Pratt and Childs trusses since these designs had various quantities of metal rods and braces in support of the wooden timbers. Other truss designs without specific names also utilized various proportions of iron and wood in several truss configurations. Later, we will discuss the Germantown and John Bright Bridges, both of which are combination trusses. There was another combination truss that was commonly-used for short spans here in Ohio and that was the simple wooden kingpost with a metal rod as the center truss vertical.

OHIO AND THE TOWN LATTICE TRUSS

A most interesting wooden truss was patented in 1820 by architect Ithiel Town of Connecticut. The Town truss design featured a web of diagonal planks which form a lattice, Figure 44. These planks are fastened at the intersections with wooden pins known as tree-nails or

trunnels for short. Mr. Town claimed that his bridges could be easily and quickly built using common plank. His agents charged builders a royalty of one dollar per foot for the use of the Town truss design. One great advantage of the Town truss was that it could be built in one continuous span over the piers from abutment to abutment, unlike other truss designs which had to be built in individual spans and fitted to the piers. This made the Town truss ideal for longer spans. It was frequently used for railroads as well as highway use and was built much heavier for railroad bridges.[28] The biggest fault of an old Town truss is that it tends to warp and twist out of line. The addition of arches and secondary chords corrects this problem.

The Town truss was quite popular in Ohio in the early days and many of the bridges built to serve the National Road and our early turnpikes were built using this design. Some of Ohio's largest Town trusses were built to span the Scioto River in Franklin and Pickaway Counties. In Pickaway County, massive Town trusses spanned the Scioto at Circleville and at South Bloomfield. The Pickaway County Commissioners were specific in ordering the "lattice" truss for many of their bridges in the 1840s and 1850s. By the 1870s, many of these early Town trusses were being replaced by new covered bridges using more "modern" truss designs. A good example of this came in 1871 when the county commissioners ordered a new Smith truss at Ashville and had the old Town truss moved to another site some two miles east of town where it served until 1952, Figure 45.

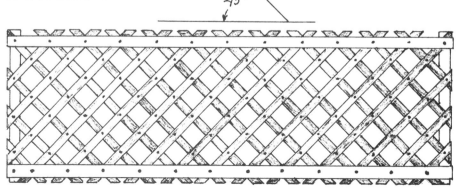

Figure 44. The Town Truss design from the 1820 patent showing the 45° angle between truss timbers and chords

Figure 45. The "old" Ashville Bridge

As mentioned earlier, many of Ohio's Town truss bridges were built by private turnpike companies and the names of the actual builders were not recorded. However, we do have the names of the firms who worked in Fairfield, Franklin and Pickaway Counties in central Ohio. The firm of Sarber and Myers was well-known for building sturdy Town trusses as was Greeno, Smith and McCready and Samuel Blake. The name David Sniveley is associated with Town truss bridges built to serve the National Road west of Columbus. Like Pickway County, Franklin county was through with the Town truss by the 1850s and seeking more "modern" designs.

The stronghold of the Town truss in Ohio is in Ashtabula County where ten of these lattice bridges still stand. These, and other Ashtabula County covered bridges are documented in a later chapter. In 1983, a fine Town truss was built to span Conneaut Creek under the supervision of County Engineer John Smolen, who drew up plans from old bridge plans he found in his office. The new bridge is known as the State Road Bridge, Figure 46. It replaced an old steel truss built in 1898 which in its turn had replaced an early covered bridge on this site some three miles east of Kingsville.

The State Road Bridge has a 140 foot clear span with a roof length of 157 feet. It is 17'6" wide and 14'6" high and can carry all legal loads. The bridge was assembled on the south side of the creek and carefully winched across into place on its modified sandstone abutments and concrete pier. Construction took five months.

The State Road Bridge cost $200,000 to build, or $1428.00 per linear foot. Contrast that with the $9.00 to $12.00 per linear foot builders were getting for a Town lattice truss bridge in the mid-1800s here in Ohio. How times have changed!

Figure 46. John Smolen's State Road Bridge

THE LONG TRUSS IN OHIO

A New Hampshire man, Colonel Stephen H. Long of the United States Army Topographical Engineers, patented all-wood bridge truss designs in 1830, 1836, 1839 and 1858. Figure 47 shows the Long truss as used here in Ohio, generally following the 1830 and 1836 designs.

The majority of Ohio's Long truss bridges were built in the southern part of the state in Washington, Lawrence, Clinton, Greene, Highland and Ross Counties. Stephen Daniels was Long's agent in southern Ohio and he was also a bridge contractor.[29] In 1850, Daniels built a large Long truss over the mouth of Symmes Creek in Lawrence County, on what is now SR 7.

In the late 1860s, the Washington County Commissioners had a set of bridge plans drawn up by Civil Engineer C.C. Lymon specifically for use in building the Cow Run Bridge over the Little Muskingum River and also to keep on file for future use. We assume that these plans

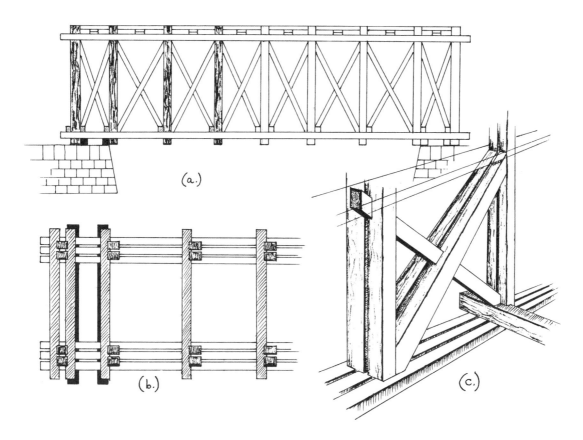

Figure 47. Sketch of the Long truss as used in Ohio: a. Side view, b. Plan view of bottom chords and floor beams, c. Oblique view of posts, braces and counterbraces of a single panel.

were for a Long truss as the Cow Run Bridge, Figure 48, was a 140 foot, 14 panel Long truss. The Long truss was also used in Washington County by bridge builder Rolla Merydith. He called it his plan Number 3.

In Highland County the Commissioners were most specific in ordering "Long's Improved Truss" for their bridges. At least 12 were built on this design in the 1870s in Highland County by John C. Gregg and Thomas Dollarhide. John C. Gregg, of Hillsboro in Highland County, had an outstanding career in southwestern Ohio where he designed and built many wooden bridges using the Long truss. Most of his career was spent working in Highland and nearby Ross County. In 1867, the Ross County Commissioners paid Gregg $130. for designing the Shotts Bridge over Paint Creek near Bourneville. That same year, Gregg designed the Kilgore Ford Bridge, Figure 17, over the Scioto River east of Chillicothe. This was a Long truss with arches that rested on the lower chords. John C. Gregg's promising career was cut short by his early death in 1880 at age 58.

The longest Long truss remaining in Ohio is Miami County's Eldean Bridge over the Great Miami River north of Troy. It is a 24 panel, 224

Figure 48. The Cow Run Bridge was a fine example of the Long truss

foot, 2 span Long truss built in 1860 by the Hamilton Brothers for $11.75 per linear foot.

Joseph J. Daniels, a son of Stephen Daniels, learned the bridge building trade from his father and moved to southwestern Ohio where he built several fine Long truss bridges in the 1850s. Daniels later moved on to Indiana where he was to reach the peak of his bridge building career.

Daniels received from $7.00 to $8.50 per linear foot for his Greene County Long truss bridges in the early 1850s. In the late 1870s, Washington County builder Rolla Merydith was getting anywhere from $6.50 to $7.17 per linear foot for Long truss bridges built of yellow poplar. At that time, a truss built of yellow poplar was a little more expensive than a truss built of oak which was 50 cents less per linear foot.

OHIO AND THE POPULAR HOWE TRUSS

The year 1840 saw a great advance in bridge design with William Howe's truss which used iron rods as the truss tension members, Figure 49. Like Burr, Town and Long, William Howe was a New Englander, from Spencer, Massachusetts.[30] The Howe truss had great advantages: it could be assembled rapidly and the tension adjusted easily by tightening the nuts on the ends of the tension rods which drew the diagonals firmly against the angle blocks set against the chords. The Howe truss was an immediate success, often eclipsing the Long truss which had appeared a few years earlier. Indeed, the Howe truss is similar to the Long truss, but uses the metal tension rods in place of the wooden truss verticals. Colonel Long claimed patent infringement, but lost his case.[31] The Howe truss was the first wood and metal combination truss to be widely used in Ohio.

The date the first Howe truss was erected in Ohio is unknown, but it was probably a railroad bridge. The railroads were expanding rapidly in Ohio in the 1840s and 1850s and they soon made the Howe truss their bridge of choice. From their earliest days in Ohio until the late 1880s, the railroads built hundreds of sturdy Howe truss bridges. Many of these bridges were left uncovered by the rail roads in their haste to lay track, build bridges and beat the competition. Often, these bridges were covered later. Figure 50 shows a fully-covered Howe truss railroad bridge with smoke vent built into the roof. Most completely covered were some of the Howe pony trusses whose sides were so well-boarded that railroad inspectors found inspection difficult. One railroad inspector in the 1860s remarked that the well-covered Howe trusses were in better condition than some of the iron bridges. The height of a full-size railroad Howe truss ran from 19 feet to 21 feet and a pony or half Howe would range in height from 6 feet to 12 feet. As mentioned earlier, the deck Howe truss, where the rails were laid on top of the trusses, was frequently used for the railroad bridges.

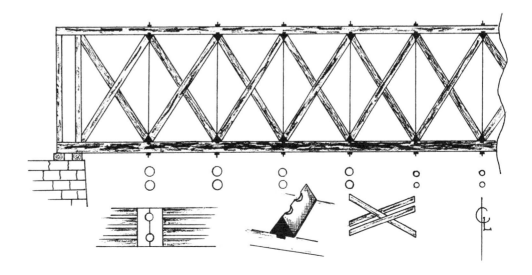

Figure 49. Detail Sketch of the Howe Truss Including the Metal Truss Block

Figure 50. Howe truss railroad bridge

A series of reports by the Superintendent of Railroads and Telegraphs to the Governor of Ohio, 1869 to 1888, contains a tremendous amount of material on the railroad bridges of Ohio. In some cases, enough information is given in these old Railroad Reports (as we refer to them here) that someone could reproduce one of these old bridges exactly. From the old Railroad Reports we learned that the Baltimore and Ohio Railroad's Central Division which ran east from Columbus through Licking, Muskingum, Guernsey and Belmont Counties to the Ohio River, had many Howe truss bridges of all types and sizes. In Belmont County alone there were 12 through Howe truss bridges, all over McMahon Creek, seven of which were fully-covered. The Railroad Reports describe Bridge #34 as an 8 panel, 80 foot Howe truss built in 1870 by carpenters of the Baltimore and Ohio Railroad. The Howe trusses were 19 feet in height. This bridge set on masonry foundations laid up on solid rock. The siding was whitewashed and extended inside to the first truss counterbrace (called a counter in the Railroad Reports).[32]

While some of the railroads like the Baltimore and Ohio and Wheeling and Lake Erie had their own crews of carpenters working year round, other rail lines had their bridges built by independent companies. Such was the case with the Columbus and Hocking Valley Railroad, some of whose bridges were built by

Dodge, Case and Company of Columbus, Ohio. The well-known Smith Bridge Company of Toledo, Ohio built many Howe and combination truss bridges for the railroads. Thatcher, Burt and Company of Cleveland built Howe trusses for both rail and highway use.

By the second half of the 19th Century, some railroad combination trusses had as much metal in them as wood. In these railroad combination trusses, the upper chords and end posts were usually wood beams while the lower chords were metal. The truss arrangements were of both metal and wooden beams, the designs differing from company to company. In 1882, the Clinton Bridge Company of Iowa built a combination wood and metal truss bridge over Honey Creek near New Carlisle in Miami County for the Cleveland, Columbus and Indianapolis Railroad. At some later and unknown date, Miami County obtained this bridge from the railroad and moved it nearby to span Honey Creek on a township road. The Honey Creek Bridge was torn down in 1979 and very few people realized at that time that the last of Ohio's combination truss railroad bridges was being removed, Figure 51.

Figure 51. The Honey Creek railroad bridge
Ohio's last combination truss railroad bridge

At times, the old Railroad Reports were very wordy and at others, quite terse, but in spite of this, one fact is very clear: the railroad bridges in Ohio were quite well-maintained and there were few reports of wooden bridge failures. No passenger deaths were recorded from 1869 to 1888 as a result of the collapse of a timber truss bridge. However, a fairly new through Howe truss collapsed under a freight train in Ross County in 1884, but it was determined that it was the failure of the wood pilings that supported the bridge and not the truss itself. The early railroad bridges were often built on wooden foundations instead of stone abutments.

Not all the Howe truss bridges in Ohio were built to serve the railroads. Indeed, it became a very popular truss design for use on our highways, even though it tended to be more expensive than an all-wood truss. Here are some examples. Ohio's longest covered bridge, the 234 foot Harpersfield Bridge in Ashtabula County, is a Howe truss built in 1868, Figure 52. Well-known Greene County bridge builder Henry E. Hebble built several Howe trusses

Figure 52. The Harpersfield Bridge

there during his career and two are still in existence today: the Glen Helen (Cemetery Road) Bridge and the Charlton Mill Bridge, both built in the 1880s. August Borneman of Fairfield County was another builder who put up sturdy Howe trusses and three of his bridges are still standing today: Hills in Washington County, Johnson in Fairfield, and Kidwell in Athens County. The Anderson Company of

Sidney, Ohio was another Ohio bridge-building firm that specialized in the Howe truss. Their McColly Bridge, built in Logan County in 1876, still serves daily traffic.

As mentioned above, the Howe trusses were more expensive to build and seldom cost less than $12.00 per linear foot. The Anderson Company was charging from $11.50 to $13.35 per linear foot for Howe trusses in the 1870s. Borneman was paid $14.50 per linear foot for the 100 foot Johnson Bridge in 1887.

The advent of the Howe truss was significant in bridge building history because of its use of iron tension rods as the truss verticals. It was one of the first steps toward the all-metal bridges that were to eclipse the building of wooden trusses by the late 1800s.

THE CHILDS TRUSS
AND EVERETT S. SHERMAN

Another wooden bridge truss that makes use of iron rods is the Childs truss, patented in 1846 by Horace Childs of Henniker, New Hampshire, Figure 53. Childs was a bridge builder and agent for the Long truss. The Childs truss is basically like the Long truss, but makes use of iron rods instead of wood for the counterbraces.

The Childs truss was never used (as far as anyone now knows) until 1883 when Everett S. Sherman, Figure 54, of Delaware County, Ohio used it in the Chambers Road Bridge in that county. In an attempt to explain Sherman's choice of the Child's truss, some bridge historians have claimed that he was a native of New England. Research has shown that he was born in Ohio in 1831, a son of David T. and Sarah Sherman, natives of Connecticut who came to Ohio between 1827 and 1831. David T. Sherman was a bridge builder who built several large bridges in Delaware County, including the two-lane, three-span White Sulphur Spring Bridge over the Scioto River in 1859 and the Lavender Bridge over the Scioto in 1869. These bridges were built on the Burr truss design.

Little is known of Everett Sherman's early career although by the late 1860s his name appeared in the Delaware County records as a bridge builder. The Delaware County records show that Sherman built a covered bridge over

Figure 54. Everett S Sherman, Builder of many Childs truss bridges in Ohio 1831 -1897

Walnut Creek at Sunbury in 1867; one over Fulton Creek in 1874; and a 240 foot two-span Burr truss over the Scioto River in 1877. He had his own bridge building business in Galena in Delaware County in the 1870s, and while living and working there, he was issued a patent for a low truss combination of wood and iron. His brochures from that period advertise that he would build covered bridges on the Howe, Burr or Sherman plan. The latter was probably the Childs truss.

The last mention of Everett S. Sherman in the Delaware County records was his contract to build the Chambers Road Bridge in 1883, Figure 55. In the late 1880s, Sherman moved west to Preble County in answer to a summons from the county engineer, Robert Eaton Lowery, who advised him of bridge contracts to be let in the wake of a disastrous storm in May 1887, which devastated roads and bridges there. Mr. Lowery, it should be mentioned here, was also a native of Delaware County and obviously knew Everett Sherman from earlier contacts. Packing up his Childs truss model, Sherman headed out for an extended career in a new environment. He built 15 Childs truss bridges in Preble County from 1887 to 1895.[33] He died in 1897 at age 66 and is buried with his family in the Berkshire Township Cemetery in Delaware County.

Figure 53. Sketch of the Childs Truss Design

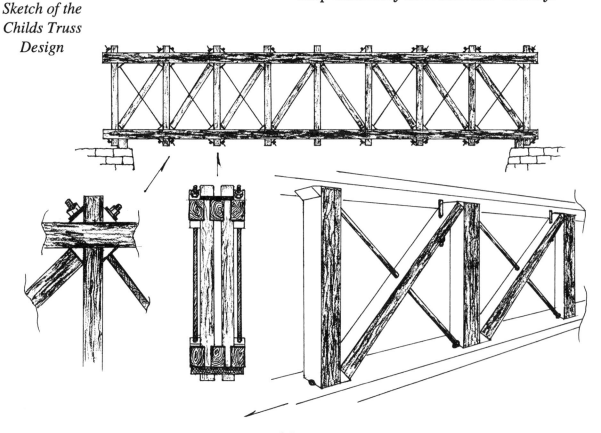

Figure 55. The Chambers Road Bridge

THE PRATT TRUSS

New Englander Caleb Pratt patented a wood and iron combination truss in 1846, Figure 56. The Pratt truss featured wooden end posts, upper chords and truss verticals. The lower chords were iron or steel. The braces, or truss diagonals were wrought iron tension rods. In the Pratt truss, the verticals are in compression and the diagonals are in tension, just the opposite of the Howe truss.[34] The Pratt

combination truss was little-used in Ohio for full-size wooden bridge construction, although it was possibly used to some extent on the railroads. We know of no full-size, covered Pratt truss in Ohio until 1986 when Ashtabula County Engineer John Smolen designed and built a 96 foot Pratt truss to span the west branch of the Ashtabula River on Caine Road in Pierpont Township, Figure 57. But, Ohio had many Pratt combination pony trusses built for highway use. As an example, Figure 58 shows the former Beasley Run bridge near Camden in Preble County.

Figure 57. Ashtabula County's Caine Road Bridge

In 1852, the first all-metal Pratt truss was built and it was widely-used for both railroad and highway bridges for many years. Some of Ohio's rapidly disappearing metal truss highway bridges are of the old Pratt design, built before 1900. These old bridges, like our covered wooden spans, are usually to be found on little-used back roads and are worthy of documentation before they are all gone.

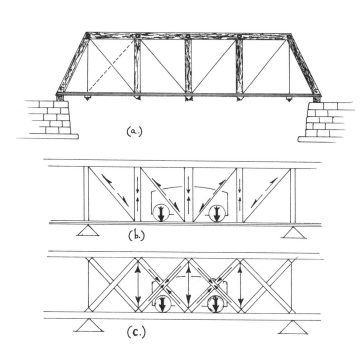

Figure 56.
a. The Pratt Truss
b. Vertical Posts in compression
c. Vertical posts in tension in a Howe truss

Figure 58. Pratt Pony Truss

ROBERT W. SMITH
AND THE SMITH TRUSS

In 1867, Robert W. Smith of Tipp City, Ohio was issued patent No.66,900 for an all-wooden bridge truss and thus began an illustrious bridge building career. Smith, Figure 59, was born in Miami County, Ohio in 1833, a son of William and Juliana Thomas Smith who had come to Ohio in 1815 from Maryland. Mrs. Smith educated Robert at home until he was 15 at which time he went to school for six weeks to study geometry which he later said was most helpful to him in his career. His brother William had a lumber yard and woodworking business where Robert worked for two years. In the mid-1850s, Smith invented a self-supporting truss for large barns and he built such a barn on his father-in-law's farm. Few details are known about this truss since it was never patented.[35]

The first mention of Robert W. Smith in the Miami County Commissioners Journals was in 1866 in reference to his rafter plan for bridges. (The rafter plan was a pony truss.) Smith built his first fully-covered bridges in 1867 in Miami County at Milton over the Stillwater River and at Knoops Crossing of Lost Creek. These two Smith trusses may have been built using the 1867 patent. In 1869, about the time Smith was issued his second bridge patent, No.97,714, he moved his business north to Toledo to take advantage of better transportation facilities. There in his bridge yards, Figure 60, he would prefabricate bridge trusses to order and then ship them to their destination via rail or canal, where they would be erected under the supervision of a Smith Bridge Company agent or foreman. The Smith truss was advertised as

Figure 59. Robert W. Smith

being light, yet strong. It featured braces set at 45 degrees and counterbraces set at 60 degrees.

The 1869 patent was used many times and improved upon several times over the years. The late Raymond E. Wilson, mechanical engineer from Swarthmore, Pennsylvania, made a thorough study of the Smith truss and divided it into four categories: Type I was the 1867 patent where the center panel was an open V; Type II was the 1869 patent and had single truss Xs with the open V center panel; Type III was quite similar to Type II, but had extra diagonal braces on the center panel; type IV had double diagonals the full length of the bridge with single diagonals intersecting the doubles. Figure 61 shows the 1869 patented

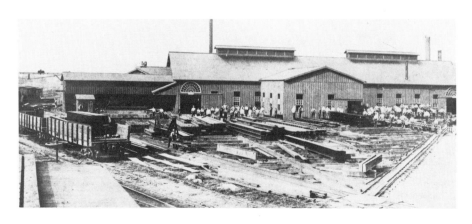

Figure 60. The Smith Bridge Company Yards at Toledo, Ohio

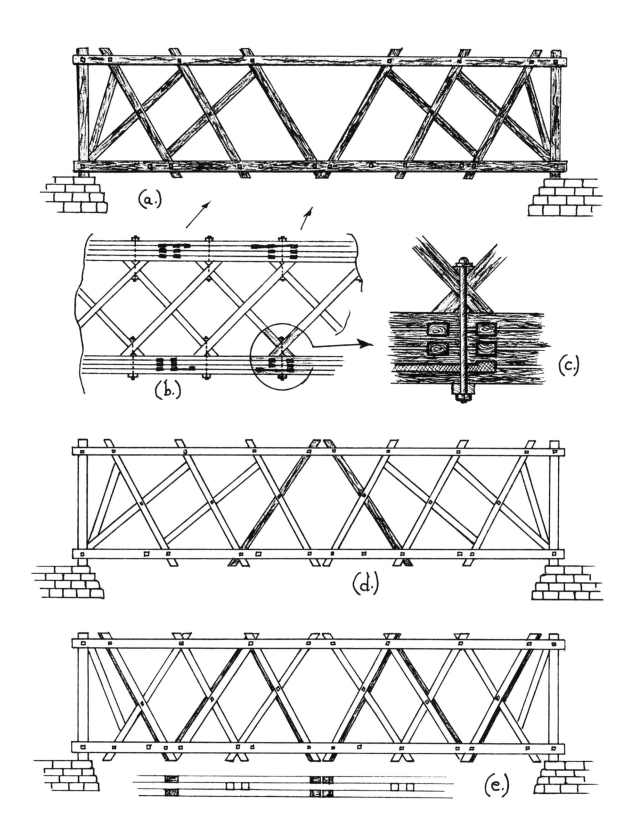

Figure 61. The Smith truss design: top is the 1869 patent with truss construction details. a. Side view of 1869 truss patent, b. Plan view of bottom chords and floor beams, c. Attatchment detail of floor beams to bottom chords, d. Side view of "improved" Smith truss with two center diagonals, e. Side view of "improved" Smith truss with single and diagonal timbers. Neither d. or e. was ever patented.

Figure 62. Smith Combination truss railroad bridge under constrution, 1873

design and the two unpatented improvements. According to Mr. Wilson, the Type IV variation was generally used after 1875. Although often used, neither Type III or IV was patented.[36]

The Smith Bridge Company built their all-wood trusses in full-height, through styles or in the low or pony design. They also built Howe and Warren trusses and were among the early builders of other combination wood and metal and all metal bridges. One of their very large combination truss bridges intended for railway use is shown in Figure 62. This bridge had trusses that were 30 feet in height; it was 80 feet above low water level and about 200 feet long.

Smith Bridge Company representatives with rights to build the Smith truss worked in Ohio and surrounding states and as far west as California and Oregon. In 1891, the Smith Bridge Company was sold and became the Toledo Bridge Company. Robert W. Smith died in 1898. Some outstanding examples of the work of his company still stand in Ohio today: the Otway Bridge in Scioto County, 1874; South Salem Bridge in Ross County, 1873; and the Stevenson Road Bridge in Greene County, 1877, to name a few.

Because it was a patented truss design, it was more expensive to build the all-wood Smith truss than the simple Buckingham truss. Smith trusses generally cost from $13.00 to $17.00 per linear foot. Ross County paid the Smith

Bridge Company $18.75 per linear foot for the South Salem Bridge--rather a high price, but other bids for the same bridge were even higher--up to $21.75 per linear foot. The giant Philo/Duncan Falls Bridge over the Muskingum River in Muskingum County cost $15.25 per lineal foot in 1874. A two-span low Smith truss built at Rockbridge in Hocking County in 1874 cost $8.00 per linear foot. A high, open double truss in the same county in 1877 cost $14.25 per linear foot.

The construction of Smith truss bridges was handled differently in Jackson County. There, in 1869, the County Commissioners contacted Robert W. Smith to purchase plans for bridges and abutments. They reasoned that they could build the bridges cheaper by paying royalties to Robert Smith for his designs and by hiring local builders to put up the structures. Jackson County paid Smith 50 cents per foot for a 60 foot bridge and 75 cents per foot for 70 foot bridges. The main reason that Jackson County turned to Smith for bridge plans was a law passed by the Ohio Legislature in 1867 which stated that any county planning to build a bridge costing $1,000. or more had to have the plans for such bridges drawn up by an architect. No doubt this law is what also prompted Washington County officials to hire Civil Engineer C.C. Lymon to draw up the bridge plans for use in that county in 1867 (see section on the Long truss).

THE PARTRIDGE TRUSS

While Robert W. Smith was establishing himself as one of this state's leading bridge builders, Reuban L. Partridge of Marysville in Union County, Figure 63, was quietly building his reputation as an excellent bridge contractor, on a more local basis. Partridge was born in

Figure 63. Reuban L. Partridge

1823 in Essex County, New York and came to Marysville in 1836 with his widowed mother to be near relatives. He went to a one room school for a short time and then began to learn the wagonmaker and carpenters trade.[37]

In 1872, Reuban L. Partridge was issued patent #127,791 for his all-wood bridge truss, which is very similar to the Smith patent. For example, the Partridge truss also features braces set at 45 degrees and counterbraces set at 60 degrees. The counterbraces of this truss are double timbers and both braces and counterbraces rest against a special metal bifurcated shoe, Figure 64, which would seem to be the main difference between the Smith and Partridge truss. It took two years for Partridge to get his bridge truss patented. Patent Office investigators felt his patent was too much like that of Robert W. Smith. According to U.S.

Patent Office Records, Partridge was rejected on his patent application three times and it wasn't until the Patent Office received a letter from the Union County Commissioners praising Partridge's "Block Bridge" as superior to Smith's patent, that the patent investigators finally relented and granted Partridge his patent.[38]

Six Partridge truss bridges remain in Ohio today and none of them follow the patent design closely and no two are alike. In Union County, where five of these sturdy bridges remain in the 1990s, the trusses have been heavily reinforced with iron rods. Two of Partridge's Union County bridges have recently been completely renovated as will be discussed in the Union County section. Perhaps the most outstanding of the six remaining Partridge truss bridges is Franklin County's Bergstresser/Dietz Bridge built in 1887 by the Columbus Bridge Company. At that time, Partridge was vice-president in charge of construction with the Columbus Bridge Company, which explains the choice of the Partridge truss. The Bergstresser Bridge is 134 feet long with a clear span of 119 feet. It is built with double and triple truss timbers making for a very sound and impressive structure, Figure 65. The Columbus Bridge Company built a Partridge truss bridge in Fairfield County in 1888, but as far as we know now, Partridge built the rest of his patented truss bridges in the 1870s and early 1880s in Union and Delaware Counties.

Figure 65. Partridge trusses of the Bergstresser/Dietz Bridge

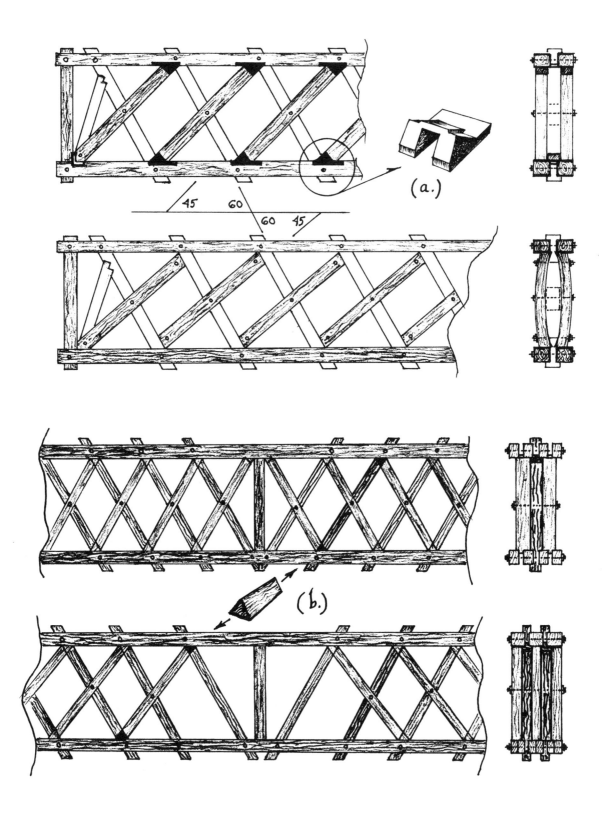

Figure 64. The Partridge Truss Design showing truss construction details and,
a. the bifurcated metal shoe truss support block of the original patent and,
b. the wooden truss support block as used in the Bergstresser/Dietz Bridge

Unlike Smith, Partridge's career kept him in central Ohio. His largest bridge was a three span, 271 foot Partridge truss over the Scioto River at Bellepoint, built in 1877, Figure 66. Reuban L. Partridge was active in his chosen career to the end of his life. In 1900, at the age of 77, he was fatally injured in a fall through the timbers of a bridge being removed in Union County.[39]

Figure 66. Partridge's Bellpoint Bridge

THE WARREN TRUSS

In the mid 19th Century, a wooden bridge truss was designed and patented by two Englishmen, James Warren and T.W. Morzani.[40] This truss, intended to be built of steel, featured a large number of braces set on an angle between the chords with no rods or truss verticals. This series of braces suggests the letter W to some while others see it as a series of inverted Vs. An American, Russell Warren, designed but never patented a wooden bridge truss very similar to the Warren/Morzani truss of 1848.[41] It is impossible for us to say at this date just how the rare wooden version of this design as used in Ohio evolved. Figure 67 shows a sketch of the Warren truss as found in Ohio bridges.

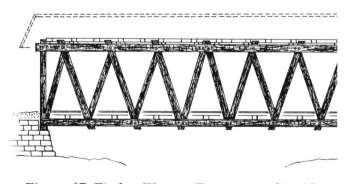

Figure 67. Timber Warren Truss as used in Ohio

The Warren truss has been used in steel bridge building for many years and is still a common sight on our highways today. The wooden Warren truss is something of an oddity, however, and it is believed that most of the covered bridges built on this plan were built here in Ohio. There were at least 13 Warren truss bridges built in Greene County, some by the Smith Bridge Company and some by Henry E. Hebble. E.B. Henderson, who built so many Buckingham trusses in Ohio, built a Warren truss in Washington County in the 1870s.

Thomas Fisher of Muskingum County built the 80 foot Warren truss owned by the Ohio Historic Bridge Association (formerly the Southern Ohio Covered Bridge Association) in 1876 for $8.00 per linear foot. He called it his Plan Number 4, Figure 68. Two other Warren trusses still stand in Ohio, the Carillon Park Bridge in Dayton, built by the Smith Bridge Company in

Figure 68. Johnson's Mill or Salt Creek Bridge, owned by OHBA

1870 in Greene County and moved to the Park in 1948. The arches were added at that time. The other Warren truss standing in Montgomery County is also a transplant from Greene County. The Jasper Road Bridge was built in 1877 and moved to the Mudlick Estates southwest of Dayton in 1964. This bridge has the arch-like reinforcing brace, with metal tension rods that were added to some of the Greene County Warren trusses after 1930.

The Warren truss bridges, close cousins of the popular multiple kingpost/ Buckingham trusses, ran about $8.00 per linear foot in the 1870s. In Greene County where most of these bridges were built, the cost ran from $6.50 to $14. per linear foot.

THE WHEELER TRUSS

In addition to the well-known bridge trusses, Ohio has had its share of the unusual types. In 1870, Isaac H. Wheeler of Sciotoville in Scioto County, patented an all-wood bridge truss, No.107,576, that is somewhat difficult to describe. It featured a horizontal timber midway between the upper and lower chords that might be referred to as a third chord. The center and end truss uprights were vertical, but uprights between center and end verticals were flared 22 degrees to look more like truss diagonals than posts. All of the uprights were tied (bolted) to each chord at each intersection and each upright was braced with additional short timbers as shown in Figure 69. The Wheeler truss as used in the bridge over Symmes Creek at Waterloo in Lawrence County seemed to have followed the patent design closely, but the McDaniel/Sulphur Spring Bridge in Scioto County was quite a conglomeration with what appeared to be pony Warren trusses added to the Wheeler trusses, Figure 70. As far as is known now, only six Wheeler trusses were built in Ohio: McDaniel, Snodgrass, Holman and White Gravel in Scioto County and Waterloo and Hanging Rock in Lawrence County.

Figure 70. McDaniel Bridge, A Wheeler truss

However, still standing in Greenup County Kentucky is the Bennett Mill Bridge, a fine example of the Wheeler Truss, built circa 1875.

Isaac Hastings Wheeler was born in Ohio, c.1815 to Luther and Rebecca Hastings Wheeler who came here from New Hampshire. Little is known of the early life of Isaac Wheeler or his bridge building career. At age 29, Wheeler became Sheriff of Scioto County, a position he held for two years. He owned and operated the Wallace Mill on Rocky Fork Creek in Madison Township and for a time, was a miller in Harrison Township. His name was first mentioned in the Scioto County bridge records in 1872 when the contract for the Snodgrass Bridge over the Little Scioto River was let to C.H. Walden at $7.99 per linear foot on the "Wheeler" plan. It is recorded that Wheeler received $1.00 per foot royalty for the use of his truss patent.

Since Wheeler was the miller at the Wallace Mill, it is quite possible that he designed and built the old covered bridge there that used the

Figure 69. Wheeler truss patented 1870 by Isaac H. Wheeler of Scioto County, Ohio

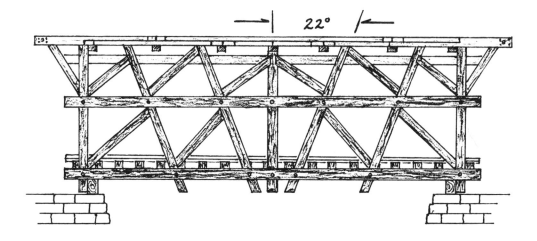

massive Warren pony trusses, Figure 71. A study of the Smith Bridge Company records reveals that Isaac H. Wheeler of Scioto County was one of that company's agents in southern Ohio. It may have been Wheeler's salesmanship that influenced the Scioto County Commissioners to build the Smith truss at Otway and the three Smith trusses over Turkey Creek in Niles Township.

While the Snodgrass Bridge in Scioto County went for just under $8.00 per linear foot in 1872, the following year Lawrence County paid Wheeler $18.00 per linear foot for the Hanging Rock Bridge. These bridges were about the same length, so the price difference in the same time period in adjoining counties is unexplainable.

Figure 72. Germantown Bridge built in 1865 over Little Twin Creek at Germantown

Figure 71. Massive Warren pony trusses of the Wallace Mill Bridge in Scioto County, Ohio

THOSE INNOVATIVE COMBINATION TRUSSES

Bridge builders with a bent towards innovation turned out some unusual combination wood and metal bridges here in Ohio. Two outstanding examples of such bridges still stand today: the Germantown Bridge in Montgomery County, Figure 72, and the John Bright #2 Bridge, Figure 73, in Fairfield County. The trusses of these bridges are quite similar. Both have wooden end posts that support wooden upper chords and the ends of the inverted arch

Figure 73. John Bright #2 Bridge built 1881

which is formed of steel eye-bars. Wooden intermediate verticals extend between the upper chord and the steel arch at regular panel intervals. The floor beams are hung from steel stirrups from the eye-bar/wooden vertical intersects. There are no lower chords. The Germantown Bridge has always been roofed, but never sided, while the John Bright Bridge has always been fully-covered.[42] Both of these unusual bridges have been moved from their original locations. The Germantown Bridge was built in 1865 to serve the Germantown-Dayton Pike and in 1911 it was moved to Center Street in Germantown. The John Bright Bridge was built in 1881 to span Poplar Creek in Liberty Township where it served until the late 1980s when it was moved to the Lancaster Campus of Ohio University on SR 37 where it was rebuilt over Fetters Run.

The Germantown Bridge has had two major renovations: in the early 1960s and in 1981. In February 1981, a speeding car out of control struck one corner post of the bridge, causing the entire bridge to collapse a few minutes later, Figure 74. The citizens of Germantown formed a Covered Bridge Committee and with generous donations of labor and money, were able to completely rebuild their old landmark. For the sake of preservation, they closed the bridge to all but pedestrian traffic.

Figure 74. Germantown Bridge lies in a creek after being struck by speeding car.

The names of three bridge builders come to mind whenever the John Bright or Germantown Bridges are mentioned: David H. Morrison, August Borneman and William B. Black. These men had outstanding bridge building careers in Ohio and while they built bridges having other truss designs, it is their combination trusses that are of special interest to us, not only due to design innovations but also because they pioneered in using considerable quantities of iron in the trusses of their structures.

DAVID H. MORRISON

David H. Morrison was one of the state's most outstanding bridge designers and contractors. He was born in 1817 and his professional life spanned the period of the 1830s to 1882. He was educated at the Dayton Academy and entered the field of civil engineering under the guidance of one of his instructors, Elijah J. Barney.[43]

During the 1850s, Morrison turned out some very innovative bridge designs in wood, metal and stone. He designed a wooden truss in 1852 which combined elements of the Howe, Burr and McCallum trusses being built for the railroads of that era. He built a bridge of this design in Dayton in 1855. Morrison built Burr truss bridges in the 1850s and in 1859 he built the best known of these bridges, his three span Burr truss aquaduct that carried the Miami and Erie Canal over the Great Miami River.[44] See Figure 14 for the artist's conception of this aquaduct with roof and sides removed to reveal the interior structure and purpose. Another Morrison design was one which he called the "Rafter Bridge". No pictures are known to exist of this design, but from the descriptions we have from the Greene County Commissioners Journals, we believe those bridges to have been a type of low wood truss with sides well-covered and capped on top. Robert W. Smith also had designs for "rafter bridges" which were used in Miami County.

Morrison's most outstanding designs were his suspension bridges. In 1858, he designed a suspension bridge with an inverted metal arch and wooden end posts and top chords. No known examples were built until 1865 with the construction of the Germantown Bridge.[45] This

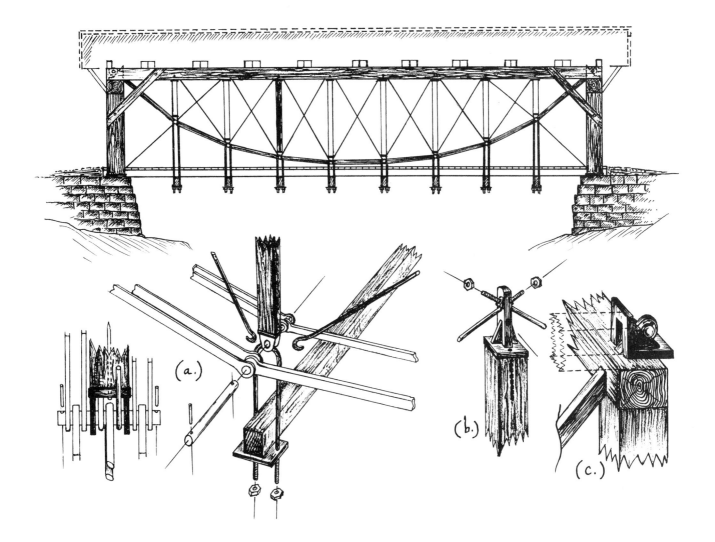

bridge as earlier described has several unique features as shown in Figure 75.

Morrison built other bridges on this plan including the English Bridge, a three span structure over the Auglaize River in Defiance County in 1875. Using this same design in all metal, Morrison built the four span Main Street Bridge over the Great Miami River at Dayton and it was considered to be one of the major bridges of his career. Morrison went on to patent an all metal bowstring truss in 1867. A fine example of this can be seen today in Putnam County, Ohio. D.H. Morrison taught his skills in bridge building and management to his son Charles Carroll Morrison who became his business partner in a company formed in 1868. The names D.H. and C.C. Morrison are found frequently in the county records of Ohio. This company became the Columbia Bridge Works. D.H. Morrison died in 1882 and his family carried on his work.[46]

Figure 75. Detailed sketch of the truss design of the Germantown Bridge. a. Vertical post, arch intersect, b. Vertical post, upper chord intersect, c. End post detail

Figure 75 d. Interior view of Germantown Bridge

AUGUST BORNEMAN AND WILLIAM B. BLACK

While much is known of the life and work of D.H. Morrison, comparatively little is known about the builder of the John Bright Bridges, August Borneman, a Prussian immigrant born February 1, 1843.[47] He came to this country circa 1864, perhaps for the freedom to pursue the career of his choice, an amenity not available to the average Prussian of the 1870s. According to his obituary, Borneman did serve in the Prussian army.

The first mention of August Borneman in the records of Fairfield County was as the partner of William Black. Black was a well-known bridge contractor in Fairfield County at that time and he operated his own bridge works in Lancaster, the county seat. His company, the Ohio Iron and Bridge Company, built all-wood and combination truss bridges and at one time, he was probably an agent for the Smith Bridge Company because we know he built one Smith truss, the Ruffner Bridge in Fairfield County in 1875. That same year, Black was granted a patent on his all-metal suspension truss, No.166,960, that is quite similar to the McGuffey Girder Patent of 1862, No.33,954. Both of these truss designs are shown in Figure 76.

In 1877, Black and Borneman announced the opening of their new bridge works in Lancaster.[48] They were bidding on bridge contracts offering their patented suspension truss, all wood or combination truss bridges, building mainly in their home county, but also in neighboring Licking and Perry Counties and in Champaign County to the northwest. Then, in 1878, August Borneman bid on and won a bridge contract in his own name. The partnership of Black and Borneman was obviously over and little more was heard of William Black in Fairfield County. In 1879, Black moved his business to Urbana in Champaign County where he continued in business into the early 1890s.[49]

August Borneman seemed to enjoy a very good relationship with the Fairfield County officials after the dissolution of his partnership with William Black as he was the premier bridge builder in the county from 1878 to 1889. Borneman founded the Hocking Valley Bridge Works in late 1878. This is the company name he used when bidding on contracts outside of Fairfield County. At home he used the name August Borneman or Gus Borneman.

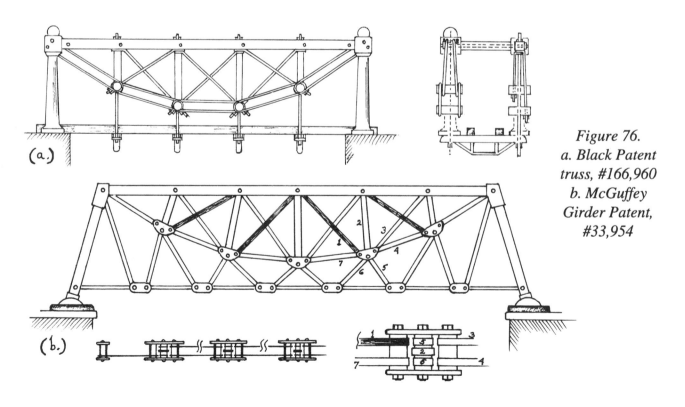

(a.)

(b.)

Figure 76.
a. Black Patent truss, #166,960
b. McGuffey Girder Patent, #33,954

In 1879, Borneman patented an all-metal suspension truss of his own, No. 219,846, a low truss with concrete or stone pillars as end posts, Figure 77. A few of these products of the Hocking Valley Bridge Works are still standing in Fairfield County today. In 1881, the Gallia County Commissioners contracted with Borneman for the plans and iron for four of his patented bridges and they were to pay him $5.00 each for these plans.

Figure 78. Metal truss support block used in all Borneman-built Howe trusses

Figure 77. Borneman's metal suspension truss

August Borneman would build any type of bridge that was wanted, Howe, combination, all-wood or all-metal trusses, in either high through trusses or low pony styles. His sturdy Howe trusses had metal angle blocks seated on the triple lower chords against which the ends of the braces rested, Figure 78. One of these fine Howe trusses still spans Clear Creek in Fairfield County, Figure 79. His Blacklick Bridge built in 1888, also featured these iron angle blocks. Probably the largest Howe truss built by August Borneman was the 472 foot Warsaw Bridge over the Walhonding River in Coshocton County, erected in 1882.

In 1881, Borneman built the John Bright #2 Bridge over Poplar Creek in Fairfield County for $13.25 per linear foot. Figure 80 shows a detailed drawing of the truss of this bridge. The John Bright Bridge was referred to in county records as a combination bridge, roofed and sided. This inverted arch suspension truss bears some similarity to Black's 1875 patent and an even greater similarity to the McGuffey Girder patented in 1862, Figure 76. It is entirely possible that Borneman developed the plans

for his suspension truss bridges from these two patents.

A unique feature of covered bridges built by August Borneman is the metal sway bracing used to stabilize the roof systems. This bracing is between side panel verticals and consists of a metal ring with four metal tension rods as shown in Figure 81. This unusual bracing is found in the four Borneman-built covered bridges still standing in Ohio today: Kidwell, Johnson, Hills and John Bright #2. In the John Bright #2 Bridge which has no lower chords, Borneman also used the sway bracing between

Figure 79. Johnson Bridge, A Borneman Howe truss

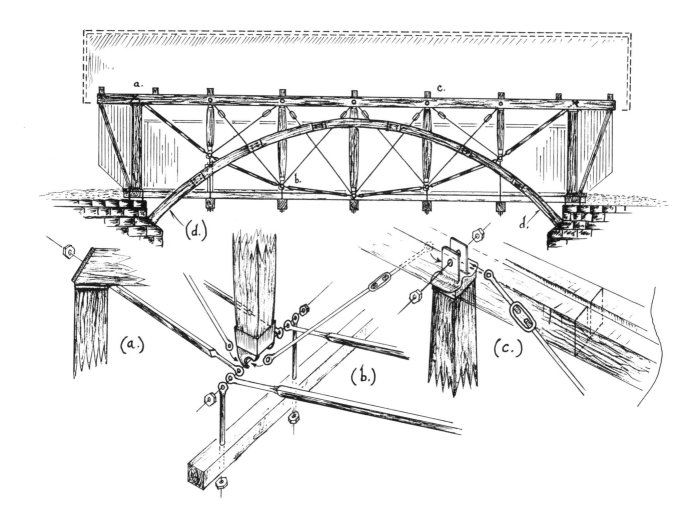

the floor beams to provide extra stability for the floor system.

Borneman was hired in 1881 by the Athens County Commissioners to build a high combination truss, covered, over the Hocking River at Athens. This may have been one of the inverted suspension trusses like John Bright #2. No pictures of this bridge are known to exist.

Figure 80. Detailed sketch of the truss design of the John Bright #2 Bridge. a. End post detail, b. Vertical post, arch intersect, c. Vertical post, upper chord intersect, d. Wooden arch, a latter addition

In 1884, August Borneman was hired to build the Smith's Mill Bridge, the all-metal suspension truss that is known today as John Bright #1 Bridge, Figure 82. John Bright #1 spanned Poplar Creek just around the corner from the John Bright #2 covered bridge. The all-metal suspension bridge replaced a covered combination truss built in 1876 by Black and Borneman. County records do not give the price per linear foot of John Bright #1, but the total price came to over $2,000.00 for a 90 foot structure indicating a price of about $22.00 per foot. In construction details, this bridge is very similar to its covered counterpart. Like John Bright #2, the all-metal bridge has been moved to Ohio University's Lancaster Campus where it will be rebuilt.

Figure 81. Detail of the Borneman roof sway bracing, also used for floor system of John Bright #2 Bridge

Figure 82. John Bright #1 Bridge

In the prime of his life, in the spring of 1889, August Borneman died of "Neuralgia Hart" to quote from his death certificate. He had been married only three years and had no children. As far as is known, he owned no property except the bridge works. August Borneman was a brilliant inventor and builder who invented and manufactured farm equipment in addition to his bridge contracting career. His final resting place is unknown, but his monuments are the bridges still standing that he designed and built, most especially the unique John Bright Bridges of Fairfield County.

After the death of August Borneman, his widow sold the Hocking Valley Bridge Works to Benjamin F. Dum, former Fairfield County Auditor. The rights to the 1879 patent obviously went with the business as Dum built several of these low metal trusses around the county. Benjamin Dum and his son, H.C. Dum, carried on the work of the Hocking Valley Bridge Works. They built a covered bridge to span Clear Creek at Written Rock in 1891 and replaced it with another covered bridge in 1900. Benjamin Dum went bankrupt in 1907 and two of his sons bought the company and continued to run it until 1911. [50]

THE FOUNDATIONS-
SANDSTONE AND LIMESTONE

Well known or obscure, educated engineer or skilled farmer/carpenter, Ohio's bridge builders contributed greatly to the development of the Buckeye State. Except to their descendants or to researchers, their names are largely unknown today, but their bridges stand as fitting monuments to these pioneer builders.

Even less remembered and honored are the masons whose fine craftsmanship provided the firm foundations for the old covered spans. While it is true that some masons traveled widely to build bridge abutments, the majority of the foundations were built by local craftsmen.

In the early days, bridges were sometimes set on foundations of wood pilings instead of cut-stone abutments. Figure 83 shows Ross County's Stockman Bridge, a tied arch structure built on wooden foundations. The railroads often built their bridges on timber pilings. However, a bridge is only as sturdy as its foundations and a bridge built on wooden pilings is more vulnerable to damage from high water than one that is built on solid masonry. While foundations of sandstone or limestone did cost more initially, they more than paid for themselves in years of service. Many of Ohio's older steel truss bridges set on masonry foundations once occupied by a covered bridge.

Figure 83. The Stockman Bridge on wood foundations

A good foundation of cut-stone could cost as much or more than the bridge itself. The total cost of the masonry for the Lindsey Ford Bridge over the Scioto River in Pickaway County was $34,000.--there were two abutments and two piers. The wooden superstructure of the Lindsey Bridge cost only $12,000. Stonework was usually priced by the perch--a perch being 24.75 cubic feet. As a general rule, the cost of stonework was from $3.50 per perch to $7.00 per perch in the second half of the 19th Century. The price could be lower if the same builder did both bridge and masonry.

Many of the men who built Ohio's covered bridges were also competant stone masons: G.W. Pilcher of Vinton County, the Shrakes of Licking County (whose names are found in county records all over southern Ohio), E.B. Henderson of Washington County and Henry E. Hebble of Greene County, to name a few. An outstanding example of the masonry work of E.B. Henderson may be found in the Hills Bridge in Washington County, Figure 84.

Figure 85. Dry-laid abutments of the former Ormiston Bridge in Washington County

Figure 84. Hills Bridge, Washington County, foundations laid up by E.B. Henderson

Ohio's covered bridges were set on abutments of either sandstone or limestone, usually quarried nearby to avoid hauling such heavy loads long distances. In the case of the Hune Bridge in Washington County, the stone was quarried right there on the Hune farm. County Commissioners seldom got specific on the details of the stonework for their bridges--just the name of the mason and price per perch. In 1881, when Fairfield County was building the John Bright #2 Bridge, the Commissioners got very specific about its foundations. They directed that the abutments were to be of "good black sandstone, well-bedded and grouted with clean, sharp sand and fresh burnt lime". Preble County officials insisted on abutments of blue limestone (a variety prevalent in that area) which was to be grouted. Many Ohio covered bridges were set on foundations that were dry laid, i.e., no grouting at all, Figure 85. Perhaps the strangest specifications in any County Commissioners Journals regarding abutments and

piers can be found in the Miami County records where they directed the masons to put up good foundations of the best quality, second-class masonry.

ROOFING AND PAINTING COVERED BRIDGES

It was the policy of some Ohio counties to specify that the new covered bridges were to be painted. Usually this added about $20. to the total cost of the bridge. It could cost from 25 cents per linear foot to paint the shorter bridges to over a dollar per linear foot for the multi-spanned structures such as the Lindsey Ford Bridge. In that particular case, the Pickaway County Commissioners agreed to pay $500. for two coats of white lead and linseed oil, or three coats of Venetian Red paint if it could be done for the same price. Evidentally, red paint was possible because another name for this bridge was the Red Bridge.

In Preble County's contracts with Everett S. Sherman it was stated that the bridges were to be given three coats of white lead and linseed oil at intervals of several days. Information on painting costs is scarce since many counties opted to leave the wooden bridges unpainted or else they simply included the cost in the bridge contract.

Of course, Ohio's early covered bridges were roofed with wooden shingles. Some contracts specified the type of shingles to be used and it was often "XXX Pine shingles". The 70 foot

National Road Bridge over Salt Creek in Muskingum County was reroofed in the 1870s with XXX Pine shingles for $822. Upstream on Salt Creek, the 80 foot Johnson Mill Bridge got its first roof in 1879 for $172. Since this was the first roof on this bridge, we must assume rafters and sheeting were included, too. When the Ohio Historic Bridge Association bought this bridge in 1960, it had a shingle roof in very poor condition that may well have been the original 1879 roof.

In 1887, Muskingum County officials decided to reroof one of their covered bridges with the new "Tulip" brand tin roof which was to be painted inside and out. Unfortunately, they failed to record the price of this new style roof.

In 1867, Pickaway County paid out a total of $1122. to reroof the three span, 612 foot West High Street Bridge. They used about 120 squares of "Michigan Sawed Shingles" at $9.30 per square. Fairfield County preferred to stick to the wooden shingles for their many covered bridges and in 1908, they were paying $5.95 per square for Oregon Red Cedar shingles. For some reason, they began using galvanized iron to reroof some of their bridges in 1891, while continuing to use the cedar shingles for others.

Perhaps the most unusual roof on an Ohio covered bridge was that found on the little Rumley Crossing Bridge, Figure 86, that was nestled between the main lines of two busy railroads over Conotton Creek in Harrison County. The proximity to these tracks may have prompted county officials to overlay the original wood shingle roof with slate. A slate

Figure 86. Slate Roof of the New Rumley Bridge

roof would have afforded more protection from the sparks of passing locomotives back in the era of the steam engine. The roof held up just fine, but in 1962, the little old bridge proved to be no match for a truck loaded with 12 tons of sand.

Our research has shown a predominant preference on the part of Ohio county officials for using shingles to roof their covered bridges even in the late 1800s and early 1900s when metal roofs were in common use for both residential and commercial buildings. The reason was that in that era the covered timber truss bridge was the economical alternative to the metal truss and this same rule of economy also applied to the choice of roofing materials. A metal roof was a sound investment for buildings whose chimneys spewed out soot and sparks that could ignite a wooden roof. This did not apply to covered bridges and so county officials with an eye towards economy always chose the reliable and cheap shingle roofs.

BRIDGE BUILDING POLICIES

In Chapter Two, the reader has learned about the trusses of Ohio's wooden bridges and about the more outstanding men who built them. We have mentioned the cost of the various wooden truss types as well as the cost of roofing and painting a bridge. The prices for masonry work have also been covered here. What we have not yet mentioned is just how the counties went about paying for the bridges. Did it all come from the county treasuries? By no means. Ohio had an agreement with the United States Government that Ohio would not tax government lands in our state and in return, the government would give 5% of the value of these untaxed lands to the state to use in building roads. Actually, 2% of this money was kept for use on the National Road and 3% went for Ohio's roads. It was not uncommon for county commissioners in the early days to petition the state government for a share of the 3% funds to use in roads and bridges. Sometimes they would get money and sometimes not.

Another way of handling bridge building petitions in the early days was for the county commissioners to offer to pay a certain amount towards a bridge. Then it was up to the petitioners to raise the rest of the necessary funds. They did this by going door to door in the neighborhood where the bridge was to be built and extracting promises or "subscriptions" from these people to help meet the costs. When the petitioners could satisfy the commissioners that the money had been promised, construction could begin. Sometimes the commissioners would appoint a man to go around and collect the money due when the bridge was completed. In some cases, this was left up to the bridge builders themselves--a thankless task one might well imagine. In the case of the Licking Dam Bridge in Licking County, subscribers in arrears were threatened with court action.

Building bridges was an expensive proposition involving not just the foundations and the bridge, but right-of-ways, excavation and embankment work. In April 1867, the Ross County Commissioners laid down some strict conditions to be met by the petitioners for the Kilgore Ford Bridge over the Scioto River. They were to: raise $10,000. towards the bridge; construct the embankments on both sides; and to procure at their own expense a perpetual right-of-way to said bridge. This was an unusual case because the foundations were so expensive: the superstructure cost was $21,892. and the abutments and pier were another $24,134. A very costly bridge indeed.

As the 19th Century drew to a close, many counties began building steel truss (they always called them iron) bridges on the major routes and were still building covered bridges on the lesser-used back roads as a matter of economy. However, Muskingum County did just the opposite in 1886 when they built the multi-span Gaysport Bridge over the Muskingum River. They contracted with the Smith Bridge Company for a fully-covered bridge for $17.50 per linear foot. This was probably a Smith truss. Within sight of this new covered bridge, the same company was hired to put up a steel truss over Dry Riffle Run

on the River Road (SR 60) to replace an old covered bridge.

No matter who built these wooden and combination truss bridges or what they cost, they proved to be a bargain. The majority of Ohio's covered bridges that are still standing today were built in the 1870s and nearly 50 percent are still carrying daily traffic. That adds up to public funds well spent.

COVERED BRIDGE INVENTORY

Facts, figures, fables and photographic documentation concerning the covered bridge in Ohio have long occupied the minds of numerous "bridgers" over quite a period of time. The author, indebtedly and with much appreciation, has drawn upon the collective knowledge of such folks, as well as on the results of her own search for information from various archives. What is believed to be the best of the above has been included in a selected inventory of Ohio's covered bridges in the next eight chapters. Ohio has 88 counties and we have decided to group these counties into eight units based on geographical location. These county groupings are shown below. While this subdivision of Ohio's covered bridges by county regions is somewhat arbitrary, it was the most convenient way to do it and we think the reader will agree. Now, on to Chapter Three and the covered bridges of central Ohio.

CHAPTER III

AT THE HEART OF THE STATE

Delaware, Fairfield, Franklin, Knox, Licking, Madison, Marion, Morrow, Pickaway and Union Counties

Figure 87. Central Ohio Counties

This chapter is devoted to a description of the wooden truss bridges found in this central area of Ohio which include the named counties. These counties lie within the glaciated section of the state known as the Central Plains or Central Lowlands. The topography is not like that found in southeastern Ohio, as it is from flat to gently rolling and is excellent farmland. The drainage in this area is largely from the Scioto, Olentangy and Licking Rivers and their tributaries such as the Alum, Big Walnut, Darby, and Deer Creeks. Columbus, the state capitol, is a hub for the major highways of the region. Many of the highways and rail lines of the area have been there since the mid 1800s. Remnants of the old Ohio and Erie Canal, which served this region from 1825 to the early 1900s, can still be seen today. Covered Bridges were built over each of these transportation arteries

FRANKLIN COUNTY

Franklin County has now been largely overtaken by the urban sprawl of Columbus which has pushed southeast into Fairfield County and north into Delaware County. Such was not the case in 1816 when the State Capitol was moved to Columbus, a rather small town on the east bank of the Scioto River. Franklinton, founded in 1797 by Lucas Sullivant, was on the west bank of the Scioto and was the larger community. In 1815, the State Legislature gave Sullivant the authority to build a tollbridge linking Franklinton and Columbus. This was the first bridge to span the Scioto in Franklin County and was probably an uncovered wood truss. Sullivant's tollbridge served until 1832 when his franchise was sold so that a new toll-free bridge could be built on the site (roughly where West Broad Street now crosses the river). This new bridge was to serve the National Road which was being built through Franklin County in the 1830s. Construction workers under the supervison of Captain Brewerton of the United States Army Corps of Engineers built a fine two-lane, two-span Town truss, 340 foot long on limestone abutments and pier, Figure 6. There were sidewalks on both sides of the bridge. When it was replaced in 1883 after almost 50 years of service, there was still from 3.5 to 6 inches of camber in the lower chords.

Other large covered bridges spanned the Scioto River in this early period of the development of the city of Columbus. One was on West Mound Street (called then the Harrisburg Pike) that was built c.1853 by the Harrisburg Turnpike Company with some assistance from the Franklin County Commissioners who promised to give $2500. towards this bridge on the condition that it NOT be a Town truss. It was replaced in 1890. Two covered bridges carried the Hocking Valley Railroad over the Scioto River in downtown Columbus. Both were three span through-Howe trusses, 369 feet long with 36 truss panels. Both were erected in 1868 by the Dodge, Case Company and both were fully-covered.

As was so often the case, the most popular truss type for early wooden bridges in Franklin County was the Town lattice. Figure 88 shows the trim Geiger Bridge over Blacklick Creek near New Albany. A fine, three-span single lane Town truss spanned the Scioto River on the east edge of Dublin. It was removed in 1885 after serving for 45 years. Near Groveport on the old Lancaster Road there was a long Town truss bridge built in 1850 by Sarber and Myers to span Walnut Creek. Just to the west of Canal Winchester an 81 foot Town truss spanned the canal at Empire Mill. Both mill and bridge burned in 1898 and no trace remains today of road, mill or bridge. In late 1851, the Franklin County Commissioners met their Fairfield County counterparts at Canal Winchester at the old bridge over Walnut Creek which had to be replaced. It was decided to build a new bridge here and the Franklin County officials voiced the opinion that it was too late in the season to put up a "trellis work" bridge. However, a Town truss is what was built the following year with both counties sharing the cost of $3,164.

Figure 88. Geiger Bridge over Blacklick Creek

The popularity of the Town truss in Franklin County declined and no more were built after 1860. Most of the wood truss bridges built in Franklin County after that time were of the multiple kingpost or Howe designs. In 1863, a three-span multiple kingpost truss bridge was built to span the Scioto River at

Fishingers Mill, Figure 89. After serving only 30 years, it was replaced by a steel truss. There were Howe truss bridges that served into the 1940s on Morse Road over Walnut Creek, at Hempy's Grove over Blacklick Creek and on Brice Road, also over Blacklick Creek. In 1948, children playing with firecrackers accidentally set fire to and destroyed the Hempy's Grove Bridge.

Figure 89. Fishinger Mill Bridge over Scioto River

Large covered bridges spanned Darby Creek in western Franklin County, too. There was one at Harrisburg on what is today US Route 62; one at Darbydale, Figure 90; and two at Georgesville. The Georgesville Bridges over the Big and Little Darby Creeks were lost to the raging floodwaters of March 1913. That same flood badly damaged the Darbydale or McKinley Bridge, but it was repaired and served into the 1930s.

In 1887, after many petitions from are a residents, the Franklin County Commissioners finally decided to build a bridge at Kramer's Ford of Little Walnut Creek south of Canal Winchester. The Columbus Bridge Company submitted two bids: one for an iron bridge at $3,875. and one for a covered wooden bridge at $2,690. In the interests of economy, the Commissioners chose the wooden bridge, Figure 91, which was built under the supervision of the Columbus Bridge Company's vice-president, Reuban L. Partridge who built a 134

Figure 90.
Darbydale Bridge
over Big Darby Creek
A survivor of the
1913 flood

foot triple Partridge truss. The bridge is known as the Bergstresser or Dietz Bridge. Eventually, the road carried by the Bergstresser Bridge became Route 674 and the State of Ohio took over both road and bridge. In 1956, Route 674 was relocated, bypassing the covered bridge and a short section of the old road which reverted back to county ownership. Both the state and the county always took excellent care of this old bridge. In 1991, it was completely renovated which included foundation work, replacement of rotted timbers, new roof and siding. In a ceremony on September 1, 1991,

the Franklin County Commissioners formally handed over ownership of the Bergstresser/Dietz Bridge to the Village of Canal Winchester. The bridge is now open only to pedestrian traffic.

There is another covered bridge in Franklin County, a transplant in 1967 from Muskingum County. Columbus Attorney Art Wesner brought the dismantled Blackburn Bridge to his property near Grove City where he rebuilt it over Big Run Creek with the help of many friends and bridgers. The cut-stone abutments on which it now sets came from the ill-fated Yankeetown Road Bridge in Fayette County.

Figure 91.
Bergstresser or Dietz
Bridge
built in 1887
by
Columbus Bridge Co.

PICKAWAY COUNTY

Pickaway County lies just south of Franklin and its major streams are the Scioto River, Darby and Deer Creeks. The county seat is Circleville, so named by early settlers because they built their town within the circular remains of mounds built by Ohio's Mound Builder Indians.

As in Franklin County, the early covered bridges of Pickaway were built on the Town lattice truss plan. There was a multi-span Town truss over the Scioto River at Circleville built in the 1830s by the Circleville Bridge Company. This group was authorized by an Act of the Legislature to build a tollbridge on the road to Washington Court House (now US 22). The bridge cost $6,000. to build and was sold to the county a few years later with the understanding that the county would complete the road. On the night of March 21, 1881, the bridge was deliberately burned by persons unknown. The burning wreckage fell into the river and lodged against the covered canal aquaduct, Figure 13, which threatened to destroy that structure, too. The floodgates of the aquaduct were opened and water poured down onto the flaming remains of the highway bridge, saving the aquaduct.

Just west of the village of South Bloomfield, another long Town truss spanned the Scioto River. This bridge was built in 1850 by Samuel Blake for over $12,000. It was torn down in 1874 and replaced by a more modern Smith truss. The covered Smith truss was destroyed by the 1913 flood.

An old Town truss over Walnut Creek at Ashville was replaced by a Smith truss bridge with massive arches in 1871 for $22.50 per linear foot, Figure 92. The old bridge was carefully dismantled and taken to a site east of Ashville where it was rebuilt over Little Walnut Creek. It served this site until 1952, Figure 45. Perhaps Pickaway County's best-known Town truss bridge was the Adelphi Bridge over Salt Creek on Route 180, Figure 93. This open-sided, one-span bridge was built c.1848 by Karshner and Hanniger for the Circleville-Adelphi Turnpike Company. By the early 1950s, local agitation for the removal of this bridge had grown to the point that someone went so far as to set a charge of dynamite on the old span. Fortunately, this was discovered before any harm was done and the bridge got a brief reprieve. The state removed it in 1954.

Figure 93. Adelphi Bridge over Salt Creek

The Crownover Mill Bridge over Deer Creek in western Pickway County was the next-to-last covered bridge in the county. It was a two-span, 175 foot Howe truss built in 1872 by the Smith Bridge Company. The flood of January 1959 caused serious abutment damage to this bridge and it was removed shortly thereafter. A small covered bridge was moved to span the millrace at Crownover Mill from the canal at Circleville in 1873. Fate of this bridge is unknown, but a member of the Crownover family remembered it well and the story was confirmed by old county records.

Figure 92. Ashville's "New" Bridge, 1871-1962

After the county removed the Ashville Bridge in 1962, Pickaway County was without a covered bridge until 1978, when William Green of near Orient acquired the old Valentine Bridge from neighboring Fairfield County. Mr. Green moved the bridge to his farm and rebuilt it over the arm of a small lake. Pickaway County once was rich in all types of wooden truss bridges from the multi-span giants over the Scioto River to the small canal bridges. Now, all are gone and only a transplant from Fairfield County remains.

FAIRFIELD COUNTY

For many years, Fairfield County was a magnet for bridgers from all over the country who came to see its many bridges. As late as 1950, there were 46 covered bridges in the county, a number that has continued to dwindle until in 1992, only 17 remain, and of these, only two carry traffic.

Fairfield County is lovely rolling land, drained by the Hocking River, Rush and Walnut Creeks. Many wooden truss bridges were built to serve the roads, railroads and canals of this county. From the research that has been done in the old county records, it would appear that Fairfield County may always have had more wooden truss bridges than any other Ohio county. The count now stands at over 270 wooden bridges of all types: multiple kingposts, queenposts, Howes, Smiths, Burrs and combinations of various designs and of course, the unique suspension trusses of August Borneman.

Figure 94. Rock Mill Bridge over Hocking River

The majority of the county's wooden bridges have been moved to new locations, giving us a number of examples of covered bridge preservation, some better than others. One example, the Hartman/Lockville Park Bridge, Figure 35, is located among some fine remnants of the old canal locks. It was moved here from its original site east of Lancaster in 1967. Another example found behind the athletic track at the Fairfield/Union School near Rushville is the Baker/Winegardner Bridge. This bridge was built in 1871 by James Arnold to span Little Rush Creek. The construction of one of the Rush Creek Conservancy Dams forced the removal of this old bridge and it was taken to the school where it now spans a small lake in a lovely wooded setting.

The Holliday/Andrews Bridge, built in the late 1890s by J.W. Buchanan to span Walnut Creek on Lake Road, was moved into Millersport in the early 1980s. The old bridge can now be seen on the Corn Festival Grounds spanning a small ravine. The covered bridge that was moved more often than any other is the little Basil canal bridge (see Figure 12) built in 1899 by Buchanan to span the canal just south of Baltimore. From Baltimore, it was moved north to span Paw Paw Creek on Roley Road. In 1974, it was moved to its present location, just inside the main gate on the county fairgrounds. A less than optimum location for a covered bridge.

Perhaps the finest example of covered bridge preservation in Fairfield County is the John Bright #2 Bridge on the Lancaster Campus of Ohio University where it now spans Fetters Run (see Figure 73).

Probably the best-known of all the covered bridges of Fairfield County is the Rock Mill Bridge, Figure 94, a 36 foot queenpost over the gorge of the infant Hocking River at Rock Mill. A covered bridge built here in 1849 by John Slife served until 1900 when the county awarded the contract for a new "house" bridge at Rock Mill to Jacob R. Brandt for $575. The Rock Mill Bridge has been heavily reinforced with steel I-beams and should last for many more years. The covered bridge and nearby mill have long been favorites with artists and photographers and at one time, the bridge was featured on a tourism promotion poster that hung in many United States Embassies abroad.

Many covered bridges spanned Walnut Creek in Fairfield County and a partial list includes: the Foust/Pope Bridge near Thurston, the Leonard Bridge just south of Baltimore, the McLeery, the Gundy, the Jackson/Ety, the Weaver, the Rainbow and the State Dam Bridges, Figure 29. In 1912, the Jackson/Ety Bridge was moved to a farm in Liberty Township from the canal at Carroll. It was an 87 foot multiple kingpost built in 1874 by A.B. Gillette. The old bridge was in very poor condition. A shortened version of the McLeery Bridge is now on private property. The Rainbow Bridge, Figure 95, was torn down in the 1950s as was the Foust/Pope Bridge. Arson claimed the Gundy and State Dam Bridges in 1967 and the county removed the Leonard Bridge the same year.

Figure 95. Rainbow Bridge over Walnut Creek

Clear Creek and Rush Creek also had their chains of covered bridges. On Clear Creek today, only the Clearport/Hannaway and Johnson Bridges remain. James Buchanan built the Clearport Bridge in 1904 to replace an earlier covered bridge. It was bypassed a few years ago and is not maintained. The 98 foot Johnson/Terry Mill Bridge was built by August Borneman in 1887, Figure 79, and is a typical Borneman Howe truss. It is scheduled to be bypassed soon.

Other covered bridges on Clear Creek were the Hutchins Bridge, dismantled in 1988 and

moved to Alley Park south of Lancaster where it may be rebuilt someday, the Landis School Bridge that collapsed under a county gravel truck in 1968, the Shaeffer/Campbell Bridge that was moved to Belmont County in 1973, and the Written Rock Bridge, an arson victim in 1969. Those of us who remember the Written Rock Bridge, Figure 96, know that it was in terrible condition for years. Its decline began when it was struck by debris from the covered bridge at Revenge that washed out in 1948.

Figure 96. Written Rock Bridge

The Written Rock Bridge served only one house and the county attempted to keep the bridge in service by shoring it up, putting on a new roof and anchoring by cables to nearby trees. None of this disguised the fact that this was a bridge in serious trouble. Arsonists destroyed the old bridge in October 1969 and now only the famed sandstone outcropping known as Written Rock still remains at what was once, many, many years ago, the intersection of two well-used Indian trails.

The last covered bridge over Rush Creek was the Hummell Bridge, a 106 foot Smith truss with arches, built by the Smith Bridge Company in 1875. Late in 1990, the old bridge was dismantled and moved into nearby Sugar Grove where it now lies piled up in the city park. The Swartz Mill Bridge, spanned Rush Creek for over 90 years before being torn down in 1962. It was in very poor condition at the time of its removal. Another Rush Creek covered bridge that is now only a memory was the Jerusalem Road or Moyer Bridge near Bremen. It was built in 1902 to replace an earlier covered bridge. In 1972, arsonists destroyed this old structure which was a landmark for those traveling east on SR 37 as it was just a few yards south of the highway.

Poplar Creek is a tributary of Walnut Creek and many covered bridges once spanned this pleasant little stream. Among those bridges were the Fultz, Hizey, Snyder #1 and Snyder #2 bridges, all on Poplar Creek Road within one township section. Not far south was the trim Macklin "House" Bridge built in 1916 by J.W. Buchanan to replace another covered bridge that had been badly damaged in the 1913 flood. The Hizey Bridge has been moved to private property to span Sycamore Creek.

Several other Fairfield County covered bridges besides the Hizey Bridge have been moved to private property. The Raab Bridge, a 44 foot queenpost built in 1891, was moved to the nearby Raab Farm on Ireland Road in 1974. The Shryer Bridge, a 65 foot multiple kingpost built in 1891 was moved to the Shryer Farm in 1987 where it stands close to the road, easily seen in its coat of bright red paint. The William Pierson Family dismantled the old Waterloo/Shade Bridge in the early 1980s and moved it to their farm south of Sugar Grove. It was rebuilt and now serves as a museum for miscellaneous artifacts. The Waterloo Bridge was built in 1871 by well-known Licking County bridge builder John Shrake to span Walnut Creek just south of of Waterloo.

Figure 98. Householder Bridge -- last covered bridge built in Fairfield County

North of the Clear Creek Valley over Arney Run, is the picturesque little Mink Hollow Bridge, Figure 97, a 53 foot multiple kingpost truss built in 1887.

It is obvious that Fairfield County was committed to the "house" bridge (the term their county officials used to describe covered bridges from about 1890 on) and they were still building them as late as 1919. In that year, the Householder Bridge, Figure 98, was built by Creager and Kober for $991. which included the foundations. That little bridge, a 34 foot multiple kingpost, served for 40 years. In addition to all the highway and canal bridges, Fairfield county had many Howe truss bridges of all types on the railroads that ran through the county.

Figure 97.
The Mink Hollow Bridge
over Arney Run in
Oil Mill Hollow
built 1887

LICKING COUNTY

Lovely Wakatomika Creek flows through northeastern Licking County and was once spanned by many covered bridges. At one time, there were five covered bridges over Wakatomika Creek on Frampton Road, but today, only the Gregg Mill Bridge remains, Figure 99. The Gregg Mill Bridge is a 124 foot multiple kingpost truss whose center pier is a later addition. It underwent major repairs in 1992. A short distance to the east of this bridge stood the Mercer/Thumwood Bridge (once known erroneously as the Johnny Little Bridge) built in 1875 by prominent builder Simon Shrake of the well-known Shrake bridge building family. This bridge was a Burr truss and the arches were removed when it was renovated in the 1960s.

*Figure 99. Gregg Bridge --
was rebuilt in 1993*

The next covered bridge (and they were ALL covered) east on Frampton Road was also known as Mercer Bridge. Perhaps we should call it Mercer Bridge #2? This six panel multiple kingpost was built in 1883 and torn down in 1948. The fact that two of these bridges on the same road had the same name is an excellent reason for the use of the bridge numbering system developed many years ago by John Diehl of the Ohio Covered Bridge Committee. While it is possible for more than one bridge to be known by the same family name, no two bridges would ever have the same number.

The next Wakatomika Creek crossing was the Dunn Bridge built c.1883 and removed in 1949. The fifth and last bridge on this road was the Frampton/ Little Bridge at the crossroads community of Frampton. It was built in 1884 to replace an earlier covered bridge and torn down in 1949.

There is still another covered bridge spanning Wakatomika Creek, the Shoults Bridge near the Girl Scout Camp about two miles north of Frampton Road. The Shoults Bridge is a 74 foot multiple kingpost that cost less than $5. per linear foot to build in 1879. This bridge has also been known as Mercer because at one time, the Mercer family owned land at this crossing.

Licking County has a good example of covered bridge preservation in the old bridge at the Boy Scout Camp in Eden Township, Figure 100. This 44 foot multiple kingpost bridge was moved to its new location from the nearby county road in 1974. To enter the Boy Scout Camp, you must cross Rocky Fork Creek on a rare example of a cast and wrought iron Post truss bridge moved here years ago from Hebron.

Figure 100. Boy Scout Bridge

In the late 1940s, the siding was removed from the old McLain or Lobdell Park Bridge, Figure 101, to make repairs to the lower chords. For some reason, the siding was never replaced and the bridge stood unhoused until it was bypassed in 1970. Then, it stood abandoned until 1977, when it was moved into Fireman's Park at Alexandria and renovated. On its original site, the bridge had a weathered

Figure 101. McLain or Lobdell Park Bridge

sign above the south portal that gave the information that it was built in 1871 by F. Phillips, followed by this poem:

All things save this
  have changed within our day,
Beside this quiet road
  nestled in these joyous hills,
You point your modest structure
  toward the sky,
Unsought and all unthanked
  you give us still,
Some fragrance of your peace
  as we go by.

The author of this poem is unknown and might have been Mr. Phillips. Unfortunately, the Licking County Commissioners Journals are missing the years 1866 to 1875, so we were unable to confirm that Phillips did indeed build this bridge. His name did not appear on any other Licking County bridge contracts.

A covered bridge that no longer depends on its wooden trusses is the decrepit Belle Hall Bridge over Otter Fork. After being badly damaged by an overloaded truck in the early 1970s, the bridge was rebuilt and heavily reinforced with steel. Some of the broken truss members were never replaced. By 1990, most of the siding was missing, too.

In 1947, Ernest Davis decided to build a covered bridge over Rocky Fork Creek to provide access off the county road to his farm. He chose multiple kingpost truss plans and proceeded to build his bridge of old barn timbers. The Davis Bridge was renovated in 1991 and is easily seen just off the main county road south of Hickman.

Like neighboring Fairfield County, Licking County once had many covered bridges spanning the rivers, creeks and canals. Our research, which of necessity omits the years 1866-1875, has turned up over 150 wood truss bridges in Licking County. There were large wood truss bridges over the Licking River at Toboso, at Stadden's Ford, and at Claylick. The Claylick Bridge, a 258 foot Howe truss, was built in 1876 by E. Anderson and Company. It was destroyed by fire in 1937. The Toboso or Licking Dam Bridge, a two-span Burr truss, was first built in 1858 and was in trouble almost immediately. Major repairs were made in 1860 and 1861 by its builder, John Shrake. That didn't prevent its collapse in late summer of 1861. The county then hired O.Z. Hilleary to rebuild the bridge. In 1862, a third span was added, a simple multiple kingpost. The other two spans were Burr trusses. The old covered bridge was razed in 1949.

The north and south forks of the Licking River come together at Newark to form the main channel of the river. There were many covered bridges over both forks including the Homer, Utica, Cemetery, and old White bridges on the north fork. On the south fork some well-remembered bridges are: the York Road/Carmelite Church Bridge, Moore's Bridge at Pataskala, and the Moscow Bridge, a two-lane Town truss on the National Road near Hebron.

Other covered bridges of recent memory in Licking County were the Concord Bridge over Lobdell Creek, the Hoover and Courson Bridges, both over Dry Creek, and the old Skinner's Ford Bridge over Brushy Fork on Buzzard Hill Road.

Just east of Kirkersville was an old Long truss bridge that carried the National Road over the Reservoir Feeder for the Ohio and Erie Canal. While the building date for this bridge is unknown, it was likely in the 1840s era and probably not the first bridge on the site.

Figure 102
Old Long truss
covered bridge
over the
Reservoir Feeder
at
Kirkersville
in Licking County

Figure 102 shows this bridge in its later years, shortly before its removal in 1917.

In 1992, an 80 foot Town truss bridge was built over a small run on the Canal Greenway bike path southwest of Hebron. Designed by Ashtabula County Engineer John Smolen, it is a pedestrian/bike bridge, eight feet wide and eight feet in height,(see Chapter XI).

In addition to the many highway and canal bridges in Licking County, there were over a dozen timber truss railroad bridges, both of the through and deck Howe designs.

KNOX COUNTY

While Knox, Marion and Morrow Counties had fewer covered bridges than surrounding areas, they still had some significant examples of wooden truss bridges. One reason that these three counties had fewer covered bridges is that they went over to the steel truss bridges earlier than some other Ohio counties.

Knox County had a large two-lane Burr truss over the Kokosing River on South Main Street at Mt. Vernon, Figure 103. This bridge was built in 1848 under the supervision of Catherinus Buckingham, builder of the famed Y-Bridge at Zanesville. The South Main Street Bridge stood until 1892. Just to the south of this large bridge, was a smaller roofed structure over Dry Creek that was also replaced in the early 1890s. Another covered bridge carried West High Street over the Kokosing in Mt. Vernon.

Figure 103.
Kokosing River
Bridge on South
Main Street at
Mount Vernon,
Knox County
Built in 1848
by
C.P.Buckingham

A sketch of Mt. Vernon in an old Knox County atlas shows the South Main Street covered bridge flanked by two covered railroad bridges. One was on the Baltimore and Ohio Railroad and the other on the Pennsylvania Railroad. Research has yielded the locations of some 34 wood truss bridges in Knox County, 19 of which were railroad Howe trusses. In addition to the large Kokosing River bridges at Mt. Vernon, there were covered bridges over the Kokosing at a long-gone community known as Zuck in the eastern part of the county, at Gambier, and over the Mohican River at Brinkhaven (Mt. Holley).

Knox and Licking County shared two covered bridges over the north fork of the Licking River. One was near Lock and the other was the Cemetery Bridge on the north edge of Utica. The latter, was built in 1864 by well-known Licking County builders, G.J. and J.B. Haggerty. Knox County took care of building the foundations.

Perhaps one reason Knox County officials began building steel truss bridges at an early date was the presence in their county of the Mt. Vernon Bridge Company. The well-known Morrison bridge builders were also active in building steel bridges here at an early date.

MORROW COUNTY

Like Knox County, Morrow County was building steel bridges in the 1860s. There were,

however, a number of covered bridges spanning the Kokosing River, Whetstone, Alum and Walnut Creeks. The last covered bridge in the county, the Stantontown/East Liberty Bridge, was torn down in 1932. A few others stood into the 1920s: the Westfield Bridge over Whetstone Creek just west of Westfield, the Johnsville/Shauck Bridge over Cedar Fork near Johnsville, and the Bartlett Bridge over the Whetstone just west of Schaaf's Corners. The Chesterville Bridge, Figure 104, spanned the Kokosing River at Chesterville. There was at least one covered bridge over the Whetstone at Mt. Gilead, the county seat. Morrow County also had a number of wood truss railroad bridges.

MARION COUNTY

John Shrake of Licking County built a covered bridge over the Scioto River at the south edge of LaRue, Figure 105, in 1867. The bridge was replaced by an iron truss in 1904 and until recently no one knew that the old covered span was still in existance (so to speak) in use as a cattle barn on a farm just south of LaRue. Our picture was taken from an old Marion County atlas and shows an uncovered Howe railroad bridge to the left and, in the foreground, an uncovered wood pony truss bridge. There was yet another covered bridge at LaRue over the Scioto at the west edge of town.

Figure 104.
Chesterville Bridge
over the
Kokosing River
in
Morrow County

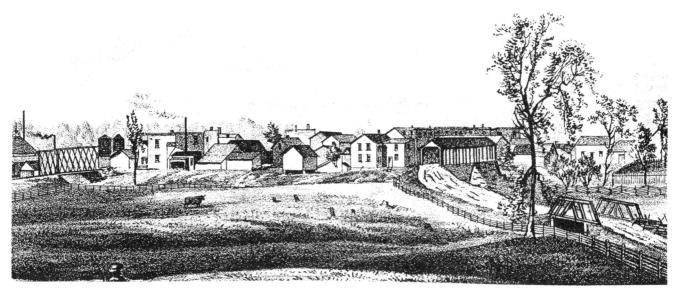

Figure 105. Woodcut of the bridges spanning the Scioto River at LaRue

So far, research has turned up the sites of 20 timber truss bridges in Marion County, five of them railroad bridges. The Newman Bridge spanned the Scioto River about 2.5 miles north of Prospect. It washed out in the 1913 flood. There was also a covered bridge over the Scioto River at Prospect, that was built in 1867 by John Shrake and carried away by the great 1913 flood. At Green Camp a covered bridge built on the "Sherman plan" (a Childs truss?), Figure 106, crossed the Scioto River from 1880 to 1914. Marion County also had covered bridges over the Olentangy River and Rocky Fork Creek.

DELAWARE COUNTY

Delaware County, which takes its name from the Delaware Indians, has only one covered bridge left out of over 60 which once spanned its rivers and creeks. The county is drained by the Scioto and Olentangy Rivers, Walnut and Alum Creeks. During the great 1913 flood, Delaware County suffered great damage and many bridges were lost, among them at least 18 covered spans. It is said that only the Lavender Bridge, Figure 107, a 151 foot double Burr truss, was left standing over the Scioto River when flood waters receded. The Lavender Bridge was built in 1869 by

Figure 106. The old covered bridge at Green Camp in Marion County -- it may have been a Childs truss

Figure 107. Delaware County's Lavender Bridge

Figure 108. Dade Terrill Bridge

David T.Sherman, father of well-known bridge builder Everett S.Sherman. Other large Scioto River covered bridges in Delaware County included: Partridge's 271 foot Bellepoint Bridge, Figure 66, which he built in 1877; the White Sulphur Spring Bridge at Rathbone built by David T. Sherman in 1859; Jarvis Landon's 1864 Marysville Pike Bridge; and the Shiveley Bridge on present-day SR 37. All of these were swept away in March,1913.

There were at least a dozen roofed bridges over the Olentangy River in Delaware County among which was the Water Hill Bridge, a 100 foot Smith truss built in 1874 and removed in 1949 due to the formation of Delaware Reservoir. In the City of Delaware, covered bridges spanned the Olentangy on Williams Street and North Street. North of town was the Norton Bridge and south were the Stratford and Powell bridges. Many of these washed out in 1913.

The last covered bridge on Alum Creek was the 138 foot Dade Terrill Bridge, Figure

108, a Howe truss built in 1874 and torn down in 1960 due to its poor condition. The Jaynes Bridge crossed Alum Creek near Cheshire. It was a 118 foot Burr truss built in 1850 (quite possibly by David Sherman). Arsonists destroyed this old structure in 1955.

South of Galena on Big Walnut Creek was the Yankee Street Road Bridge, a covered bridge remembered fondly by the author. Family trips between Mt. Vernon and Columbus in the 1940s led through this bridge if the "back road" was taken. David T. Sherman built this two span Burr truss in 1859 and the county paid him over $1600. for it. The bridge was slated for removal when Hoover Reservoir was completed. However, an overloaded coal

Figure 109.
Yankee Street Bridge
over
Big Walnut Creek
in
Delaware County
1859-1953
Victim of an overloaded
coal truck

truck caused the collapse of the east span in 1953 and the rest of the bridge was removed at that time. Figure 109 shows the old bridge circa 1950 in a sadly deteriorated condition.

Yankee Street was but one of the colorful names attached to Delaware County covered bridges. There was Monkey Hollow, Lavender, Mink Street and Begger Louse Hill, too. In addition to all the highway covered bridges, Delaware County had its share of timber truss railroad bridges, including the 240 foot deck-Howe truss at White Sulphur Springs.

The last covered bridge in Delaware County is on Chambers Road over Big Walnut Creek near the village of Olive Green. Everett S. Sherman built this bridge in 1883, his first use of the Childs truss, Figure 66. Extensive renovations were done to this bridge in 1982/83. The foundations were rebuilt of concrete and a concrete center pier was added. A steel substructure now carries the weight of the bridge. The renovation was completed with a wood shingle roof and new siding.

UNION COUNTY

Mention Union County to a covered bridger and it immediately evokes thoughts of that county's premier bridge builder, Reuban L. Partridge. Marysville, the county seat, was Partridge's home and it is said that he built over 100 bridges in his home county. The County Commissioners Journals fail to bear out this story, but they do tell us that he built at least 33 wooden bridges in Union County, many of which were full-size covered Partridge trusses. All five of the remaining covered bridges in Union County are Partridge trusses built in the late 1860s to 1884 by Partridge.

Big and Little Darby Creeks flow through Union County and these two streams, with the smaller creeks such as Blues, Mill, Fulton and Rush, needed many bridges. Bridge maintenance is excellent in Union County and as far as can be determined, no covered bridge has been removed since the 1930s, which is quite a record. Roofed windows were cut into the sides of the five remaining covered bridges in the 1930s as a safety measure to improve visibility. It might be well to mention again at this point that the steel rods and cables found in the

Figure 110. Reed Bridge over Big Darby Creek -- very poor condition 1993

Union County Partridge truss bridges are not a part of the original construction, but were added later to strengthen the old trusses.

The Reed Bridge, Figure 110, over Big Darby south of Marysville, was built in 1884 (and not 1838 as the sign inside the bridge maintains) and bypassed in 1963. The county historical society and the county commissioners now maintain the old span.

Just off SR 161, on the old Post Road, is the Axe Handle Road Bridge, a familiar sight to motorists in this area. Built in 1873, this sturdy old bridge recently underwent a complete renovation by the county highway department that included foundation work and the addition of heavy laminated arches. This work should ensure the continuing service of this bridge for years to come.

On Wingett Road, there is a 100 foot Partridge truss bridge over Treacle Creek that was moved here many years ago from an unknown location. It serves only light traffic and a concrete ford has been built beside the bridge to handle any extra wide or heavy vehicles.

There are two covered bridges at the west end of the county. The Upper Darby/Beltz Mill Bridge crosses Darby Creek. This 105 foot Partridge truss was built in 1868 and will be bypassed soon due to increasingly heavy traffic. Not far from the Upper Darby Bridge is the much smaller, 75 foot Spain Creek Bridge over a branch of Darby Creek. The Spain Creek Bridge building date was never found, but we presume it was in the 1870s. In 1988 and 1989, this bridge was completely rehabbed under direction of County Engineer Steve Stolte and his crew. The work included the installation of glu-lam beams at floor level on each side that are attached to the base of the trusses, a new floor system and floor beams, new siding and new roof. The east abutment was rebuilt in concrete and the west abutment was reinforced with concrete (see further details and picture in Chapter XI).

Reuban Partridge built several covered bridges over Mill Creek, Blues Creek and Rush Creek. His Byhalia Bridge, removed in the 1930s, is shown in Figure 111.

A few of Union County's covered bridges were not Partridge trusses—such as John Fleck's 1868 Burr truss over Mill Creek near Raymond, and a few Howe truss railroad bridges.

Figure 112. Amity Bridge over Big Darby Creek in Madison County

MADISON COUNTY

Madison County lies south of Union and west of Franklin Counties and is crossed by the National Road. Big and Little Darby Creeks and Deer Creek form the main drainage of this county. The last covered bridge in Madison County was the two span Partridge truss over Big Darby at Amity, Figure 112. This bridge was built by Reuban Partridge in 1873 for $2,825. The masonry alone cost another $2,966. In 1957, the county removed this last covered bridge and planned to use some of its timbers to build a storage shed.

Southeast of London on Glade Run Road the Holway or Pancake Bridge spanned Deer Creek, Figure 113. This 110 foot Howe truss was an 1874 product of the Anderson Company of Sidney, Ohio, who specialized in the Howe truss. The Anderson Company built another

Figure 111. Byhalia Bridge over Rush Creek

Figure 113.
Pancake or Holway Bridge
over Deer Creek
in
Madison County
1874-1950

Howe truss in Madison County over Deer Creek on Anderson Road northwest of Mt. Sterling in 1875. This 245 foot, two-span structure cost $13.95 per linear foot. It served less than 50 years.

Noted builder John Shrake built a covered bridge near West Jefferson in 1866 and the county ordered that it be covered inside and out and roofed with pine shingles. Unfortunately, the old county records neglected to state the exact location of the bridge which we believe was on the National Road over Little Darby Creek.

Madison County shared some important bridges over Big Darby Creek with Franklin County. One was on the National Road, and others were on Beach and Roberts Roads. All were replaced many years ago with steel truss bridges and today, only the 1888 Beach Road Bridge steel Pratt truss is still standing.

There were several through-Howe railroad bridges in Madison County and a large deck-Howe truss over Big Darby Creek on the Franklin County line. The latter was built in 1872 to replace an earlier deck-Howe truss bridge.

EXISTING BRIDGE LOCATIONS

Delaware County:
35-21-04 Chambers Road Bridge, 73' Childs, 1883, Chambers Road over Big Walnut Creek in Porter Twp., 1.5 m NE of Olive Green.

Fairfield County:
35-23-07 Hizey Bridge, 83' QP/MKP, 1891, 12549 Tollgate Road over Sycamore Creek on the James Visitine property in Violet Twp., 3 m NE of Pickerington. Moved here in 1986.

35-23-10 John Bright #2 Bridge, 75' Suspension truss,1881, off SR 37 on the Ohio University Campus over Fetters Run, north of Lancaster. Moved here in 1988.

35-23-15 Clearport/Hannaway Bridge, 86' MKP, 1901, CR 24 over Clear Creek in Madison Twp. just S of Clearport. Bypassed.

35-23-16 Johnson Bridge, 98' Howe, 1887, CR 69 over Clear Creek, in Madison Twp., 5 m SE of Amanda.

35-23-19 Zeller/Smith Bridge, 79' MKP, 1906,over Sycamore Creek in Sycamore Creek Park, Violet Twp. at Pickerington. Moved here in 1986.

35-23-20 Waterloo/Shade Bridge, 122' MKP, 1871, off Sullivan Road on the Pierson property in Berne Twp., 1.5m SE of Sugar Grove.Moved here in 1979.

35-23-25 McLeery Bridge, 52' MKP, 1864, 5905 SR 158 on the Walters property in Greenfield Twp., 1 m south of Baltimore.Moved here in 1983.

35-23-27 Shryer Bridge, 66' MKP,1891, 4750 Basil Road on the Shryer Farm in Liberty Twp., 3 m west of Baltimore. Moved here in 1987.

35-23-30 Holliday/Andrews Bridge, 98' MKP, 1897, on the Corn Festival Grounds in Walnut Twp. at Millersport. Moved here in 1982.

35-23-33 Baker/Winegardner Bridge, 66' MKP, 1871, on the Fairfield/Union School property behind the athletic track in Richland Twp., 2 m west of Rushville. Moved here in 1981.

35-23-37 John Raab Bridge, 44' QP,1891, on the Raab Farm at 5695 Ireland Road in Pleasant Twp. 5.5m E of Lancaster. Moved here in 1974.

35-23-38 Hartman/Lockville Park Bridge, 48' QP, 1888, over the Ohio and Erie Canal in Violet Twp., at Lockville 4.5m S of Pickerington. Moved here in 1967.

35-23-43 Mink Hollow Bridge, 51' MKP, 1887, off CR 28 over Arney Run in Hocking Twp., 5 m SSW Lancaster. Bypassed

35-23-48 Rock Mill Bridge, 37' QP, 1901, CR 41 over the Hocking River, 6.5m NW Lancaster.

35-23-49 Roley School Bridge, 49' MKP, 1899, on the County Fairgrounds at North Broad St. gate, in Lancaster. Moved here in 1974.

Franklin County:
35-25-03 Bergstresser/Dietz Bridge, 125' Partridge, 1887, over Walnut Creek in Madison Twp., on South edge of Canal Winchester off SR 674. Closed.

35-25-65 Wesner/Blackburn Bridge, 50' MKP, off Big Run Road east of US 3/62 over Big Run in Franklin Twp., 2 m N of Grove City. Moved here 1967 from Muskingum County.

Licking County:
35-45-01 Belle Hall Bridge, 56' MKP, TR 56 over Otter Fork, 3 m E of Croton.

35-45-04 Boy Scout/Rainrock Bridge, 49' MKP over small creek and ravine in the Boy Scout Camp off CR 210 in Eden Twp., 5 m SW of Fallsburg. Moved here in 1974.

35-45-05 Girl Scout/Shoults Bridge, 68' MKP, 1879, TR 225 over Wakatomika Creek in Fallsbury Twp., 2 m NNW Fallsburg.

35-45-06 Gregg/Pine Bluff Bridge, 124' MKP, 1881, CR 201 over Wakatomika Creek in Fallsbury Twp., 1 m NNW Fallsburg.

35-45-17 McLain/Lobdell Park Bridge, 47' MKP, 1871, in Fireman's Park in St. Albans Twp., off SR 37 at south edge of Alexandria. Moved here 1977.

35-45-25 Davis Farm Bridge, 50' MKP, 1947, off CR 210 over Rocky Fork in Mary Ann Twp. on Davis Farm 1.5m S of Hickman and SR 79.

35-45-80 Maple Run Bridge, 24' KP on Fairgrounds at Croton. in Hartford Twp. Moved here in 1975.

35-45-160 Canal Greenway Bridge, 80' Town, 1992, over small creek off Canal Road in Union Twp.on abandoned railroad right-of-way 2.5m SW Hebron. Bike and pedestrian use only.

Pickaway County:
35-65-15 Bill Green Bridge, 36' MKP, 1887, over pond off Thrailkill Road on Green Farm in Scioto Twp., 2.5 m SE of Orient. Moved here from Fairfield County in 1978.

Union County:
35-80-01 Upper Darby/Beltz Mill Bridge, 105' Partridge, 1868, CR 164 over Big Darby Creek in Allen Twp., 2 m NE of North Lewisburg.

35-80-02 Spain Creek Bridge, 75' Partridge, CR 163 over Spain Creek in Allen Twp., 2 m ENE North Lewisburg, off SR 275.

35-80-03 Treacle Creek Bridge, 100' Partridge, 1868, CR 82 over Treacle Creek in Union Twp., 3 m S of Milford Center. Dead-end Road.

35-80-04 Little Darby/Axe Handle Road Bridge, 114' Partridge 1873, CR 87 over Little Darby Creek in Union Twp., off SR 161, 4 m S of Milford Center.

35-80-05 Reed Bridge 160' Partridge, 1884, over Big Darby Creek just off SR 38 in Darby Twp., 3.5 m S of Marysville. Bypassed. Bridge collapsed in August 1993.

Jaynes Bridge over Alum Creek in
Delaware County (pg.61)

Pickaway County's Crownover Mill Bridge over
Deer Creek (pg.52)

Chapter IV

A VISIT TO THE HANGING ROCK IRON REGION

Gallia, Hocking, Jackson, Lawrence, Pike, Ross, Scioto and Vinton Counties

Figure 114, Ohio's Hanging Rock Iron Region

ROSS COUNTY

When Ohio became a state in 1803, Chillicothe, on the banks of the Scioto River at the falls of Paint Creek, was chosen for its first capitol. Nathaniel Massie, early Ohio surveyor, had laid out this town and named it Chillicothe, a Shawnee word for village or tribal unit. The Great Seal of the State of Ohio depicts the view Thomas Worthington, early Ohio governor, saw from his estate, Adena, near Chillicothe.[51] The capitol was moved to Columbus in 1816, but Chillicothe remained the county seat of Ross County and is a thriving city today.

There were many large timber truss bridges built to span the Scioto River and its tributaries, Paint and Deer Creeks, in Ross County. One of the first, if not the first, was the Bridge Street Bridge over the Scioto River at Chillicothe built in 1817, Figures 42 and 43.

Six other covered bridges spanned the Scioto in Ross County including three railroad Howe trusses. The Kilgore's Ford Bridge, Figure 17, was built in 1867 approximately at the point where US 50/35 crosses the river today. This large bridge lasted only 10 years before being destroyed by arson and the county replaced it with a metal truss structure.

The Silvey's Ford Bridge was another multi-span crossing of the Scioto River at Chillicothe. It stood close to the site of the present East Main Street bridge. The B.L.Pugh Company built this four span Howe truss, Figure 115, in 1870 for $16,490. The plans were drawn up by John C. Gregg. In the southern part of the county, the Higby Road Bridge spanned the Scioto not far off the old Jackson to Gallipolis Pike, now US 35. The Smith Bridge Company built this four span, 430 foot Howe truss in 1877. Figure 116 shows the Higby Bridge during repairs after a flood in 1893 washed out one span. Both the Silvey Ford and Higby Bridges were destroyed in the 1913 flood.

Paint Creek is a good-sized stream which necessitated the construction of large bridges to span it. Just below Chillicothe on the old Portsmouth Pike (now US 23) there was a two-span multiple kingpost truss bridge built in 1863 to replace an earlier covered bridge. In July 1863, Confederate General John Hunt Morgan was leading his cavalry through southern Ohio, looting towns, stealing horses, burning bridges and generally giving the citizens of Ohio a thorough fright. People were seeing Morgan everywhere, and in order to stop the Raiders from crossing Paint Creek in Chillicothe, the local militia burned the covered bridge. It didn't take them long to realize how foolish this act was because the creek was only a foot deep at the time and could have been forded easily. Also, Morgan wasn't really coming through Chillicothe, so their bridge burning bravado was all in vain.[52] Later that year, another covered bridge was built on this

*Figure 115.
The Silvey Ford
Bridge mirrored
in the waters of
the Scioto River*

site. About one mile east of the old Portsmouth Pike Bridge was the Ohio and Erie Canal Aquaduct over Paint Creek, Figure 15.

Upstream from Chillicothe, the next covered bridge over Paint Creek was the the Shotts Bridge, a 278 foot, two span Long truss designed by John C. Gregg and built in 1867, Figure 117. At the time of its removal in 1960, it was the last covered bridge on Paint Creek.

Two miles east of Bainbridge was the well-known Seymour Bridge on US 50 over Paint Creek, Figure 39. (See Chapter II for more details on the Seymour Bridge.) A large covered bridge known as Benner's Bridge spanned Paint Creek just north of Bainbridge. Built in

the 1850s, this two-span multiple kingpost washed out in the great 1913 flood. As did the next Paint Creek Bridge upstream, the Rapid Forge or Lost Bridge.

Ross County also had smaller covered bridges and wood pony trusses over such creeks as Kinnikinick (an Indian word meaning tobacco), Buckskin, Twin, Deer, Salt and Walnut and over the Ohio and Erie Canal. A Long truss bridge spanned Deer Creek at the site of the old Hall's Mill on Westfall Road. John C. Gregg built this bridge in 1866 for $25. per linear foot, a very high price for a Long truss. It was still in good condition when it was destroyed by arsonists in 1968. The loss of the Westfall Road

*Figure 116,
Repairs underway
on the Higby
Road Bridge over
the Scioto River in
Ross County,
1893*

Figure 117. Shott's Bridge -- last covered bridge over Paint Creek

Bridge left only one covered bridge in Ross County, the Buckskin or South Salem Bridge over Buckskin Creek at the west edge of South Salem, Figure 118. The Smith Bridge Company built this 100 foot Smith truss in 1873. It is in good condition and still carries rather heavy traffic.

Figure 118. Buckskin or South Salem Bridge built in 1873 by the Smith Bridge Company

PIKE COUNTY

Pike County lies south of Ross County along the Scioto River. There were at least 55 wooden truss bridges in this county, including some two dozen over the Ohio and Erie Canal. A chain of small covered bridges carried both public and private roads over the canal from the Ross County line down through Waverly to the Scioto County line. Most of them were single kingpost structures, fully-covered, although there were a few covered pony trusses.

The last of these privately-owned canal bridges was the Barger Farm Bridge off SR 335 northeast of Waverly, Figure 11. Forgotten for many years, it was rediscovered in the early 1960s. The bridge had the typical single kingpost truss with the unusual feature of a trapdoor in the floor to facilitate the loading and unloading of canal boats below. There was no concerted effort to retain this important bit of Pike County history, and the old span collapsed into the dry bed of the canal about 1972.

Just south of Waverly, the Scioto River was spanned by the Gregg Hill Bridge, a five-span, double Burr truss built in 1859 by Barney Stone for the Waverly-Beaver Turnpike Company, Figure 119. The county bought the bridge from the turnpike company in 1870 for $18,000. which was payable in installments of $3600. over five years. In 1907, the two south spans were destroyed by a flood and replaced by steel trusses. The three north spans were in use until 1935 when they were also replaced by steel trusses.

The Jasper Bridge, Figure 120, carried old SR 124 over the Scioto River at Jasper. It was built in 1868 by T. Nesmith and Company to replace an earlier wood bridge. It cost the county over $9,000. to build. Note the ruins of the pony truss canal bridge in the foreground of Figure 120. The 1913 flood wrecked the Jasper Bridge.

In 1842, a fine six-span double Burr truss covered bridge, Figure 121, was built to span the Scioto River at Piketon. The Piketon Bridge served the Portsmouth Pike (US 23) traffic for many years.

Pike County had wooden truss bridges over the smaller streams such as Sunfish, No Name,

*Figure 119.
Pike County's
Gregg Hill Bridge
over the Scioto
River -- built
originally for a
turnpike company*

Pee Pee Creeks, Bakers, Morgans and Chenowiths Forks. Local legends say that Morgan's Raiders burned a Pike County covered bridge during their mad dash across the state. Although we cannot be entirely certain, this was probably the old Sunfish Creek bridge at Alexander's Mill on the old SR 124. A new bridge was built here in 1863.

Pike County had five timber truss railroad bridges of the through and pony truss varieties. Two of them spanned the Scioto River and both were over 450 feet in length. There was one 100 foot through Howe truss that crossed the canal just a few yards from the Barger Farm Bridge. The other two Pike County timber railroad bridges were small pony trusses.

SCIOTO COUNTY

Scioto County is just south of Pike County and, like the counties to the north, is divided by the waters of the Scioto River. Both county and river take their name from an Indian word for deer. This area was settled early because the river was a natural highway for the settlers coming in from the Ohio River.

Scioto County's last covered bridge is the fine Smith truss spanning Scioto Brush Creek at Otway, Figure 122. The Otway Bridge was built in 1874 by the Smith Bridge Company for $14.30 per linear foot. The massive arches and tension rods were added during an 1896 renovation. The low steel truss on the east end of

Figure 120. Jasper Bridge over Scioto River in Pike County, 1868-1913

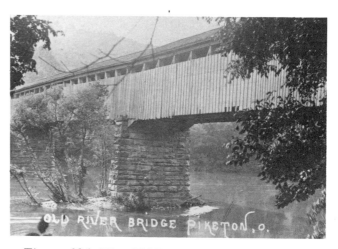

Figure 121. The Old River Bridge at Piketon

Figure 122. Scioto County's Otway Bridge

the bridge is a replacement for the original low wood Smith truss. The relocation of SR 348 in the early 1960s bypassed the Otway Bridge which reverted to the care of a local group.

There were, at one time, over 80 wooden truss bridges built to serve the highways, railroads and canals of Scioto County. However, there were no large, fully-covered bridges over the Scioto River, but references in the old county records indicate the existance of one or two pony truss bridges (county records are confusing on this point) that were built in the early days of the county. One that seemed to be of special importance was built over the "old bed" of the Scioto River near Portsmouth and was to serve as a model for other county bridges.

Many of Scioto County's covered bridges were built with massive kingpost trusses of varying heights. The county was also home to the strange-looking Wheeler trusses (see Chapter II) and at least four of them were built here. The McDaniel Bridge, Figure 70, the Snodgrass Bridge, the Holman and White Gravel Road Bridges were all built on the Wheeler truss patent.

We know of 10 covered bridges built to span the Little Scioto River, including the one at the mouth of the creek at Sciotoville (New Boston today), Figure 123. The Sciotoville Bridge was the third wooden truss bridge on the site. It was built in 1874 by the Smith Bridge Company to replace one of their own covered bridges which had collapsed suddenly in January 1874 due to abutment failure. The blame seemed to point to the masons, E.H. and L. Wishon, but they in turn, pointed the finger at the county commissioners and the engineer in charge, stating that the engineer deviated from the rules of masonry despite their protests and that the abutments were not given a proper base. Fortunately, the bridge collapsed at night and there were no injuries.[53]

Upstream on the Little Scioto north of Sciotoville were covered bridges at Dixon's Mill, Wheeler's Mill, and Harrison's Mill. The Harrison Mill Bridge was also known as the Bennett Schoolhouse Bridge, a 112 foot double multiple kingpost with arches built in 1867 by

Figure 123. Sciotoville Bridge over the Little Scioto River 1874-c1924

Figure 124. Massive timber trusses of the former Shuter Bridge in Scioto County, c1940

Van Buren Farney to replace an earlier covered bridge. This first covered bridge at Harrison's Mill was taken down after serving only a few years, dismantled and made into two bridges which were rebuilt at two different sites on Long's Run. One of these bridges, the Shuter Bridge, stood into the 1940s. Figure 124 shows the interor of this bridge and its massive timber trusses so typical of Scioto County's wooden bridges. Farney's 1867 Bennett Schoolhouse Bridge was dismantled in 1984 after standing abandoned for years. It is now in storage at South Webster, Ohio.

There was a fine old multiple kingpost truss bridge built to span Scioto Brush Creek at Rushtown in 1864 on what is now SR 104. R.S. Wynn built this bridge and several others in Scioto and Pike Counties. Figure 125 shows the Rushtown Bridge and the uncovered wooden aquaduct of the Ohio and Erie Canal beside it as they looked in 1903. The covered highway bridge was removed in 1931.

Figure 125. Rushtown Covered Bridge and wooden canal aquaduct over Scioto Brush Creek

The Norfolk and Western Railroad (known earlier as the Cincinnati and Eastern Railroad) had a 990 foot, six span combination truss over the Scioto River just north of Portsmouth built in 1884. This same railroad had Howe truss bridges of both the through and deck truss designs over Scioto Brush Creek.

LAWRENCE COUNTY

Lawrence County is located along the Ohio River to the east of Scioto County in the heart of what was once known as the Hanging Rock Iron Region. Commercial deposits of coal and iron ore in this area (which in Ohio included Lawrence, Scioto, Gallia, Hocking, Jackson and Vinton Counties) led to the establishment of the highly successful iron furnaces which employed so many of this area's people from the mid-1800s to the 1880s. The name Hanging Rock came from an impressive sandstone outcropping along the Ohio River west of Ironton, the county seat.[54]

A small Wheeler truss covered bridge spanned Osbourne's Run at the base of Hanging Rock on the old River Road, Figure 126. I.H. Wheeler built this bridge in 1873. In the late 1920s, the highway was relocated and widened. To do this, the state highway crews blasted away the old Hanging Rock. The covered bridge was removed at that time, too.

Figure 127. Scottown Bridge over Indian Guyan Creek

The Hanging Rock Iron Region produced much of the iron used for armament during the Civil War, including the ironplate used on the Union ironclad boat, the Monitor. Soon after the great war, the iron industry began to decline in this area and in December 1916, the last iron furnace was closed.[55]

Lawrence County's last covered bridge is the trim Scottown Bridge over Indian Guyan Creek just east of Scottown, Figure 127. This 1877 structure has been described by some as a "mongrel" truss, but close examination shows that it is a multiple kingpost. It has been greatly strengthened over the years by the addition of steel channels, gussets, cables and tension rods, making one stop and think before declaring a truss type here. William Thompson built this bridge for $547. to replace an earlier wooden structure.

Early in 1991, the Windsor Grange made a gift to the county of $2,000. to pay for the materials needed to replace the rusty corrugated siding and paint the rusty metal roof. County Engineer David R.Lynd decided that the bridge needed more than just cosmetic work and so the county hired a consulting firm to do an analysis to show what was needed to keep the bridge in service. The report showed that only the floor system was weak. The trusses (with all that steel added in the 1930s) were in good condition and adequate to carry schoolbuses. Mr. Lynd decided to replace the floor system with steel floor beams and stringers and a new laminated timber strip floor.

Figure 126. The Hanging Rock Covered Bridge

The project was completed with new siding and roof. The Scottown Bridge now can safely carry 12 tons and the cost of the project was only $10,000. with the county work force doing the labor. A new 80 foot bridge here would have cost at least $130,000.

Stephan Daniels, who was an agent in this part of Ohio for Stephan Long, inventor of the Long truss, built a covered bridge over the mouth of Symmes Creek in 1850. It is logical to assume that this was a Long truss bridge. It served the public until it was replaced in 1884. Several other Long truss bridges were built in Lawrence County including the bridge over Symmes Creek at Aid, built in 1855 by William Knowlton. This bridge stood for 95 years. Two Long truss covered bridges spanned Pine Creek in Elizabeth Township. One was at Gold Camp Station and the other was at Fox Hollow. William Hosey built the Gold Camp Station Bridge in 1877. It was removed in 1952. Hosey also built the Fox Hollow Bridge in 1880. It served until 1968.

The covered bridge over Symmes Creek at Waterloo was another of the Wheeler patent trusses built in 1872. The Waterloo Bridge was a well-known landmark that stood until 1940. Near the village of Getaway a 100 foot Smith truss spanned Symmes Creek. This bridge was built in 1878. The timbers for its trusses were pre-cut in the Smith Bridge Company yards at Toledo and shipped to the bridge site. The last water leg of the journey was made on the Ohio River steamer Lizzie Bay which carried the timbers to Chesapeake. There they were unloaded and taken by wagon north to the construction site where they were erected under the supervision of James Templeton.[56] The old bridge stood unhoused in its later years, Figure 128, and was torn down in 1955.

Altogether, over 70 wooden bridges were built for highway use in Lawrence County, but there were no wooden truss railroad bridges that could be documented.

GALLIA COUNTY

Beautiful Gallipolis, City of the Gauls, was settled by refugees from the horrors of the French Revolution. Promises made to these people by representatives of the Scioto Com-

Figure 128. Getaway Bridge over Symmes Creek

pany never materialized and these folks, many of them aristocrats unused to any type of manual labor, faced very hard times getting settled.[57] Lovely homes were eventually built, including Our House Tavern in 1819, which is now a museum owned by the Ohio Historical Society. Gallipolis is a river town, boasting a lovely town square with an old-fashioned bandstand. The principle stream draining the county is Raccoon Creek with its tributaries, Little Raccoon, Symmes and Sand Fork Creeks.

Many covered bridges spanned Raccoon Creek in Vinton and Gallia Counties. This creek, at over 100 miles in length, is the longest stream in Ohio. There were at one time many mills in operation on the Raccoon in these two counties, but only one is still standing, the old Cora Mill south of Rio Grande in Gallia County. Today it houses an antiques and craft business. In 1868, Aaron Davis, miller at Cora Mill, built a three-span multiple kingpost truss bridge over the falls of the Raccoon at his mill. The bridge was the first bridge on this site and it served until the early 1930s. Figure 129 shows the Cora Mill Bridge, the falls of the Raccoon and the old mill.

Upstream at Garner's Ford, R.D. Edwards built a multiple kingpost bridge in 1872 for $9.99 per linear foot. He was told by the commissioners that he would get $500. when "all materials were on the ground" and the balance

*Figure 129.
Old mill and covered
bridge over Raccoon
Creek at Cora in
Gallia County*

due on completion. At some later date, an inverted wooden arch was added to the trusses of this bridge.

Downstream from Cora Mill where SR 775 crosses the Raccoon was the Koontz Bridge. There were several covered bridges built to serve this important crossing, the last in 1880 by Graves and Scott, well-known bridge builders in this area. The county commissioners specified a "double Burr truss" for the new Koontz Bridge for $10. per linear foot. Graves and Scott put up a fine double multiple kingpost truss with arches, Figure 130. This bridge also had an inverted wooden arch added in later years. At some unknown point in time, a Gallia County Engineer added inverted arches to strengthen weak covered bridges. Some of these arches were of wood and some were made of steel.

Morgan's Raiders spent a warm July night in 1863 at the little town of Vinton in northern Gallia County. Before they left on their way to Vinton County the next morning, they burned the covered bridge over Raccoon Creek. It was replaced that same year by a double timber multiple kingpost truss built by J.G. Henshaw, Figure 131. This second Vinton covered bridge was torn down in the 1920s. There was also a covered bridge upstream at Ewington which was another of the double multiple kingpost truss bridges favored by Gallia County. It served until 1934.

Gallia County had only one large through Howe railroad bridge, the 144 foot Hocking Valley Railroad Bridge over the Raccoon at Vinton. It was destroyed by fire in the late 1880s. When the Harrisburg Bridge was torn down in 1954, the covered bridge era passed from Gallia County. The bridges were all gone and few noted or mourned their passing.

JACKSON COUNTY

Many of the early settlers of this area were Welsh and they felt right at home in these lovely hills, farming and working in the coal mines. Some helped to build and maintain the county's main artery, the Chillicothe-Jackson and Gallipolis Pike (now US 35).[58] As early as 1817, an Act of the Legislature provided $500. towards the construction of two bridges over Salt Creek on this important road. There is no

*Figure 130. Koontz Bridge over Raccoon Creek
was third covered bridge on site*

*Figure 131.
The second covered
bridge at Vinton in
Gallia County built
in 1863*

Figure 132. The Buckeye Furnace Covered Bridge

doubt that these were substantial timber trusses and probably covered.

The Jackson County officials were sold on the Smith truss which they used exclusively from 1869 on for all their wooden bridges (see Chapter II). With only two exceptions, county officials hired local contractors to build these Smith trusses. One of those exceptions was Ebenezer B.Henderson who built two Smith truss bridges in Jackson County, and the other was R.D. Edwards who was a well-known builder in Gallia and Vinton Counties. The local firm of Cutter and Souers built the three covered Smith trusses in the town of Jackson.

Three covered bridges remain in Jackson County, one at Buckeye Furnace built in 1871 by Dency, McCurdy and Company; one at Byer over Pigeon Creek built in 1872 by T.J. Dency; and the Enoch Crabtree Bridge built to span the Little Scioto River in 1870 by J.G. Stengall. The Buckeye Furnace Bridge, Figure 132, is 59 feet long and is just west of the restored Buckeye Furnace complex. The Byer Bridge, Figure 133, carried the main road over Pigeon Creek until SR 327 was relocated in the mid-1930s. The Crabtree Bridge is the last survivor of three Smith truss bridges that once spanned the Little Scioto on Johnson Road in Scioto Township.

Figure 133. The Covered Bridge at Byer

Not far from the Crabtree Bridge on SR 776 over the Little Scioto was the Keller Bridge, a 60 foot Smith truss built in 1871. It didn't last too long—it was replaced in 1902. Also gone for many years are these Little Raccoon Creek bridges: the Goddard Bridge on SR 124; the Burt Bridge on Mulga Road; the Hollingshead Bridge; the Fitzpatrick Road Bridge, the Perkins Bridge and the Keystone Furnace Bridge. Figure 134 shows the Goddard Bridge circa 1932.

Jackson County had a few wooden truss railroad bridges on the Baltimore and Ohio Railroad over Pigeon Creek near Byer. All were Howe trusses built in the early 1880s.

VINTON COUNTY

In 1850, Vinton County was partitioned off from Athens, Jackson, Hocking and Gallia Counties. The majority of what is now Vinton County was originally a part of Athens County. It is necessary to study the old bridge building records of the neighboring counties to fully understand the history of bridge building in this area before 1850.

Vinton County lays claim to one of the most beautiful covered bridges in Ohio, the lovely old Humpback or Ponn Bridge, Figure 135, spanning Raccoon Creek southwest of Wilkesville. The Humpback Bridge was built

Figure 134. The Goddard Bridge

in 1874 to replace the Barnes Mill Bridge which had been burned by arsonists that May. A substantial reward was offered by the county commissioners to apprehend the arsonists, but no one came forward with information.

The county hired Martin McGrath and Lyman Wells, contractors from McArthur, to erect a new bridge for $1898. They built a 174 foot, three-span multiple kingpost truss with arches on the center span. The entire structure arches up high above the waters of Raccoon Creek with a camber of at least 3.5 feet. Even so, floodwaters from the creek leave debris inside on the floor of the bridge at its highest point above the water.

A family named Ponn once lived close by the bridge and some folks gave this name to the

*Figure 135.
Ohio's famed
Humpback covered
bridge over Raccoon
Creek in Vinton
County*

bridge. Earlier on, the miller here was Jacob Geer and the bridge was known for many years as the Geers Mill Bridge. Most of us prefer to call it old Humpback for obvious reasons.

Upstream a few miles from the Humpback Bridge stands the abandoned Eakin Mill Bridge, Figure 136, which was also known as the Arbaugh Bridge for the tiny community that

Figure 136. Covered bridge at Arbaugh

used to exist near it and also as Geers Mill Bridge because Henry Clay Geer, brother of Jacob, was the miller here for many years. Contracts for the construction of this bridge referred to it as the Eakin Mill Bridge. It is a single-span, double multiple kingpost truss with arches. Although the arches in this bridge rest on the lower chords, we feel certain that they were part of the original structure.

This oldtimer was built in 1870/71 by Gilman and Ward of McArthur, Ohio. The Appalachian Highway (SR 32) runs close to this bridge and was the cause of its being closed. Trucks carrying materials for the construction of this new road in the early 1970s caused such damage to the bridge that the county had to close it and it has been abandoned ever since. Plans are being made in 1992 to repair it.

Less than two miles upstream from Arbaugh was the little town of Vales Mills and the old Vales Mill Covered Bridge over Raccoon Creek. There are no records pertaining to the construction of the Vales Mill Bridge in the Vinton County records, but an 1836 entry in the Athens County Commissioners Journals mentions a bridge at this site.

On the College-Township Road (US 50) over Raccoon Creek was the Bolen's Mill Bridge built in 1841/42. Jacob Lentner lived close by the bridge site and superintended construction of the bridge for Athens County officials, but the name of the actual contractor is unknown. The bridge was a simple, one-span multiple kingpost truss that served this important highway into the 1920s.

More than 60 covered bridges served the traffic needs of Vinton County and many were built on the queenpost (QP) truss design. This was obviously the bridge truss preferred by the county officials. George Washington Pilcher (see Chapter II) built several queenpost bridges in Vinton County. He also was a master mason and built many bridge foundations in the area as well as working on buildings at Ohio University at Athens. The Mt.Olive Road Bridge, Figure 34, near Allensville, is one of Pilcher's queenpost truss bridges, built in 1875.

Figure 137. The Cox Bridge on its new site

In northern Vinton County just off SR 93 over Brushy Fork Creek is the 40 foot Cox Bridge built in 1884 by Diltz and Steel. It is a variation of the usual Vinton County QP truss because for some reason, the extra upper chord was eliminated. In late August 1992, workers from the Vinton County Engineer's office moved the Cox Bridge 20 feet north onto new concrete foundations.

The relocation and preservation of the Cox Bridge was handled in a very unique and innovative way. The ends of the bridge were jacked up and metal runners were placed under them. Strips of plywood were laid down both banks of the creek between the old and new locations. These plywood strips were then nailed together and liberally coated with heavy grease. Steel cables were fastened to the runners under the ends of the little covered bridge and attached to front loaders which then slowly pulled the little bridge onto its new site.[59] Figure 137 shows the Cox Bridge shortly after the move.

Near Creola on SR 93 over Brushy Fork, there once was a a flat-roofed Town lattice truss bridge built in 1919 by the Ohio Highway Department. Like so many of Ohio's covered bridges on the state highway system, it was removed in the 1950s (See Chapter XI). Also serving traffic on a road that became a state route was the old covered bridge near Ray over the middle fork of Salt Creek on what is now SR 327. Alex Ward built this double multiple kingpost truss with arches in 1873. For several years prior to its removal, the Ray Bridge stood unhoused, its old trusses open to the weather. The state removed it in 1956.

In 1966, Vinton County officials moved the old Bay or Tinker Bridge from Clinton Township where it had spanned Little Raccoon Creek near Hamden, to the Junior Fairgrounds north of McArthur just off Route 93. Graves and Scott built the Bay Bridge, a double multiple kingpost truss, in 1876 for $9.50 per linear foot. It cost $2,000. to move it north to the fairgrounds, less than 10 miles away.

As stated in the Gallia County section, there were many mills operating on Raccoon Creek and the majority of them were in Vinton County. On old SR 124 there was a bridge known as the Curry Mill or Hawk Bridge, Figure 138, another double timber multiple kingpost truss with arches that stood for a number of years after it was bypassed in the 1920s by a new steel truss bridge. Upstream on the Raccoon were the Worthman's Mill Bridge in Brown Township and the Hartley Mill Bridge and the Kecks Mill Bridge, both in Wilkesville Town-

Figure 138. Hawk or Curry Mill Bridge over Raccoon Creek

ship. Close to the tiny community of Moonville in Brown Township near the Moonville Tunnel of the Baltimore and Ohio Railroad, there were two wooden truss bridges over Raccoon Creek. Both were replaced circa 1900.

Vinton County had few railroad Howe trusses. Two through Howe truss bridges spanned the middle fork of Salt Creek near Ray and the same railroad had a deck-Howe over the Little Raccoon near Hamden.

HOCKING COUNTY

With its beautiful caves, rock outcroppings, miles of hiking trails, camping and fishing, Hocking County is truly the Wonderland of Ohio as proclaimed on a sign at Logan, the county seat. Logan was named for the great Mingo Chief Logan, and the name Hocking, also an Indian word, is from the Delaware for bottleneck. The Indians and early settlers called the river that flows through this county the Hockhocking.

Research has turned up close to 100 timber truss bridges in Hocking County, many of which were of the low or pony truss design with trusses separately-covered. The single kingpost truss was favored for the shorter spans and the multiple kingpost for the longer bridges. In 1856, Hocking County was building fully-covered bridges for under $300. References to combination bridges of wood and metal were also found in the county records for a somewhat later period.

The Smith Bridge Company was on the scene in Hocking County and built large Smith trusses over the Hocking River at Millville (todays Rockbridge) and at Enterprise. The Millville Bridge was a low (pony) Smith truss built in 1874. It failed just a few years later and the company replaced it with one of their pony metal truss bridges. The original cut-stone foundations of the wooden bridge are still in use here. The bridge at Enterprise was a full-size wooden truss built in 1875 and left uncovered until 1878.

Another familiar name in old Hocking County bridge building records is that of August Borneman and his Hocking Valley Bridge Works. Borneman built several combination truss bridges in Hocking County, including the high combination truss over Laurel Run on the north edge of Laurelville at Albins Mill.

G.J. and J.B. Haggerty of Licking County built the first covered bridge at Logan over the Hocking on Mulberry Street in 1855. In 1856, this bridge collapsed and was replaced by a two-lane multiple kingpost truss built by A. Dickens for $2,780. The next summer, this bridge had to be rebuilt at a cost of $2,000. By 1862, the same story of near collapse and rebuilding was unfolding again. The county insisted that Dickens and Gottlieb Bunz (another contractor involved) make immediate repairs as they had guaranteed their work. They added arches; two on each side and two on the center trusses. In 1864, a center pier was added for another $1195. A study of the picture of this bridge, Figure 139, shows these obvious additions. The bridge was finally replaced by a steel truss in the 1890s.

The Columbus and Hocking Valley Railroad built fully-covered Howe trusses in this area to serve the coal fields in the eastern part of the county. They built at least eight through Howe trusses over Monday Creek, Little Monday Creek and the Hocking River. Three of the new Howe trusses on the Monday Creek Division of the Hocking Valley were burned in 1884 by striking coal miners. It was at this time that coal miners set mine fires that smolder to this day.

Hocking County was one of those Ohio counties that began building the new metal truss bridges in the 1870s, while surrounding counties were still building the wooden truss bridges. The Motherwell Iron and Steel Company, located at Logan, may have been one of the reasons for this early interest in metal bridges. Floods in the 1870s and 1880s in the Hocking Valley destroyed many wooden bridges which were then replaced by modern metal trusses.

Figure 139. Mulberry Street Bridge at Logan in Hocking County -- 1856/57 - c1900

Figure 140.
Scene on Clear Creek
at the old Pine Grove
Covered Bridge,
c1900

When Ohio lost so many covered bridges in the great 1913 flood, Hocking County had already replaced most of its wood bridges with metal trusses. One county historian believed that the last wooden bridge in the county was over Clear Creek near the old Camp Wyandot (Camp Fire Girls) and that it was removed in the 1920s. There is an old picture, taken in the early 1930s, of a Hocking County covered bridge stripped for removal, site unknown. This proves that at least one of these bridges survived into the 1930s.

Figure 140 shows a family group wading in Clear Creek at the abandoned Pine Grove Bridge. This site was near present day US 33. The old tied arch bridge had been abandoned for many years before this picture was taken, circa 1900.

EXISTING BRIDGE LOCATIONS

Jackson County:
35-40-06 Johnson Road Bridge, 71' Smith, 1870, 4 m SW Petersburg, .5m ENE SR 776 over Lt. Scioto R.in Scioto Tp.

35-40-08 Byer Bridge, 74' Smith, 1872, over Pigeon Creek at Byer in Washington Tp.

35-40-11 Buckeye Furnace Bridge, 59' Smith, 1871, TR 165 off CR 58 over Little Raccoon Creek at Buckeye Furnace in Milton Tp.

Lawrence County:
35-44-05 Scottown Bridge, 79' MKP, 1877, 1.m E of Scottown and just S off SR 217 over Indian Guyan Creek in Windsor Tp.

Ross County:
35-71-02 Buckskin/South Salem Bridge, 99' Smith, 1873, CR 54 over Buckskin Creek on W edge of South Salem in Buckskin Tp.

Scioto County:
35-73-15 Otway Bridge, 127' Smith w/arches, 1874, over Scioto Brush Creek in Brush Creek Tp., off SR 348 just W of Otway. Bypassed.

Vinton County:
35-82-04 Mt. Olive Road Bridge, 48' QP, 1875, over mid fork of Salt Creek on TR 8 in Jackson Tp., 1.5m N of Allensville via CR 18.

35-82-05 Bay/Tinker Bridge, 63' double MKP, 1876, over pond on Junior Fairgrounds in Elk Tp. W off SR 93, N edge of McArthur. Pedestrian use only. Moved here 1966.

35-82-06 Humpback Bridge, 175' 3 span double MKP w/arches, 1874, over Raccoon Creek on TR 4 in Wilkesville Tp., 2.5m S of SR 124, 4m SW Wilkesville.

35-82-07 Eakin Mill Bridge, 108' double MKP w/ arches, 1870/71, over Raccoon Creek in Vinton Tp. on CR 38 (dead end),.3m off SR 32. Closed.

35-82-10 Cox Bridge, 40' QP, 1884, over Brushy Fork in Swan Tp. just W of SR 93,.8m S of junction of SR 56 and SR 93. Pedestrian and bike use only. Moved 20' off CR 20 in 1992.

Dixon Mill Bridge over the Little Scioto River in
Scioto County (pg 71)

Hall's Mill Bridge over Deer Creek in Ross
County (pg. 68)

CHAPTER V

IN THE APPALACHIAN HILLS

Athens, Meigs, Monroe, Morgan, Noble, Perry and Washington Counties

Figure 141. Ohio's Appalachian Hills

PERRY COUNTY

The dashing cavalry figure of Little Phil Sheridan dominates the town square at Somerset, a quiet and historic little town in Perry County, Sheridan's birthplace. Not far from the equestrian statue, an 82 foot covered bridge spanned the railroad cut on what is now SR 13, Figure 142. John Shrake built this bridge in 1862. The sign on the portal advises passersby: "For Choice Dry Goods Go To A.H. Yost". Note the figure on the church steeple.

One of Perry County's four remaining covered bridges spanned Rush Creek west of Somerset until 1987 when it was moved into the county fairgrounds at New Lexington. This is the Bowman Mill Bridge, an 81 foot multiple kingpost built in 1859 by Hocking County's Gottlieb Bunz. The formation of the Rush Creek

Dam that necessitated the moving of Fairfield County's Baker Bridge was also responsible for the moving of the Bowman Mill Bridge. It was completely renovated when moved to the fairgrounds.

A study of the Perry County Commissioners Journals revealed that, with few exceptions, all the covered bridges built for public highway use were on the Buckingham (multiple kingpost) truss plan. The majority of these simple bridges were built by a local man, William A. Dean who erected at least 24 covered wood and wood pony trusses from 1874 to 1884. As noted above, John Shrake and Gottlieb Bunz also built bridges in Perry County as did the firm of Black and Borneman and later,

Figure 142. Old covered bridge over the railroad cut at Somerset built by John Shrake in 1862

August Borneman. Another well-known local builder was Hiram Dennison. Many bridge foundations were laid up by Isaac Cotterman.

One of the earliest wooden bridges in Perry County was built to span Rush Creek at the foot of the Main Street hill in New Lexington in 1818. Just two years later, it was replaced by another wooden truss structure. There was a number of covered bridges built in the 1850s and 1860s including the Bowman Mill Bridge, Clum's Saw Mill Bridge and the Guinton Mill Bridge, all over Rush Creek.

There was a very old covered bridge over Jonathon Creek at the old mill in Glenford, Figure 143. There was no mention of this old bridge in the early county records so we think it may have been built by a turnpike company. Like so many other Ohio covered bridges, the Glenford Bridge was a victim of the great 1913 flood.

Figure 143. Glenford Covered Bridge

In addition to those bridges already listed, Perry County had covered bridges over Jonathon Creek at Glass Rock, at Mt. Perry, and at the Rousculp Mill west of Mt. Perry. The Kendall Farm/Chalfont Bridge just off SR 204 at Chalfont was over a branch of Jonathon Creek known as Painters Run. The Kendall Farm Bridge was for many years a landmark for those traveling Rt 204. The owners kept a model T Ford truck parked in the bridge for years. The Kendall Farm Bridge was bypassed in the late 1920s and despite years of neglect, it managed to stand until the winter of 1978 when it finally collapsed into the creek.

One-half mile below Chalfont on Painters Run is the trim Hopewell Church Bridge built in 1874 by Hiram Dennison for only $4.85 per linear foot. About one mile below the Hopewell Church Bridge on Painters Run is the old Parks or South Bridge, an outstanding example of the multiple kingpost truss built in 1883 by Dean. (See Chapter II for details of the Parks Bridge.) A third covered bridge spanned Painters Run south of the Parks Bridge at the Love Farm. Dean built this bridge in 1874 and it was removed by the county many years ago.

The fourth covered bridge still standing in Perry County is the Jacks Hollow Bridge, Figure 31, which spans Kents Run in the extreme northeastern section of the county, northeast of Mt. Perry. This is another of Dean's bridges, built in 1879. A few years ago, vandals set fire to the bridge, causing damage to some of the trusses and the bridge had to be closed for months. It was repaired and has been reopened to traffic.

In 1976, Perry County officials sanctioned the painting of their covered bridges red, white and blue in honor of our country's Bicentennial. The paint job looked good for a year or so, and then the colors began to fade. We regret that in the course of this painting, the distinctive gingerbread trim was removed from the Parks Bridge and never put back in place.

Other Perry County covered bridges that stood into the 1930s were: the Wigton School Bridge near Roseville, the Conway Bridge near Crooksville, and the Rehobeth Bridge just south of Rehobeth.

Perry County had many Howe truss railroad bridges on the old Zanesville and Western, the Cincinnati and Muskingum Valley and the Baltimore and Ohio Railroads. The Cincinnati and Muskingum Valley Railroad had many fully covered through-Howe truss bridges over Moxahala Creek in the Roseville and Crooksville area. There were both covered highway and railroad bridges in the village of Crooksville.

In 1986, another covered bridge joined the list of Perry County wooden bridges. Carroll Moore moved Fairfield County's Ruffner Bridge to his farm on SR 13 seven miles south of Interstate 70. It has been rebuilt over a small lake where it can be seen from the highway in a beautiful setting, Figure 144.

MORGAN COUNTY

Unlike other counties split by the Muskingum River, Morgan County had only one large covered bridge spanning that great waterway. It had taken the citizens of Morgan County years to get to the point where a bridge was actually under construction to span the Muskingum River between Malta and McConnelsville. There had been so many setbacks and delays, but finally the iron bridge on stone abutments and piers was coming along well and due for completion in December, 1866. However, more delays occured and in February 1867, rapidly rising floodwaters tore out the two completed iron spans. In despair, the stockholders of the Morgan Bridge Company told their Directors to erect a wooden bridge on the site without delay.[60] And so, the McConnelsville Bridge was built in 1867 by two contractors from Washington County, Fouts and Grubb. The long-awaited bridge they built was a three-span, 565 foot long structure, Figure 145. Although we cannot be certain, we think this was probably a multiple kingpost truss. After serving only 34 years, the covered bridge was replaced by the present steel truss in 1901.

Figure 144. The Ruffner/Moore Bridge

We know that the rest of the county's covered bridges were small, one-span multiple kingposts. One of the loveliest of these little bridges is the old Barkhurst Mill Bridge, Figure 146, back on a narrow township road over Wolf Creek northeast of Chesterhill. Nearby is the decrepit old Barkhurst Mill, built in 1830 and unused for many years. The 84 foot covered bridge was built in 1872 and the three-ply laminated arches were probably a later addition. Due to flooding problems here, the bridge is anchored to its abutments by iron rods, Figure 147. Both road and bridge are seldom used.

*Figure 145.
Old covered bridge
at McConnelsville
over the
Muskingum River,
built 1867*

Figure 146. Barkhurst Mill Bridge spans Wolf Creek in Morgan County

Another very scenic Morgan County covered bridge is the Helmick Mill or Island Run Bridge near Eagleport, Figure 148. This old bridge is a 72 foot multiple kingpost truss which now has a center pier added sometime after the 1940s. Our picture shows the bridge before the pier was added. A natural falls below the bridge makes this a favorite spot for artists, photographers and swimmers. The original wooden siding was replaced by corrugated metal many years ago. The Helmick Mill Bridge was built in 1867, four years after a band of Morgan's Raiders made a dash down the valley of Island Run to the Muskingum River where they crossed at Eagleport.

Strip mining has changed the face of eastern Morgan County and many covered bridges have disappeared from this area. The Ohio Power Company (OPC) has reclaimed much of the land and turned hundreds of acres into recreation land where boating, fishing, camping and hiking can be enjoyed. The OPC has also salvaged a covered bridge from nearby Noble

Figure 147. Barkhurst Mill Bridge abutment detail

Figure 148. Helmick Mill Bridge over Island Run

County and brought it to the Campsite D where it now spans Brannons Fork. However, no effort was made to save four covered bridges in the OPC strip mine area in Manchester Township in the 1960s. Gone are the Foster, Fowler, Woodgrove and Gilliland Bridges.

Morgan County lost six small covered bridges in the late 1940s when the east branch of Sunday Creek was dammed up to form Burr Oak Lake. Lost were the Quill Ervin, Frank Bishop, Dave Roberts, Mark McDonald, Wes Akers and Andy Williams Bridges, all single-span multiple kingpost trusses.

Preserved on the county fairgrounds at McConnelsville is the covered bridge moved from Rosseau in the southwestern part of the county where it had spanned a branch of Wolf Creek. The county moved this bridge in 1953, the first Ohio covered bridge to be preserved in this manner.

There is one more covered bridge still standing in Morgan County, the Adams or San Toy Bridge over a branch of Sunday Creek near the Perry County line. It was built in 1875 and is now in very poor condition. The little bridge has been closed to traffic for several years and is now the property of the County Historical Society who hopes to move it to a park at Malta. Area residents want the old bridge to stay where it is, possibly to be restored in place. No timber truss railroad bridges have been recorded for Morgan County.

NOBLE COUNTY

Forty years ago, a trip down almost any road in Noble County, state highway, county road or township lane would have taken you across at least one old covered bridge. The total of known covered bridges for this youngest and smallest Ohio county stands at 110, including seven Howe and combination truss railroad bridges. With few exceptions, the highway bridges of Noble County were built on the multiple kingpost truss plan.

Exhaustive research work was done in the area by Anita Knight, John Diehl and Earnest Bates and much of what is now known of the covered bridges of Noble county is due to the hard work of Mrs.Knight who took the 1940 Bates and Diehl list and added to it several times over. We are privileged to have the black and white photos taken in 1940 by the late Mr.Bates as he traveled the back roads of his home county, recording the bridges that were left at that time.

The efforts mentioned above were important because work was going forward at that time on the construction of Seneca Lake and many Noble County covered bridges fell victim to that project in the late 1930s and early 1940s.

The ravages of time, strip mining and oil well drilling have taken their toll here and by the early 1990s, only four covered bridges still remain in Noble County. Two of the county's covered bridges, Rich Valley and Park Hill Road, were torn down in 1970 and parts of both went into the little covered bridge now on the fairgrounds at Caldwell, Figure 149. The covered bridge spans a small ravine near an old country church and log cabin. This is one of the best examples of what can be achieved by moving old buildings to the right site on a county fairgrounds.

Figure 149. Caldwell Fairgrounds Bridge built from the remains of two Noble County covered bridges

The Wood/Huffman Bridge carries a private farm lane over the mid fork of Duck Creek just off SR 564 south of Middleburg. This bridge was built circa 1914 to replace a bridge destroyed by the 1913 flood. It was bypassed by a road relocation less than 20 years later and has been privately owned ever since.

Bypassed a few years ago, the Parrish Bridge over Olive Green Creek, south of Sharon and SR 78, is now a part of the county's park system. Nearby in Sharon Township is the Manchester Bridge, Figure 150, the last covered bridge carrying public highway traffic in Noble County. Local legends say that the Manchester and Parrish Bridges were both built after the 1913 flood to replace earlier bridges destroyed by that great catastrophe.

Figure 150. Manchester Bridge

As mentioned previously, strip mining and the formation of Seneca Lake have taken their toll of the covered bridges of Noble County. Among those bridges removed for Seneca Lake were: the Beaver/Stephans, Wells, Rich Wilson, Mose Bates and Laymon Wilson Bridges. The Crumtown Bridge was among those lost to the ravages of strip mining. It spanned the east fork of Duck Creek just off SR 260 near Elk. In 1972, it was finally removed after standing abandoned for many years. The old Crumtown Bridge was but one of many covered bridges that spanned Duck Creek and its forks in Noble County.

At Belle Valley, on the old turnpike that was known as the Marietta and National Road Plank Road (later US 21 and now SR 821), there was a covered bridge over Wolf Run, Figure 151. This bridge featured sidewalks for pedestrian safety.

Two railroads served Noble County and there were a total of eight wooden Howe truss bridges on these lines. The Ohio River and Western (also known as the Bellaire, Zanesville and Cincinnati) Railroad had a 70 foot pony Howe truss over the west fork of Duck Creek at Caldwell, the county seat. The Wheeling and Lake Erie Railroad's Marietta Division had through-Howe trusses, deck-Howes and combination wood and metal trusses on their route down the valley of the west fork of Duck Creek. The Wheeling and Lake Erie Railroad's Marietta Division was 96 miles long and according to the old Railroad Reports, six percent of this line was in trestles and wood bridges. They kept a crew of carpenters busy year round, building and repairing these structures. A typical through-Howe truss on this railroad was 14 feet wide and 22 feet high.[61]

Figure 151. Covered bridge at Belle Valley on the old Marietta and National Road Plank Road

MONROE COUNTY

Monroe County is known as the Switzerland of Ohio because of its ruggedly beautiful landscape. The principal streams of Monroe County are the Little Muskingum River and its tributaries. Two covered bridges still stand in Monroe County in the early 1990s, the Foraker Bridge and the Knowlton Bridge. Both span the Little Muskingum River.

The Knowlton Bridge, Figure 152, also known as the Long or Old Camp Bridge, is a three span, 192 foot multiple kingpost truss with arches on the center span. It sets high above the river on cut-stone abutments and piers. The Knowlton Bridge, built in 1887, has been abandoned for many years. There is a small rural park at the north end of the bridge.

The Foraker Bridge, Figure 153, is a single span, 92 foot multiple kingpost truss that was

Figure 154. The Jericho Bridge
- they partied here at night

also built in 1887. It has been heavily reinforced over the years and steel I-beams running from abutment to abutment now carry the load. The steel cables on the trusses were installed in 1938 by Louis S. "Stock" Bower who also did extensive work on the Knowlton Bridge that same year.

At Jericho over the Little Muskingum River on the Jericho-Low Gap Road was a covered bridge built about 1866, Figure 154. Like many covered bridges, it was a community gathering place and dances were sometimes held in the old bridge at night.[62] It goes without saying that night-time traffic on this rough, unpaved road was light in those days. In 1936, the old Jericho Bridge was replaced by a concrete structure in a WPA project.

A partial list of other Monroe County covered bridges that are now only memories: Burkhart Station, Calais, Clarington, Clifty, Cranenest, Earlwine, Marr and Sycamore Valley.

Monroe County had only two wooden truss railroad bridges that we can document and both were on the county's only rail line, the old Bellaire, Zanesville and Cincinnati (Ohio River and Western) or, as it was known to the locals, the Bent, Zigzag and Crooked Railroad. One of these bridges was a 90 foot deck-Howe truss over Sunfish Creek near Coats, and the other was a 100 foot, two-span pony Howe truss over the south fork of Wills Creek at Burkhart Station.

Figure 152. The Knowlton Covered Bridge

Figure 153. The Foraker Bridge

WASHINGTON COUNTY

The oldest continuing city in Ohio and certainly one of the loveliest and most historic, is Marietta at the confluence of the mighty Muskingum and Ohio Rivers. Many settlers entered Ohio at this point, traveling on upstream on the Muskingum River. They replenished supplies at Marietta before continuing on their journeys. Campus Martius Museum has many artifacts of pioneer life as it was lived in the early days of this area. The 1788 Ohio Land Company Office at Campus Martius is the oldest building in the Northwest Territory.[63]

The Muskingum River flows through Washington County and as might be expected, there

bridges which were Smith trusses built on Mr. Stultz's Plan #4. The Beverly Bridge had two 151 foot covered spans, plus one 149 foot open span, a 35 foot wood pony truss span, a 60 foot trestle and a 129 foot swing bridge over the canal. The Beverly Bridge cost $20,500. The bridge at Lowell was built in three spans of 155 foot each with a 15 foot roadway and open approach spans on each end, Figure 155.

In June of 1883, a great windstorm severely damaged the Lowell Bridge which had to be rebuilt at a cost of $3,000. In 1884, the Ohio River flooded to 44 feet at Marietta and this of course, caused flooding on the Muskingum River which caused further damage to the bridge at Lowell which had to be repaired

*Figure 155.
Covered Bridge
over the
Muskingum River
in Washington
County at Lowell,
1881 - 1913*

were a number of large wooden truss bridges built to span this magnificent stream. One of the first covered bridges to span the Muskingum River in Washington County was built in 1859 to link Marietta and Harmar, the settlement on the west bank of the river. This was known as the Butler Street Bridge and was a four-span Burr truss built by private investors. It was rebuilt as a railroad bridge in 1873 and served until 1880 when it was replaced by an uncovered Howe truss.

In 1881, two large covered bridges were built to span the Muskingum River north of Marietta at the river towns of Lowell and Beverly. Stultz and Townsend were the contractors for both

again. Both the Beverly and Lowell Bridges were lost in the great 1913 flood.

Turnpike companies were building covered bridges at an early date in Washington County. One such bridge was at the Little Muskingum Mills over Duck Creek where SR 26 crosses that stream today. An 1815 Act of the Legislature authorized construction of this bridge which was known as the Farmers Duck Creek Bridge. In the early 1860s, Washington County officials bought a bridge and tollhouse at this site for $3,000. and then spent over $1,000. more in repairs to the bridge which was probably not the original structure on this site.

Before construction of Interstate Route 77, the most important road in eastern Washington County was US 21, now known as SR 821. In the early days of the county, this was the old Marietta and National Road Plank Road, a privately-owned toll pike that connected Marietta with the National Road. There were many covered bridges on this road in Washington County: Boyce's Mill, Cedar Narrows, Lower Salem and Macksburg. The only known picture of a covered bridge on this old road is Noble County's Belle Valley Bridge, Figure 151.

Western Washington County had many covered bridges built at an early date, too. There were covered spans at Wolf Creek Mills (oldest mill site in Ohio), at Watertown, Figure 156, at Woodruff's Ford and Bartlett's Ford. All of these bridges were on what is now SR 339 over Wolf Creek and its branches.

Figure 156. Watertown Bridge built by Henderson

Three of the county's remaining covered bridges span branches of Wolf Creek: the Harra Bridge, a 96 foot Long truss built in 1878 by Rolla Merydith, the Bell Bridge, a 63 foot MKP built in 1888 by E.B. Henderson, and the Shinn Bridge, also built by Henderson, Figure 32. The Shinn Bridge was built in 1886 as the direct result of a near-drowning which occured when the Shinn family was crossing Wolf Creek in a rowboat and as they docked, the youngest child, a three year old girl, lost her balance and fell into the swiftly moving water. Only the

quick action of an older brother saved this child. Petitions were presented to the County Commissioners asking for a bridge at Shinn's Ford. E.B.Henderson built this bridge for $7.70 per linear foot.

In the late 1960s, the Marietta Jaycees undertook the moving of the Schwendeman or Bennett Bridge from Warren Township where it spanned Halfway Run to Jackson Hill Park at Marietta. This old bridge, built in 1894 by Henderson, now spans a ravine in the park.

Another Washington County covered bridge was moved in 1980 from Belpre Township where it had spanned Mill Branch Creek, to the Barlow Fairgrounds at the junction of SR 550 and 339.

A number of covered bridges were built to span the West Branch in western Washington County and two of those bridges are still in existance in the early 1990s. The Henry or Goddard Bridge, Figure 157, was built by Henderson in 1894 after a small child slipped off of a shakey footbridge on her way to school and drowned in the flood swollen waters of the creek. Not far from the Henry Bridge is the Root Bridge, a 70 foot Long truss built by Rolla Merydith in 1878. Both the Henry and Root Bridges are now bypassed.

Figure 157. The Henry Bridge over West Branch

In 1961, the late Dr. H.B. Hune, then 90 years old, reminisced with a friend about his life as a boy on his father's farm on the Little Muskingum River in the 1870s. He well remembered the surveyors coming to select the site for a bridge over the river on the Hune Farm. The year was 1879 and the builder, Rolla Merydith of Marietta, came to board at the Hune Farm while the bridge was under construction. He brought his young son with him to play with the little Hune boy. Dr. Hune remembered that the stone for the abutments was quarried right there on the farm and the yellow poplar used to build the sturdy Long trusses also came from the family farm.[64] The Hune Bridge as it looks today is seen in Figure 158.

linear foot. It was bypassed in 1990. Other Little Muskingum River covered bridges were: Wilsons Run, Bloomfield, Scottown, Cow Run (Figure 48), Archers Ford, Bear Run and Mackey's Ford.

Other well-known Washington County covered bridges now gone these many years were: Belpreville over the Little Hocking River, Figure 159, Ransom Lane, Ormiston, Williams, and Twin Bridges to name just a few.

The Wheeling and Lake Erie Railroad's Marietta Division served eastern Washington County and they had at least three Howe trusses over Duck Creek in the Macksburg and Whipple areas. The Baltimore and Ohio Railroad had a three-span Howe truss over the Muskingum River at Marietta.

Figure 158. The Hune Bridge over the Little Muskingum River in Washington County, built 1879 by Rolla Merydith

Upstream from the Hune Farm was the Rinard Bridge built to span the Little Muskingum River in 1871. Four years later Dr. Hune said he saw the wreckage of the Rinard Bridge float past their farm during a flood.[65]. The present Rinard Bridge was built in 1876 by the Smith Bridge Company to replace the flood-wrecked span. The 140 foot Rinard Bridge is now bypassed.

One other covered bridge still crosses the Little Muskingum today, the fine old Hills Bridge built in 1878 by the Hocking Valley Bridge Works, Figure 84. This outstanding example of the Howe truss system cost $13. per

Figure 159. Belpreville Bridge

ATHENS COUNTY

The City of Athens lies in a curve of the Hocking River which surrounds the town on three sides. This much river frontage demanded substantial bridges at an early date and there were some interesting humpback bridges built to span the Hocking at Athens in the 1830s.

On the east edge of town was the East or Stewart's Mill Bridge, built in 1834, a two lane multiple kingpost truss. This bridge was modeled after the bridges at Zanesville built by the Buckinghams. There was an Athens County connection to the Buckingham Family of Zanesville, Ohio. Ebenezer Buckingham, Sr., settled in Carthage Township, Athens County in 1801.[66]. He was the father of Ebenezer Buckingham, Jr., one of the owners of the Y Bridge Company. His son, Catherinus, built the famed Y Bridge at Zanesville in 1832. (See Chapter II)

On the west edge of Athens at Joseph Herrold's Mills, was a fine, two lane multiple kingpost truss bridge built in 1834 by Isaac Jackson. Close by was the two-span covered Howe truss of the Marietta and Cincinnati Railroad. Figure 160 shows these two bridges and the fine brick home of Mr. Herrold who was a prominent businessman and also a bridge builder and designer. He designed and/or built many bridges in Athens County.

At the south edge of Athens was a bridge over the Hocking known, naturally, as the South Bridge, built in 1839. In 1876, this bridge was dismantled and taken to Millfield where it was rebuilt over Sunday Creek. A new covered South Bridge was built by the Smith Bridge Company that same year. It served until its destruction in the 1907 flood. The original East, South and West Bridges in Athens were all built in the 1830s by private companies and were toll bridges until the county bought them in the 1850s.

Another early Athens County covered bridge built with a pronounced camber was the Margaret Creek Bridge, Figure 161. It spanned Margaret Creek on what is now SR 56 southwest of Athens. It was torn down in the 1930s. The Bingham Mill Bridge crossed Margaret Creek close to Herrolds Mill on SR 683. Joseph Herrold built this bridge in 1845.

Figure 161. The Margaret Creek Bridge

Figure 160. The covered bridges over the Hocking River at Joseph Herrolds west of Athens

There were covered bridges over the Hocking River on the highways and railroads at Nelsonville in northern Athens County. The highway bridges were at Brooks Mill (where SR 278 crosses today) and at Robbins Mill at the southwest edge of Nelsonville. Both of the covered railroad bridges were on the Hocking Valley Railroad.

The Brooks/Nelsonville Bridge was built in 1873 by the Smith Bridge Company and served this crossing until 1944. Just how many bridges did span the river at this site is unknown, but we do know that an uncovered timber truss was built here in 1827, first bridge across the river in Athens County. It collapsed the following year and was replaced immediately. In 1870, W.B. Brooks, local businessman who owned the Brooks Coal Works at Nelsonville, asked the county to help him build a bridge over the Hocking there. The county agreed to pay half, or $400. The bridge was built and must have turned out to be a very substantial covered structure because, after it washed out in 1873, Mr.Brooks approached the County Commissioners asking for $2,513. which he claimed the county owed him for building the bridge. After much haggling, the county decided not to pay any more money on this bridge as they had already paid $428. and figured they did not owe the unfortunate Brooks another cent.

The Robbins Bridge at Nelsonville was privately owned and the county reached an agreement with the owner, Mr.Robbins, that would allow the traveling public to use the bridge. It was built in 1868 and survived the 1873 flood which destroyed the Brooks Bridge. When it was finally removed is unknown.

Other major covered bridges spanned the Hocking River in Athens County at Courtalls Ford near Nelsonville, at Beaumont, at Webster Mill five miles east of Athens, at Guysville, at Frost Station and at Coolville. The Coolville Bridge was a 14 panel Howe truss built by private investors in 1840. In 1869, the county bought the bridge for $2,842. The great flood of March 1913 brought the waters up to the eaves of the Coolville Bridge (see Chapter XI), but it held fast and continued to serve the public until the early 1930s.

The Guysville or Savannah Bridge was a 163 foot Smith truss built in 1869 by the Smith Bridge Company for $18.50 per linear foot to which was added an extra $50. for two coats of paint. The Guysville Bridge carried the heavy traffic of US 50 until its replacement in 1951.

Athens County also had important covered bridges over Federal Creek northeast of Stewart (the Federal Creek Tollbridge) on SR 329, built in 1842, and the Amesville and Big Run Bridges.

Athens County has three covered bridges still standing: the Palos or Newton Bridge over Sunday Creek off SR 13, the Kidwell Bridge also over Sunday Creek off SR 13, and the Blackwood Bridge over a branch of the Shade River. The Palos Bridge, Figure 162, is an 81 foot multiple kingpost truss built in 1876. There are counterbraces on the end truss members of this bridge. In 1977, the bridge was completely boarded up on the inside to keep vandals from stealing the siding boards and to prevent the accumulation of trash along the lower chords.

The Kidwell Bridge, Figure 163, is an 1880 product of the Hocking Valley Bridge Works of

Figure 162. Palos Bridge

Lancaster, Ohio. The bridge is a 96 foot Howe truss. It has been closed since 1978 when an overloaded truck caused extensive damage.

The Blackwood Bridge is located in Lodi Township over a branch of the Shade River far off the beaten path. It was built in 1879 by E.B. Henderson for $6.75 per linear foot. In 1905, steel tension rods were added to strengthen the old MKP trusses, and in 1975, a steel pier was

Figure 163. Borneman's Kidwell Bridge, a Howe truss built over Sunday Creek in 1880

placed under the old structure. All three of Athens County's remaining covered bridges are on the National Register of Historic Places.

Coal mining was one of this area's leading industries and as a result, the county was well supplied with railroads. On these railroads there were at least 17 through-Howe truss bridges, some of which were fully covered. The Toledo and Ohio Central Railroad had 11 timber truss railroad bridges in Athens County, all of which were through-Howe trusses except for three queenpost trusses over Margaret Creek.

The Columbus and Hocking Valley Railroad had six through-Howe truss bridges in Hocking County.

MEIGS COUNTY

None of the covered bridges of Meigs County that were built in yesteryear remain today and no one is certain how many there were. We believe the last covered bridge in the county was removed before 1930. Research has turned up only a few timber truss bridges for this Ohio River county. However, we know that major highway covered bridges spanned the Shade River at Chester and at Keno.

There were two wooden truss bridges at Chester. The first was burned by Morgan's Raiders in July 1863 and was replaced by a Long truss with arches, Figure 164. This covered bridge was replaced in 1926 by a concrete arch bridge.

Raccoon Creek flows through the extreme northwest corner of Meigs County in Columbia Township. A covered bridge spanned the creek at Starr Mill. Local legend says that the bridge washed out in the 1913 flood.

The Toledo and Ohio Central Railroad traversed Meigs County and crossed Margaret Creek and Leading Creek on small queenpost truss bridges. This rail line also had a large through-Howe truss over the mouth of Leading Creek south of Middleport.

Figure 164. Shade River bridge at Chester in Meigs County, built 1863 to replace a bridge burned by Morgan's Raiders

EXISTING BRIDGE LOCATIONS

ATHENS COUNTY:

35-05-01 Palos Bridge, 75' MKP, 1875, over Sunday Creek 1m NE Glouster & SR 78 on TR 347, in Trimble Tp. sec 4.

35-05-02 Kidwell Bridge, 96' Howe, 1880, over Sunday Creek 1.75m N Millfield on TR 332 in Dover Tp. sec 18. Closed.

35-05-06 Blackwood Bridge, 64' MKP, 1881, over mid branch Shade River 4m ESE Shade & US 33 on CR 46 off CR 44 in Lodi Tp. sec 1.

MONROE COUNTY:

35-56-14 Foraker Bridge, 92' MKP, 1886, over Lt. Muskingum River 3m E Graysville on CR 40 in Perry Tp. sec 28.

35-56-18 Knowlton Bridge, 192' 3 span MKP+arches, 1887, over Lt. Muskingum River 1.5m N Rinard Mills on TR 384 in Washington Tp. sec 6. Closed.

MORGAN COUNTY:

35-58-15 Barkhurst Mill Bridge, 81'MKP+arches, 1872, over Wolf Creek 2m ENE Chesterhill on dead-end TR 21, in Marion Tp. sec 4. Road closed south of bridge.

35-58-32 Rosseau Bridge, 58' MKP on county fairgrounds at SE edge of McConnelsville, off SR 376, .5m S junc SR 60. Moved here from Rosseau in 1953.

35-58-35 Helmick Mill/Island Run Bridge, 74' MKP, 1867, over Island Run 2.25m SW Eagleport on TR 269 off CR 74, in Deerfield Tp. sec 2.

35-58-38 Adams/San Toy Bridge, 58' MKP, 1875, over branch of Sunday Creek .5m W SR 555 on TR 16, in Union Tp. sec 6. Closed.

35-58-41 Milton Dye Bridge, 41' MKP, c. 1923/24, over Brannon's Fork 3.25m NE Bristol, in the Ohio Power Company Campsite D off SR 83, in Manchester Tp. sec 7. Moved here in 1965 from Noble County. Closed.

NOBLE COUNTY:

35-61-33 Manchester Bridge, 49' MKP, 1915, over branch of Olive Green Creek 2m S Olive Green & SR 78 on TR 3, in Sharon Tp. sec 14.

35-61-34 Parrish Bridge, 81'MKP, 1914, over Olive Green Creek 2.5m SSW Sharon & SR 78, off CR 8, in Sharon Tp. sec 24. Bypassed.

35-61-40 Park Hill/Rich Valley Bridge, 44' MKP, on county fairgrounds off SR 78 at SW edge of Caldwell. Moved here in 1970.

35-61-57 Wood/Huffman Bridge, 59' MKP, c.1914, over mid fork Duck Creek 1.5m SE Middleburg, on private farm lane just off SR 564 in Jefferson Tp. sec 36. Private.

PERRY COUNTY:

35-64-02 Parks/South Bridge, 58' MKP, 1883, over Painter Run 1.5m S Chalfont & SR 204 on CR 33, in Hopewell Tp. sec 26.

35-64-03 Hopewell Church Bridge, 55' MKP, 1874, over Painter Run .5m S Chalfont & SR 204 on CR 51, in Hopewell Tp. sec 22.

35-64-05 Jacks Hollow Bridge, 60' MKP, 1879, over Kents Run 3m NE Mt. Perry & SR 204 on TR 108, in Madison Tp. sec 3.

35-64-06 Bowman Mill Bridge, 82' MKP, 1859, on county fairgrounds off SR 37 on W edge of New Lexington. Moved here in 1987 from Reading Tp.

35-64-84 Ruffner/Moore Bridge, 78' Smith, 1875, over pond on private farm lane on the Carroll Moore Farm on SR 13, 7m S I-70, in Thorn Tp. sec 26. Moved here from Fairfield County in 1986. Private.

WASHINGTON COUNTY:

35-84-03 Shinn Bridge, 98' MKP+arches, 1886, over west branch Wolf Creek 2m S SR 676 on TR 447, in Palmer Tp. sec 14.

35-84-06 Henry Bridge, 45' MKP, 1894, over West Branch, 2m N Cutler off TR 61, in Fairfield Tp. sec 20. Bypassed.

WASHINGTON COUNTY
(CONTINUED)

35-84-08 Root Bridge, 65' Long, 1878, over West Branch .5m N Decaturville & SR 555 off CR 6, in Decatur Tp. sec 11/17. Bypassed.

35-84-11 Harra Bridge, 95' Long, 1878, over south branch Wolf Creek 2m NW Watertown off TR 172, in Watertown Tp. Bypassed.

35-84-12 Bell Bridge, 63' MKP, 1888, over sw branch of Wolf Creek 2m NW Barlow on TR 39, in Barlow Tp. sec 29.

35-84-17 Mill Branch Bridge, 59' MKP, over brook on Barlow Fairgrounds at junction of SR 550 & SR 339 in Barlow Tp. Moved here in 1980 from Belpre Tp.

35-84-20 Schwendeman Bridge, 44' MKP, 1894, in Jackson Hill Park at Marietta off SR 60 on N. Washington St. which becomes Cisler Dr. Moved here in 1967 from Warren Tp.

35-84-24 Hills/Hildreth Bridge, 122' Howe, 1878, over Lt. Muskingum River 4m E I-77, S off SR 26 on CR 333, in Newport Tp. sec 36. Bypassed.

35-84-27 Hune/Gallagher Ford Bridge, 128' Long, 1879, over Lt. Muskingum River off SR 26 on TR 34 at Lawrence in Lawrence Tp. sec 6.

35-84-28 Rinard Bridge, 130' Smith, 1876, over Lt. Muskingum River, off SR 26 off CR 406, 1m E Wingett Run, in Ludlow Tp. sec 26. Bypassed.

The Parks Bridge as it looked c.1970

*Brooks or Nelsonville
Bridge over Hocking
River in Athens County,
1873-1944 (pg.94)*

*Calais Bridge over
Seneca Fork of Wills
Creek on St. Rt. 379 in
Monroe County (pg. 89)*

*Crumtown Bridge over
the East Fork of Duck
Creek in Noble County
off St. Rt 260 near Elk
(pg 88)*

CHAPTER VI

THE EAST CORRIDOR ALONG
THE NATIONAL ROAD

Belmont, Carroll, Coshocton, Guernsey, Harrison, Holmes, Jefferson, Muskingum, and Tuscarawas Counties

Figure 165. East Corridor Along the National Road

The topography of east central Ohio is much like that of the southeastern section, rugged and hilly with deep valleys and many small streams. Large rivers such as the Walhonding and Tuscarawas which come together at Coshocton to form the mighty Muskingum River are a major part of the drainage system of this area. The Licking and Mohican Rivers and Wills and Killbuck Creeks were also of great importance to the settlers in this region as they depended on the larger streams for transportation and on all of them for power for their mills.

BELMONT COUNTY

In 1953, an overloaded truck caused the collapse of the last covered bridge in Belmont County. Twenty years after this accident, Belmont County Engineer, R.J.Boccabella who had long wanted a covered bridge for his county, managed to get one from Fairfield County. The Shaeffer/Campbell Bridge over Clear Creek south of Amanda was scheduled to be torn down and Fairfield County officials were only too happy to let it go to Belmont County. The bridge, Figure 166, was rebuilt over a small lake (created by the construction of nearby Interstate 70) on the Belmont Campus of Ohio University. It sets on wooden piers with open approach spans on both ends. Mr.Boccabella designed the railings on these approach spans after those found on the summer home of Mark Twain.

Perhaps the best-known of the covered bridges of Belmont County was the Bridgeport Bridge over the west channel of the Ohio River, Figure 2, at Bridgeport (see Chapter I). Belmont County built many wooden bridges for very nominal amounts of money in the 1830s, 1840s

Figure 166. Schaeffer/Campbell Bridge

and 1850s, most of which we have to assume were of the pony truss variety. However, the county did build three major covered bridges in the 1830s and 1840s: at Bridgeport over Wheeling Creek on the River Road (now SR 7), at Bellaire over McMahon Creek, also on the River Road, and at Steinersville over Captina Creek west of Powhatan Point. These three bridges were all battered by frequent flooding and all had to be rebuilt at least once. We have a clue from reports of a rebuilding job at the Bellaire Bridge, that it and the Bridgeport Wheeling Creek bridges were Town trusses. All three of these early covered bridges were replaced by iron trusses in the 1860s.

Belmont County began building iron bridges in 1859 and only the less important crossings got wooden spans. Then, for some reason, in 1877, county officials hired the Smith Bridge Company to build a covered Smith truss at Captina. This was known as the Dover Bridge, Figure 167. The following year, the Smith Bridge Company built the Grahams Crossing Bridge over Captina Creek, a 131 foot multiple kingpost truss, for $14. per linear foot. This is the bridge that collapsed under the coal truck in 1953.

For the most part, local builders took care of the wood bridge business in Belmont County with but few exceptions which included the Smith Bridge Company and the well-known

Figure 167. Dover Bridge over Captina Creek

Shrake family of Licking County. Many of the wooden truss bridges of Belmont County were to be found on its railroads. There were 14 Howe trusses over McMahon Creek on the Baltimore and Ohio's Central divison from just west of Warnock to the Ohio River. Seven of these bridges were fully-covered. The old Bent, Zigzag and Crooked Railroad had a number of wooden truss and combination bridges in Belmont County, too.

GUERNSEY COUNTY

The principle stream of Guernsey County is Wills Creek with its major tributaries of Salt Fork and Seneca Fork. Many bridges were necessary to carry the public over all these creeks and our research shows that over 100 wooden truss bridges were built in Guernsey County.

In the 1830s, bridge builders in Guernsey County were putting up what they termed "self supporting" bridges, no doubt some type of wooden truss. In his Sketches of a Tour to the Western Country, author and traveler Fortescue Cumings tells of crossing an unsafe old wooden bridge over Wills Creek at Cambridge in 1810.[67] This was a predecessor to the well-known, two-lane covered bridge built there in 1828. This was probably one of those early "self supporting" bridges.

Most of Guernsey County's covered bridges were built by local contractors, but a notable exception was Ebenezer B. Henderson who built two small multiple kingpost truss bridges here in 1878 over Salt Fork: the Dr.Clark Bridge and the Hackley Bridge. As in all Ohio counties, time has winnowed out these oldtimers until only three remain in the early 1990s: the Armstrong, Indian Camp and Reservoir Bridges.

When Salt Fork Reservoir was under construction in the 1960s, it was decided by county officials to save the four covered bridges that stood within its boundaries: the Gunn, Armstrong, Leeper and Milligan Bridges. As it turned out, only one was saved. The Leeper Bridge collapsed under an overloaded truck in 1964 and the Milligan Bridge was burned by vandals in 1966. Efforts to save the Gunn Bridge went to naught and the waters of Salt

Fork Reservoir rose up around the old structure where it stood. A portion of the trusses can still be seen above the waters today.

In 1849, the county hired Abraham Armstrong to build a covered bridge over Salt Fork at his mill at Clio for $510. The date of 1849 makes the Armstrong Bridge one of the oldest covered bridges in Ohio. Clio was one of those little villages once so vital to rural citizens with its post office, general store and mill. Unfortunately, Clio was one of the sites in the way of Salt Fork Reservoir and had to be destroyed. Fortunately, the Armstrong Bridge, Figure 168, was saved and moved into Cambridge City Park in the winter of 1966/67.

Figure 169. Indian Camp Bridge

Figure 168. Armstrong Bridge in Cambridge City Park

The Indian Camp and Reservoir Bridges are Guernsey County's other two covered bridges still in existance. The Indian Camp Bridge is the last such bridge to carry traffic, Figure 169. It is a 40 foot multiple kingpost which has been heavily reinforced with steel beams. The Reservoir Bridge was built circa 1900 by the Baltimore and Ohio Railroad to provide access to their reservoir. This bridge is a 43 foot multiple kingpost in very poor condition. Ownership is in doubt and unless some action is taken very soon, the bridge will collapse into Leatherwood Creek. (Collapsed - May, 1993)

Nearby, at Quaker City, there was once a covered bridge over Leatherwood Creek at the center of town, Figure 170. This bridge was probably built by a turnpike company as it is

not mentioned in old county records. We know it was in service in 1874 because there is a record of a wedding taking place there in December of that year. Rather a cold and drafty wedding site! In 1885, the Quaker City bridge was badly damaged by a flood and it was decided to take it down and rebuild it over Leatherwood Creek between Quaker City and Salesville. The bridge served here until its removal in 1958.

Many highway and railroad wooden truss bridges spanned Wills Creek in Guernsey County. A partial list of the highway bridges would include: the Kennedy Bridge, the Tyner or Narrows Bridge at the junction of Wills and Salt Creek, the Barnes Mill Bridge, the Oldham Bridge, the Byesville Bridge, the DeHart Bridge, the Birds Run Bridge and of course, the National Road Bridge on the west edge of Cambridge, Figure 3.

The last covered bridge over Wills Creek was the Kennedy Bridge, a two-span multiple kingpost truss built in 1883 to replace an earlier covered bridge. To honor our state's sesquicentennial observance in 1953, Guernsey County officials decided to renovate the old Kennedy Bridge. This included replacement of the west span with an open steel beam bridge. In 1962, the county quietly removed the old bridge.

Figure 170. Leatherwood Creek Bridge at Quaker City in Guernsey County -- scene of a December wedding in 1874

Spanning Wills Creek on the west side of Cambridge was an 87 foot Howe truss railroad bridge, Figure 18, known as the Tunnel Hill Bridge because of the nearby railroad tunnel. The Tunnel Hill Bridge was a nine panel Howe truss built in 1868 by the Baltimore and Ohio Railroad. It was removed in 1883. Over a dozen other through-Howe truss railroad bridges served the rail lines in Guernsey County. The Wheeling and Lake Erie Railroad's Marietta Division wound south through Guernsey County, crossing and recrossing Wills Creek frequently on through-Howe and combination-truss bridges.

MUSKINGUM COUNTY

Situated at the confluence of the Muskingum and Licking Rivers, Zanesville, the county seat of Muskingum County, has always been a hub for highway, canal and railroad traffic. The National Road passes through Muskingum County and the Ohio and Erie Canal follows the Muskingum River south through this region. Several railroads crisscrossed the county, too. Important multi-span bridges were built to span the Muskingum River from the northern edge of the county at the Stillwell Bridge (see Chapter II), the steel suspension bridges at Dresden, the Upper and Lower Bridges at Zanesville, and the Philo/Duncan Falls and Gaysport Bridges below Zanesville. All but the Dresden Bridge were covered timber trusses as were many of the early railroad bridges over the mighty Muskingum River.

Although the National Road crossed over the Y Bridge (also known as the Upper Bridge) at Zanesville, this unusual bridge (see Chapter II) was not a part of the old Pike. Although it was a link on the National Road, the Y Bridge was a privately-owned toll bridge until 1868 when it and the Lower Bridge were bought by Muskingum County. Muskingum County records referred to it as the Upper Bridge for many years and the Lower Bridge was the old Putnam or Third Street Bridge below the Y Bridge. The Third Street Bridge was built in 1845 to replace an earlier covered bridge at this site destroyed by arson. According to one source, a disgruntled workman set fire to the first bridge to make work for unemployed workers. He got his work alright — in the Ohio Penitentiary.[68]

The second covered bridge at Third Street, Figure 171, was a five-span Buckingham truss that stood until destroyed by the 1913 flood.

Near the Third Street Bridge was the four-span, 592 foot covered Howe truss of the Cincinnati and Muskingum Valley Railroad. The bridge was built in 1877, arches were added to its trusses in the 1880s, and in 1891 it was replaced by a steel Pratt truss bridge. This same railroad had another wooden Howe-truss bridge upstream on the Muskingum at Ellis near Jackson Island, Figure 172. The first wooden bridge here was built in 1871 and had three deck Howe trusses plus a through-Howe truss on the west end. The 1882 Railroad Reports said that this was a new bridge (1881/82) and that it had a 560 foot deck-Howe truss. The bridge was badly damaged in the 1884 flood and replaced by pony steel Pratt trusses that washed out in 1913.

Below Zanesville at Philo over the Muskingum River was a five-span, 797 foot Smith truss covered bridge built in 1875 by the Smith Bridge Company. They rebuilt the bridge in 1884 after an ice dam seriously damaged a large part of the bridge. In 1908, the two western spans were ripped out by a windstorm and were replaced by metal trusses. The 1913 flood swept the entire structure away. Figure 173 shows the Philo/Duncan Falls Bridge as it looked circa 1896. Unlike some of the other Muskingum River bridges, no pictures exist today of two large covered bridges that once spanned this mighty river, the Stillwell and the Gaysport Bridges.

While the Y Bridge was certainly the most unusual covered bridge in Muskingum County, the old bridge at Pleasant Valley, Figure 174,

Figure 171. Third Street/Lower Bridge

was also unusual in appearance. The Pleasant Valley Bridge over the Licking River, was a two span structure with a distinctly uneven roof line where the two spans met at center pier. The shorter span had a queenpost truss and was part of the original structure. The longer span was a Smith truss built in 1875 to replace one span of the original bridge. The Pleasant Valley Bridge was the last covered bridge over the Licking River and was scheduled for demolition due to the formation of Dillon Reservoir, but it went out ahead of schedule in the flood of January 1959.

Figure 172. Muskingum River railroad bridge near Ellis, north of Zanesville

Figure 173. Philo/Duncan Falls Bridge over the Muskingum River, built 1874, rebuilt 1884, destroyed in 1913 flood. Note wooden truss swing bridge over canal in foreground

Most of Muskingum County's highway covered bridges were built on the Buckingham truss plan with few exceptions. One is the Johnson's Mill/Salt Creek Bridge owned by the Ohio Historic Bridge Association, Figure 68. This 80 foot Warren truss was built in 1876 at Johnson's Mill by Thomas Fisher for $8. per linear foot. In the early 1950s, over 20 covered bridges in Muskingum County were scheduled to be bypassed or demolished and the Johnson Mill Bridge was one of them. It was bypassed and ownership reverted to the nearby landowner in return for the right-of-way for the new bridge. In 1960, the covered bridge and two thirds acre of land were sold for $300. to the

newly-formed Southern Ohio Covered Bridge Association (known now as the Ohio Historic Bridge Association). This group has renovated the old bridge and maintains it as a historic landmark; it is site of their annual picnic. The Johnson Mill/Salt Creek Bridge is now the last covered bridge in Muskingum County.

Other Muskingum County covered bridges that stood into the 1950s were: Bliss/Tracey over Williams Fork and the Moorehead over Buffalo Fork at Chandlersville, Burnt Mill over Salt Creek (built by Washington County's Rolla Merydith), Krafft/Thompson over Kent Run near White Cottage, White Cottage Bridge, Big Run/Fowler's Mill, and the Museville Bridge over Meigs Creek. Like Fairfield County, it would take an entire book to tell the full story of the wooden truss bridges of Muskingum County.

JEFFERSON COUNTY

Jefferson County lies along the Ohio River and once had major wooden truss bridges on the River Road over the mouths of Cross, Short, Island and big Yellow Creeks. These bridges were replaced at an early date by steel trusses.

The first wooden truss bridge in Jefferson County was built to span Short Creek in 1812 for $195. Another was built in 1817 and roofed in 1819. Other well-known Jefferson County covered bridges spanned Cross Creek at Reed's Mill, Fernwood and Broadacre.

Figure 174. Pleasant Valley Bridge -- last covered bridge over Licking River

104

After the Civil War there was a marked decline in the construction of wooden truss bridges in Jefferson County when it seemed that the county officials wanted only metal truss bridges. The last recorded highway wooden truss bridge construction in Jefferson County was in 1860 when a new covered bridge was built to span Yellow Creek at Moore's Mill near Provo. However, the railroads built numerous wooden Howe truss bridges in Jefferson County throughout the 1870s.

In 1936, Jefferson County officials removed their last covered bridge, a 100 foot Burr truss over Short Creek at Adena, Figure 175. The Adena Bridge was built in 1858 by Joseph and William Hale.

Figure 175. Jefferson County's last covered bridge, spanned Short Creek at Adena

HOLMES COUNTY

Holmes County is largely rural with beautiful rolling farmland. There is a high concentration of Amish in the area and tourism is one of the most important industries. Surprisingly enough, we know of only one highway covered bridge in Holmes county, over Killbuck Creek at Millersburg, the county seat. The old Railroad Reports tell us that there were two pony Howe truss bridges on the railroads in Holmes County. There is no doubt that there were many more highway and railroad covered bridges than can be presently documented for Holmes County and perhaps additional research will show where they were.

COSHOCTON COUNTY

Coshocton and Tuscarawas Counties have a far different story than that for nearby Carroll and Holmes Counties regarding covered bridges. Coshocton County had over 90 wooden truss bridges and Tuscarawas had 107. Research was done in both counties by Terry E. Miller who took his data from the county commissioners journals and interviews with older residents. Many well-known bridge builders worked in these two eastern Ohio counties including the Haggertys and Shrakes of Licking County. Both counties usually built the Buckingham truss with a sprinkling of Burrs, Howes and Smiths.

In May, 1991, one of the last two Burr truss covered bridges in Ohio fell with a resounding crash into the waters of Wills Creek. The Sandles/Hamilton Farm Bridge was built in 1879 by F. Mayer for $1,188, Figure 176 That was just for the superstructure. The foundations cost another $1,578. By the mid-1950s, strip mining had all but closed the roads on the east side of this bridge and a flood in this time period tore out some of the wooden supports under it. The county decided to close the Hamilton Farm Bridge and it was used for many years for the storage of farm machinery. Naturally, with no maintenance, the old structure began to deteriorate steadily until it finally gave up and fell into the creek.

That left the Helmick Bridge, Figure 33, over Killbuck Creek at Helmick as Coshocton County's last covered bridge. It is a two-span Buckingham truss built in 1863 by John Shrake.

Figure 176. Hamilton Farm or Sandles Bridge

County records show contracts for both bridge and foundations going to Shrake, but on the abutments we find carved the name of F. Victor, and the date, 1863. Mr. Shrake undoubtedly subcontracted the foundation work to Mr. Victor who was a well-known mason in this area. Mr. Victor was obviously determined to leave his mark here. The Helmick Bridge was closed in the 1980s and deteriorated into very poor condition. The county finally turned it over to the Helmick Bridge Restoration Committee in 1990 and this group is attempting to restore the old structure.

There were many covered bridges built to span Wills Creek in Coshocton County including: the Wills Creek Village Bridge (actually three covered bridges were built to serve this site), the Frew's Mill Bridge, the Linton Mills Bridge, and the Plainfield Bridge. An old cast and wrought iron Whipple truss bridge still spans Wills Creek on an abandoned road east of SR 83. It is the 1872 Roderick Bridge built by the Coshocton Iron works. We mention it here because it is such a unique historic structure.

In 1867, Jonas Asire was hired by the county to build a 10 panel Buckingham truss covered bridge over Doughty Creek at Power's Mill, southwest of Clark, Figure 177. He built the superstructure for $690. This was originally just one span, but a center pier was added at some later date. The flood of July, 1969 tore the bridge off of its foundations and deposited it lengthwise in the creek with the water roaring through it. The county decided not to put the bridge back in place, so they had it taken out of the creek, dismantled and placed on the creek

bank. In 1976, the county Bicentennial Committee decided to move the remains of the bridge to Roscoe Village where it was to be rebuilt. (Roscoe Village is a rebuilt canal town on the north edge of Coshocton.) The Doughty Creek Bridge was successfully moved but the timbers lay rotting on the banks of the canal and are probably beyond reassembly at this time.

Two large covered bridges spanned the Muskingum River south of Coshocton. In 1876, the county contracted with the Smith Bridge Company to build two bridges, one at Moore's Crossing and the other at Conesville. The Conesville Bridge, Figure 178, was a four-span, 400 foot Smith truss built with double truss timbers at a cost of $7,110. In 1955, after nearly 80 years of service, the Conesville Bridge was closed to traffic after much hassle with concerned citizens, especially parents of schoolchildren riding buses over the old bridge. Due to legal snarls, the bridge stood abandoned until 1958 when a contractor disposed of it by pouring 150 gallons of gasoline over it and setting it afire. This was probably the cheapest and easiest way to get rid of a wooden bridge of this size, but one cannot help but think what use could have been made of those old timbers.

The Moore's Crossing Bridge over the Muskingum became known as the Jack Randles Bridge and just a few feet west of the bridge stood the Jack Randles Canal Bridge, Figure 179. Both bridges were destroyed in the 1913 flood.

Coshocton County also had large covered bridges over the Walhonding and Tuscarawas Rivers. The Smith Bridge Company built a three-span, 340 foot Smith truss in 1877 to span the Walhonding at Walhonding Village, Figure 180. It was the third covered bridge on this site and was destroyed by the 1913 flood. August Borneman built the Warsaw Bridge to span the Walhonding River in 1872. It was a four-span, 472 foot Howe truss. The Warsaw Bridge was also destroyed by the great 1913 flood. The Haggerty Brothers built the Miskimmens Bridge over the Tuscarawas River near the east county line in 1856. It was a double lane, 200 foot long Buckingham truss. A fire destroyed the Miskimmens Bridge in 1910.

Figure 177. Doughty Creek Bridge over Killbuck Creek

Figure 178. Conesville Bridge over the Muskingum River built in 1876 by the Smith Bridge Company

Figure 179. Randles or Moore's Crossing Bridges, one spanned the river and the other spanned the canal

Figure 180. Walhonding Village Bridge over the Walhonding River, 1877 - 1913

Coshocton County had only one recorded railroad Howe truss, a 441 foot, three-span through-truss over the Muskingum River, just north of Conesville.

TUSCARAWAS COUNTY

Tuscarawas County once had over 100 wooden truss bridges spanning its many rivers and creeks. The largest of these streams is the mighty Tuscarawas River and at least 18 major highway covered bridges were built to span this waterway. Among these bridges were: the Lockport Bridge, the Trenton Bridge, the Port Washington Bridge, the Zoar Bridge and the Blicktown Bridge, Figure 181. John Shrake built the 445 foot Blicktown Bridge in 1867. It served for over 30 years.

Figure 182. Zoar Station Bridge

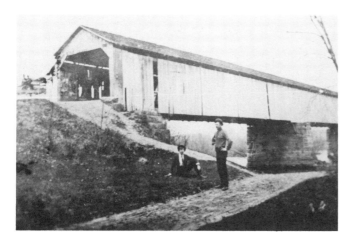

Figure 181. Blicktown Bridge

Jacob Morgan built the three-span Buckingham truss Zoar Bridge at the southwest edge of Zoar in 1863 for $3,068.(Zoar was a religious commune started in 1817 by Wurtenburg Separatists from Germany.) In 1884, the Zoar Bridge was taken down (to be replaced with the steel bridge on that site today) and moved to Zoar Station, Figure 182, where it spanned the Tuscarawas River until its removal in 1903.

Conotton Creek (also known as One-Leg Creek) had its share of covered bridges, too. One was the well-known New Cumberland Bridge, Figure 183, which was built in 1860 and rebuilt in 1870. It stood into the 1920s. There were covered bridges over Conotton Creek at Zoar Station (not to be confused with the

Tuscarawas River bridge at Zoar Station) and at Scott's Mills. Many of Tuscarawas County's covered bridges were built to span the Ohio and Erie Canal, Sugar Creek and Big and Little Stillwater Creeks.

Tuscarawas County had over 20 wooden truss railroad bridges over the Tuscarawas River, Conotton and Sugar Creek and the Ohio and Erie Canal.

CARROLL COUNTY

Strange as it may seem, research so far has turned up no wooden truss highway bridges for Carroll County. And this is a county bordered by Columbiana and Tuscarawas Counties where so many wooden bridges were built. Carroll County did have at least 10 wooden Howe truss bridges on the railroads, only one

Figure 183. New Cumberland Bridge

of which was designated as a pony truss. All the others were noted as through trusses in the old Railroad Reports. It is quite possible that further research will reveal a greater extent of wooden truss highway bridges in Carroll County.

HARRISON COUNTY

Small covered bridges were all that was needed to span the little creeks and runs of Harrison County. There is a recorded total of nearly 50 timber truss bridges, including four uncovered Howe truss railroad bridges.

For the most part, building dates are unknown for Harrison County's covered bridges. Our research in the County Commissioners Journals began with 1870 and by that time they were building steel truss bridges. We deduce from this that the little Buckingham truss bridges of Harrison County were products of the 1850s and 1860s.

Over Skull Fork south of the village of Freeport stands the county's last covered bridge. It is the 44 foot Skull Fork Bridge, a typical small Harrison County Buckingham truss with projected portals and high-boarded siding, Figure 184. The Skull Fork Bridge served a township road and was bypassed in the early 1970s. It was renovated by the county and is now maintained as an historic site. Part of this renovation was the replacement of its metal roof with one of wood shingles.

Figure 184. Skull Fork Bridge

Many years ago, a photographer caught an interesting picture of two Harrison County covered bridges near Freeport, Figure 185. In the foreground is the Clark Bridge over Stillwater Creek and in the background can be seen the second Clark Bridge which spanned the backwaters of Stillwater Creek.

An essay on rural America around the turn of the century can be found in our picture of Bowerstown, Figure 186, which shows the covered bridge, its steel replacement, the mill with W.B. Penn Clothing Company ad and the path through the snow to the old outhouse.

Figure 185. Clark Bridges near Freeport in Harrison County

Figure 186. Bowerstown in Harrison County, c 1900 -- an essay on life in rural America

EXISTING BRIDGE LOCATIONS

Belmont County:

35-07-05 (formerly 35-23-46) Shaeffer/Campbell Bridge, 68' MKP, 1875, over small lake on Ohio University Campus, just N of I-70 off SR 331 in Richland Tp. sec 28, 4 W of St. Clairsville. (Moved to this site 1973.)

Coshocton County:

35-16-02 Helmick Bridge, 166' 2-span MKP, 1863, over Killbuck Creek on TR 343 just off CR 25 ESE of Blissfield and SR 60 in Clark Twp. sec 18. Closed.

Guernsey County:

35-30-04 Indian Camp Bridge, 36' MKP, over Indian Camp Creek on TR 68 just E of SR 658, 3 S Birds Run, in Knox Twp. sec 12

35-30-12 Armstrong Bridge, 76' MKP, 1849, over ravine in Cambridge City Park (moved here 1966 from Clio), 1 N US 22/40 between 6th and 8th Streets. Pedestrian & bike use only.

35-30-33 Reservoir Bridge, 42' MKP, c.1900, over Leatherwood Creek, just off the abandoned B&O RR right-of-way, 1.5 ESE Quaker City, .5 W of TR 949 in Millwood Twp. sec 13. **COLLAPSED MAY, 1993**

Harrison County:

35-34-19 Skull Fork Bridge, 45' MKP, over Skull Fork, off TR 123, 2 S Freeport via CR 27 in Freeport Twp. sec 16. Bypassed.

Muskingum County:

35-60-31 Salt Creek/Johnson's Mill Bridge, 87' Warren, 1876, over Salt Creek off Arch Hill Road, 2 N US 40 & 3 WNW Norwich in Perry Twp. sec 2. Owned by the OHBA. Bypassed.

CHAPTER VII

THE WESTERN RESERVE AND THE LATTICE TRUSS:

Ashtabula, Columbiana, Cuyahoga, Geauga, Lake, Lorain, Mahoning, Medina, Portage, Stark, Summit, Trumbull and Wayne Counties

Figure 187. Ohio's Western Reserve and Northeastern Ohio

Northeastern Ohio lies within what is known as the Western Reserve, land that once was claimed by the colony of Connecticut. Connecticut ceded most of her lands to the government in 1786, reserving a section north of the forty-first parallel and extending 120 miles west from the Pennsylvania border. This area is bounded on the north by Lake Erie. These lands were reserved by Connecticut to be granted to those people of her state whose property had been destroyed by Tory raids during the Revolutionary War.[69]

The Western Reserve was covered by dense forest when the first settlers arrived and the land had to be cleared so that crops could be planted and houses built. Now this region includes the great steel industries of the Mahoning Valley, thousands of acres under cultivation, and the busy lake ports of Ashtabula Harbor and Conneaut Harbor, Fairport Harbor, Cleveland and Lorain.

For purposes of this study of Ohio covered bridges, we have chosen to include Columbiana, Stark and Wayne Counties with the Western Reserve counties even though these three counties were not a part of that area.

ASHTABULA COUNTY

Ashtabula County lies in the extreme northeastern corner of Ohio bordered on the east by Pennsylvania and on the north by Lake Erie. The New England tradition of the Town lattice truss is still strong here where at least 29 of these bridges were built. The actual figure is undoubtedly higher since this county was settled before 1800 and some of the Town trusses in use today have to be replacements for earlier covered bridges. Today, the traveler can still see 10 Town truss covered bridges in Ashtabula County including the State Road Bridge, Figure 46, built in 1983 (see Chapter II).

In March 1831, the State Legislature authorized the Ashtabula County Commissioners to pay $100. from the 3% fund (see page 37) to Ira Benton and David Niles to reimburse them in part for the bridge they had just built over Conneaut Creek on the State Road in Monroe Township. This may have been the first covered bridge on this site which stood until 1898 when it was replaced with a steel truss bridge. When the steel truss bridge could no longer carry traffic safely, it was replaced by the new Town truss bridge, Figure 46, in 1983.

Fourteen covered bridges still dot the landscape of Ashtabula County giving this area a

*Figure 188.
The Warner
Hollow Bridge
over Phelps Creek
in Ashtabula
County*

distinct flavor of a bygone era. Perhaps the most scenic of these bridges is the Warner Hollow Bridge, Figure 188, over Phelps Creek in the southern part of the county. This Town truss was built in 1867 on abutments and piers of fieldstone and sandstone, high above the creek. The sandstone came from quarries that once flourished in the Windsor area. The Warner Hollow Bridge is now closed to all but pedestrian traffic.

Two covered bridges still span Conneaut Creek: the Middle Road Bridge, Figure 189, east of Farnham, and the Creek Road Bridge near Conneaut. The Middle Road Bridge is a 131 foot Howe truss built in 1868. Major renovation was needed to save this old bridge in 1984 when a broken timber caused it to sag dangerously. The county budget was tight, but John Smolen, the County Engineer, drew up the plans and three volunteers came forward to do much of the work with the aid of county employees. Various truss members were repaired or replaced and the foundations were rebuilt and two concrete piers were added. New floor, siding and roof completed the renovation. The volunteers saved the county money and made it possible to preserve another Ashtabula County covered bridge. The Creek Road Bridge is an attractive 124 foot Town truss whose history is unknown.

Spanning the Ashtabula River are the Root, Olin/Dewey, and Benetka bridges. The Root Road Bridge is a 76 foot Town truss built in 1868 southwest of Monroe Center. The Benetka Road Bridge, Figure 190, is a 127 foot Town truss said to date to circa 1900, but it is believed to be much older than that. In 1985, the Benetka Bridge underwent major repairs that included the rebuilding of one abutment, laminated arches added to the trusses, new floor beams and deck planking, new siding, roof and gable ends. Rehabilitation of the 1873 Olin/Dewey Bridge which spans the Ashtabula River east of Ashtabula began late in 1992. The on-

Figure 189. Middle Road Bridge

112

Figure 190. Renovated Benetka Road Bridge

Figure 191. Doyle Road Bridge over Mill Creek

going renovation of the older covered bridges in Ashtabula County is part of John Smolen's master preservation plan for the county's historic bridges.

One other covered bridge that used to span the Ashtabula River is the Graham Road Bridge which was moved into a nearby field some years ago. A small rural park now surrounds the old structure.

Spanning Mill Creek southeast of the county seat of Jefferson is the trim 94 foot South Denmark Road Bridge, a Town truss built in 1868. The county bypassed this bridge in the late 1970s. Northeast of Jefferson over Mill Creek is the Doyle Road Bridge, Figure 191, a 98 foot Town truss built circa 1876. Major renovation work was done on this bridge in the late 1980s, reinforcing it with massive laminated arches, new deck, siding and roof among other improvements.

The major stream of western Ashtabula County is the Grand River. Three covered bridges still span this waterway: the Mechanicsville Bridge, a Howe truss with arches, built in 1867, the Harpersfield Bridge and the Riverdale Road Bridge. The Mechanicsville Bridge, Figure 192, was bypassed in the late 1980s. The Harpersfield Bridge, Figure 52, once carried SR 534 over the Grand River. The state road was relocated in the 1950s and the old road and covered bridge reverted to county ownership. The bridge, a two-span Howe truss, was built in 1868. The

steel span on the north end was added after the 1913 flood cut a new channel around that end of the bridge. The Harpersfield Bridge has recently undergone a complete renovation.

The Riverdale Road Bridge stretches its 140 foot Town trusses across the river just northwest of Rock Creek. This bridge, too, has been extensively renovated in recent years.

At the village of Rock Creek there was once a two lane Town truss covered bridge over Rock Creek. Ackley and Crowell built this bridge, Figure 193, in 1832 for the Trumbull and Ashtabula Turnpike Company. The old bridge stood for over 100 years and was finally replaced in 1948.

Figure 192. The Mechanicsville Road Bridge over the Grand River

Figure 193. Ackley and Crowell's Rock Creek Bridge

On old SR 7 at the south edge of Conneaut was an old covered bridge over Mill Creek (a different Mill Creek than the one near Jefferson) that was the twin of the Mechanicsville Road Bridge. It, too, was a Howe truss with arches, built in 1867, probably by the same builder. In 1924, a violent windstorm struck Conneaut and tore the roof off of this bridge. It was replaced the following year by a concrete rainbow arch bridge, which though bypassed, is still standing today.

Other Ashtabula County covered bridges that are but a memory today were the twin bridges at Farnham, the Kelloggsville Bridge over the Ashtabula River, the Prim's Sawmill Bridge over Mill Creek, and the Foreman Road Bridge over Mill Creek. The truss timbers of the latter have been incorporated into the interior design of a pizza parlor at Kingsville in Ashtabula County.

Northwest of Rock Creek an old covered bridge once spanned the Grand River on Fobes Road. This 130 foot Howe truss was moved here in 1911 from New Hudson Road. In the early 1960s, the Fobes Road bridge had deteriorated to the point where it had to be closed and the county finally burned it in 1971.

Ashtabula County Engineer John Smolen has received nationwide recognition for his dedication to the maintenance of his county's covered bridges and great praise for his two new covered bridges, the State Road Bridge

and the Caine Road Bridge, a 96 foot Pratt truss built in 1986, Figure 57 (see Chapter II).

There were a number of railroad Howe trusses in Ashtabula County including a 780 foot deck-Howe truss over the Ashtabula River gorge built in 1852 for the Lake Shore and Michigan Southern Railroad. This bridge was replaced in 1863 by the ill-fated, cast-iron, Howe truss bridge that collapsed under a passenger train in a snowstorm on December 29, 1876 with a loss of over 90 lives.

TRUMBULL COUNTY

Trumbull County was formed in 1800 and named for Connecticut Governor Jonathon Trumbull. The major streams of the county are the eastward flowing Mahoning River and its branches. In the early 1800s, two covered bridges were built to serve the village of Newton Falls, one over the west branch of the Mahoning and the other over the east branch. The East Branch Bridge still stands today, known as the Stedman or Newton Falls Bridge. It is a sturdy Town lattice truss built in 1831, making it the second oldest covered bridge in Ohio. Figure 194 shows the bridge as it looked circa 1907 before the addition of the sidewalk. This walk was added in 1921 when a school opened on the east side of the bridge and parents were afraid for their children to walk on the roadway of the bridge.[70] The Newton Falls Bridge has been reinforced with steel beams and piers were added in 1962. The people of Newton Falls and Mahoning County take great pride in this bridge, Figure 195. It is well maintained and in daily use.

Newton Fall's West Bridge spanned the west branch of the Mahoning on what is now SR 534. The first covered bridge (probably a Town truss) was built here in 1832 and it served until 1856 when it was replaced by a two lane, open sided Howe truss, Figure 196, with a roofed sidewalk on both sides. This was one of the covered bridges chosen to be included in the Historic American Building Survey in the 1930s, at which time detailed drawings were made of the structure. The West Branch Bridge was replaced in 1943 by a modern bridge.

The Diehl/Braceville Bridge spanned the Mahoning River west of Warren. The contract

114

Figure 194. 1907 View of Newton Falls Bridge

Figure 195. Newton Falls Bridge today

for the "new" bridge at Mrs. Diehls was let to Robert Stewart in August of 1878 for $12. per lineal foot for a Howe truss. It was one of the last, if not the last, fully-covered wooden bridge built in Trumbull County. The Diehl Bridge was destroyed by arson in 1959.

Other well-known Trumbull County covered bridges included the South Street Bridge which crossed the Mahoning at Warren and the Center of the World Bridge, Figure 197. This bridge crossed the Mahoning River on SR 82 and was so named because the proprietor of the nearby general store and gas station called his store the Center of the World. It was the Center of his World! This covered bridge was removed in 1934.

The Erie Railroad had 10 Howe truss bridges in Trumbull County including a 300 foot through-Howe truss bridge over the Shenango River on the Ohio-Pennsylvania state line built in 1870.

MAHONING COUNTY

The Western Reserve Chronicle published a notice to bridge builders in November 1832 announcing that the Trumbull County Commissioners would take bids for a new bridge over the Mahoning at Price's Mill on the line between Milton and Newton Townships. (This is now the Trumbull/Mahoning County line.) The newspaper said that the Price's Mill Bridge was to be built on the same plan as the new

Figure 196. The West Bridge at Newton Falls spanned the West Branch of the Mahoning River on SR 534

Figure 197. Center of the World Bridge

bridge at Labaw's Tavern.[71] Since the Price's Mill Bridge was a 132 foot two lane Town truss, Figure 198, we know that the Labaw's Tavern Bridge was also a Town truss. The center truss of the Pricetown Bridge was set back a few feet in the dark interior of the bridge, making it a traffic hazard for the unwary. In 1846, Mahoning County was formed and Milton Township became part of the new county and a small community grew up around Price's Mill on the county line known as Pricetown. The old covered bridge at Pricetown survived floods and ice jams and served the public well for over 110 years before its removal in the 1940s.

Figure 198.
The old Pricetown
Bridge, a two-lane
Town truss over the
Mahoning River at
Pricetown

Side view of
Pricetown Bridge
below

116

In addition to the bridge at Pricetown on the Trumbull County line, Mahoning County had at least five other major covered bridges that spanned the Mahoning River. There were covered bridges over the Mahoning at Lowellville, two in Milton Township (one of which was the Labaw's Tavern Bridge built c.1830. The other was where CR 18 crosses the river today), one in Youngstown at Mahoning Avenue (the Spring Common Bridge) and at South Avenue (the Presque Isle Bridge). The Lowellville Bridge was built in 1841 to carry Washington Street over the river at Lowellville. Building dates of the other Mahoning River covered bridges are unknown.

The last covered bridge to carry traffic in Mahoning County was the Meander Creek Bridge near Ellsworth. This was a 42 foot pony-queenpost-truss bridge, building date unknown, that was torn down in the 1950s. In the 1970s, a covered bridge was discovered serving as a barn near North Benton. It had been built in 1878 to span Island Creek. When it was moved to become a barn is unknown, but shortly after it was found again, it was torn down by its owner.

There were many railroads serving Mahoning County and at least six wooden Howe-truss bridges were built to carry these rail lines, including two over the Mahoning River, one of which was in Youngstown and the other some three miles southeast of town. The other four railroad bridges were over smaller streams.

COLUMBIANA COUNTY

Well over 100 small highway covered bridges and at least 16 through Howe truss railroad bridges spanned Little Beaver Creek and its small branches in Columbiana County. Most of the highway bridges were quite short and built on the popular and economic Buckingham truss plan.

It was in Columbiana County that the shortest covered bridge ever built for public highway use in the country was built in the 1870s. The little Church Hill Road Bridge, Figure 199, was built to span Middle Run east of Lisbon. It has a clear span of only 19 feet and is supported by a single kingpost truss on each side. In 1963,

Figure 199. Church Hill Road Bridge

the bridge was bypassed and a small rural park was established at the site. Vandaliam became a serious problem and it was feared that it was only a matter of time before someone destroyed the old bridge. So, the local historical society at nearby Elkton undertook the project of moving and rebuilding the bridge at Elkton near the Lock 24 Restaurant where it stands today. Lock 24 is a remnant of the locks of the Sandy and Beaver Canal, a branch of the Ohio and Erie Canal, that once served this area.

A small covered bridge spanned the Sandy and Beaver Canal on Tunnel Hill Road, Figure 200. Like many covered bridges, this one was used as a billboard. It had full side coverage advertising Estep Clothier, Hanover, Ohio.

Figure 200. Tunnel Hill Canal Bridge

There are still five covered bridges in Columbiana County in the early 1990s: the Sells, McClellan, Teegarden, Miller Road and Malone Bridges. The Sells Bridge, built in the 1870s, spanned the west fork of Little Beaver Creek just off Trinity Church Road. It deteriorated into such bad condition that the county dismantled it in 1989 and stored it until it could be rebuilt. In 1991/92, the Sells Bridge was rebuilt at Scenic Vista Park southwest of Lisbon.

Just off Trinity Church Road is the Jim McClellan Bridge over the west fork of Little Beaver Creek. There was talk of establishing a small rural park here when the road was closed some years ago, but nothing ever came of the idea and the McClellan Bridge joined the ranks of abandoned covered bridges.

There were several covered bridges on and just off of Trinity Church Road, and one many people will remember is the McKaig Mill Bridge, Figure 201, destroyed by arson on a June afternoon in 1988. This was an especially lovely area and the perfect setting for a covered bridge.

Figure 201. McKaig's Mill Bridge

Recently bypassed is the 65 foot Teegarden or Centennial Bridge, Figure 202, built in 1875 by Robinson and McCracken. This is another lovely rural area with a small park nearby.

The Miller Road Bridge, a 32 foot multiple kingpost truss, built in 1867, spans Mill Seat Creek north of Lisbon. It has been heavily reinforced with steel beams and these now carry the load of daily traffic.

There is a little covered bridge in Beaver Creek State Park north of East Liverpool that has an interesting history. The late Tom Malone, county historian and bridge buff, discovered this little bridge in use as a shed in Elk

Figure 202. Teegarden Bridge

Township. He began to trace the history of the bridge and found that it had been built originally to span Middle Run in Elk Township and that it was moved circa 1900 to a farm where it stood for about 12 years until SR 154 widening was planned and it was determined that the bridge was in the way. The Elk Township Trustees then took the bridge and moved it to Pine Hollow Road where they rebuilt it for use as a storage shed. At that time, the structure was widened and a new roof was installed.

Mr. Malone began a campaign to get this bridge moved to Beaver Creek Park and in the early 1970s, the move was made. The bridge was dismantled and moved to the park where the timbers were extensively renovated and then rebuilt over the old Sandy and Beaver Canal bed, Figure 203. The bridge now bears the name of the man who worked so hard to see it moved and preserved. Unfortunately, Mr. Malone did not live to see. the project completed.

Figure 203. The Tom Malone Bridge

Not far from Beaver Creek Park in section 36 of Liverpool Township was the first covered bridge built in Ohio (see Chapter I). At this site, John Bever built a paper mill in 1807. It was to Mr. Bever and his associates that authority was given by Act of the Legislature to build a bridge at his mill in 1807 (bridge not built until 1809). One abutment of this bridge still stands today.

There are some very interesting excerpts from the old "Bridge Book" from the Columbiana County Engineer's Office, which were compiled by the late B.M. French, County Engineer from 1906 to 1915 and which contains material of interest about the county's covered bridges. In most cases, the engineer had noted that the abutments of the bridges were weak and this included all still standing today.

Most of the county's railroad Howe trusses were on the Cleveland and Pittsburgh Railroad (later Pennsylvania). For the most part, these were small bridges that were probably pony trusses. Some were described as having separately covered trusses while a few had roof and siding. These bridges were built in the 1860s and 1870s and were being replaced in the 1880s with steel structures.

Recent research in the old Columbiana County records have added substantially to our knowledge of the wooden truss bridges of this northeastern Ohio County and the men who built them. Foremost among the bridge builders of Columbiana County was West Croft, who built many of that county's covered spans in the 1860s and 1870s. Robert McClellan was another well-known Columbiana County bridge builder during this era.

A partial listing of the long-gone covered bridges of this eastern Ohio county would include: Donaldson's Bridge; the Willard Bridge and the Aunt Rosa Willard Bridge, both over Brush Run on what is now SR 518; Gaston's Mill; Nichols; Culbertson's Mill; Fredericktown; Elkton; Pumping Station and Andrew Smith. It would not be difficult to devote an entire volume to the covered bridges of Columbiana County, Ohio.

SUMMIT COUNTY

One stormy night in May 1975, the rains poured down and the waters of Furnace Run in Summit County became a raging torrent. The force of the swollen waters caused one abutment of the Everett Road Bridge to collapse, sending the old Smith truss structure into the creek. The remains of the bridge were soon pulled from the creek and the timbers were marked to aid in rebuilding. Then the timbers were taken to the nearby Hale Farm (a restored pioneer farm) where they were stored until rebuilding could begin. Years passed while controversy raged on as to whether or not it was the right thing to do to rebuild a narrow covered bridge or to put up a modern structure capable of carrying any legal load. Meanwhile the bridge remained in storage and most folks thought it never would be rebuilt.

The area where the bridge was located became part of the Cuyahoga Valley National Recreation Area and the future of the covered bridge rested with the National Park Service. The wrecked abutment was rebuilt in 1980 and work on the reconstruction of the bridge itself got underway in the mid-1980s, the work being done by National Park Service personnel. They soon discovered that very little of the original truss timbers could be reused and they had to study what they had and build a new Smith truss. The result is a fine, almost new Smith truss covered bridge that spans the creek on its original site, Figure 204. No vehicular traffic is

Figure 204. Everett Road Bridge

allowed, but less than a year after it was rebuilt, a speeding car, out of control, smashed into the west portal, causing minor damages (now repaired).

During reconstruction of the bridge, Park Service officials made an effort to find the correct building date, but the best they could come up with was the 1870s. Years ago, the Everett Road Bridge had a sign over one portal which gave the building date as 1856. Since the bridge is a Smith truss, this is impossible and had to refer to an earlier bridge on the site.

There is a relatively short list of recorded covered bridges for Summit County. Four of the six known highway covered bridges spanned the Cuyahoga River. There were covered bridges at Botzum, at Chagrin Falls, on Babb Road and at Boston. The Boston Bridge, Figure 205, was built in 1883 and was destroyed by the 1913 flood.

LAKE COUNTY

Lake County is, as its name suggests, located on Lake Erie between Cuyahoga and Ashtabula Counties. Very few covered bridges are known to have existed here and all are long gone. The last covered bridge was the Blair Road Bridge, a 148 foot Howe truss over the Grand River, which was torn down in the early 1950s. Elsewhere in Lake County, there were covered highway bridges at Painesville, Willoughby, Kirtland and Trumbull's Mills.

The old Railroad Reports listed no timber truss bridges for Lake County, but we know that at least one did exist because an old postcard shows an uncovered deck-Howe truss at Painesville.

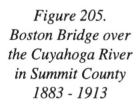

Figure 205. Boston Bridge over the Cuyahoga River in Summit County 1883 - 1913

Summit County was served by three railways that listed Howe truss bridges in the old Railroad Reports: the Cleveland, Lorain and Wheeling; the Erie; and the Valley Railroad. The latter was a line that ran south from Cleveland to Canton, via Akron. This line had nine Howe truss bridges including two deck-Howe structures over the Cuyahoga River. All told, the railroads of Summit County had 12 Howe truss bridges of all types.

GEAUGA, LORAIN, MEDINA, PORTAGE, STARK AND WAYNE COUNTIES

The railroads accounted for the majority of the covered bridges in the rest of the counties that make up this chapter covering the northeast section of Ohio. In Geauga, Medina and Portage Counties, all timber truss bridges have been gone for many years. Only railroad Howe trusses, including a few on the Interurban lines, are recorded for Geauga County, while Medina and Portage Counties did have both highway and railway timber truss bridges. In Kent in Portage County, there was a 200 foot Burr truss bridge that spanned the Cuyahoga River on Main Street from 1837 to the late 1870s.

The same bridge situation applies also to both Stark and Wayne Counties where all covered bridges have been gone for nearly 50 years. A large covered bridge carried SR 212 over the Tuscarawas River west of Bolivar in Stark County until the 1930s. There was also a very early highway covered bridge built on the west edge of Louisville in 1828 to span Nimishillen Creek.

A tragic accident occured many years ago where the Buck's Hill Bridge crossed the railroad tracks on the west edge of Canton in Stark County roughly where SR 791 crosses the tracks today. As a freight train was entering the yards at Canton, a careless brakeman walked along the tops of the boxcars, completely forgetting about the covered bridge coming up ahead. His head struck the bridge and he was killed instantly.[72]

Wayne County had only two known highway covered bridges, both of which were removed in the 1890s. One spanned Killbuck Creek on the southwest edge of Wooster, and the other was just south of town over Apple Creek. Wayne County did have seven railroad Howe trusses.

All but one of the known wooden truss bridges of Lorain County were railroad bridges. The one highway bridge was a 117 foot uncovered Howe-pony truss over the railroad tracks on Highbridge Road. This bridge was built in 1910 and was slated for removal in the late 1980s.

CUYAHOGA COUNTY

The northern terminus of the Ohio and Erie Canal was at Cleveland. From that city, the canal coursed southward following the valley of the Cuyahoga River. There were at least eight timber truss bridges over the canal in Cuyahoga County. Perhaps the best known of the Cuyahoga County covered bridges was the Columbus Street Bridge, Figure 206, built in 1835 to span the Cuyahoga River by James S. Clark. The Columbus Street Bridge was 200 feet long over all and was built in three spans with a drawbridge in the center for large ships to pass through. The builder gave the bridge to the city and stipulated that it always be toll free.

Figure 206. Cleveland Bridge over Cuyahoga River -- center of the Great Cleveland Bridge War

Instead of gratitude for this new, free bridge, there arose heated disagreements between the citizens of Cleveland and the citizens of Ohio City, a small town across the river. The new bridge directed traffic away from Ohio City which was the basis for the problem. This discontent led to what has become known as the "Cleveland Bridge War".[73]

The Ohio Canal Plat maps show the locations and truss designs of the many bridges that spanned the Ohio and Erie Canal in Cuyahoga County. Some of the county's railroad bridges can also be seen on these old maps. One quite interesting railroad bridge spanned a city street, the canal and the Cuyahoga River at Cleveland. The bridge was a combination of truss designs and materials. The span over the street was a 122 foot uncovered Howe truss, the span over the canal was a 90 foot through-metal-truss bridge, and the remaining three spans over the river were uncovered Howe trusses with arches, totaling 184 feet. There were many other timber truss railroad bridges in Cuyahoga County of the Howe design, both deck and through trusses, full height and pony trusses. Like Geauga County, Cuyahoga also had a few Howe trusses on the Interurban lines.

The sprawling industrial complex of Cleveland now takes up much of Cuyahoga County and it has been many years since the last covered bridge disappeared from this scene.

EXISTING BRIDGE LOCATIONS

Ashtabula County:

35-04-03 Dewey/Olin Bridge, 115' Town, 1873, over Ashtabula River on TR 334, 3m E Ashtabula in Plymouth Twp.

35-04-05 Creek Road Bridge, 112' Town, over Conneaut Creek on TR 443, 4m ENE Kingsville in Conneaut Twp.

35-04-06 Middle Road Bridge, 136' Howe, 1868, over Conneaut Creek on TR 425, 4m SSE Conneaut in Conneaut Twp.

35-04-09 Root Road Bridge, 97' Town, 1868, over w. branch Ashtabula River on TR 414, 2.5m WSW Monre Center in Monroe Twp.

35-04-12 Benetka Road Bridge, 115' Town, c. 1900, over Ashtabula River on TR 350, 2.5m NW Sheffield in Sheffield Twp.

35-04-13 Graham Road Bridge, 85' Town, 1867, off TR 343, 3m NW pierpont in Pierpont Twp. Moved to field by road 1972.

35-04-14 South Denmark Road Bridge, 80' Town, 1868, over Mill Creek off CR 291, 3.5m SE Jefferson in Denmark Twp. Bypassed.

35-04-16 Doyle Road Bridge, 84' Town, 1876, over Mill Creek on TR 287, 1.5m NW Jefferson in Jefferson Twp.

35-04-18 Mechanicsville Bridge, 154' Howe+arch, 1867, over Grand River off CR 9, 3m SW Austinburg in Austinburg Twp. Bypassed.

35-04-19 Harpersfield Bridge, 234' 2-span Howe, 1868, over Grand River on CR 154 just S Harpersfield in Harpersfield Twp.

35-04-22 Riverdale Road Bridge, 120' Town, 1874, over Grand River on TR 69, 1.5m NW Rock Creek in Morgan Twp.

35-04-25 Warner Hollow Bridge, 120' 3-span Town, 1867, over Phelps Creek off TR 357, just SW of Windsor Mills. Bypassed.

35-04-58 State Road Bridge, 157' 2-span Town, 1983, over Conneaut Creek on CR 354, 3m E Kingsville in Conneaut Twp.

35-04-61 Caine Road Bridge, 96' Pratt, 1986, over w branch Ashtabula River on TR 579, 8m NE Jefferson in Pierpont Twp.

Columbiana County:

35-15-01 Sells Bridge, 50' MKP, 1870s, in Scenic Vista Park off TR 764, 4m SW Lisbon in Center Twp. sec 33. Fell to Arson, 1993

35-15-02 McLellan Bridge, 53' MKP, 1870s, over w fork Little Beaver Creek on abandoned road off Trinity Church Road, 5m ESE Hanoverton in Center Twp. sec 32. Abandoned.

35-15-05 Teegarden Bridge, 66' MKP, 1875, over mid fork Little Beaver Creek, 3m W Lisbon at Teegarden in Salem Twp. sec 32. Bypassed.

35-15-07 Miller Road Bridge, 37' MKP, 1870s, over Mill Seat Creek on TR 862, 2.5m N Lisbon in Center Twp. sec 2.

35-15-08 Church Hill Road Bridge, 19' KP, 1870s, W edge Elkton off SR 154 at Lock 24 Restaurant in Elk Run Twp. sec 21. Moved here in 1982.

35-15-96 Tom Malone Bridge, 42' MKP, 1870s, over Sandy & Beaver Canal in Beaver Creek State Park 6m N East Liverpool in St. Clair Twp. sec 6.

Summit County:

35-77-01 Everett Road Bridge, 100' Smith, c. 1870s, over Furnace Run on CR 42, 3m SW Peninsula. Rebuilt 1986. Closed.

Trumbull County:

35-78-01 Newton Falls Bridge, 117' Town, 1831, over e branch of Mahoning River on Arlington Street in Newton Falls.

Fobes Road Bridge over the Grand River

*Spring Street
Bridge over
Ashtabula River
at Ashtabula -
removed 1896*

*Interior of
Doyle Road
Bridge
(pg, 113)*

CHAPTER VIII

IN THE NORTHERN FLATLANDS

Allen, Ashland, Crawford, Defiance, Erie, Fulton, Hancock, Hardin, Henry, Huron, Lucas, Ottawa, Paulding, Putnam, Richland, Sandusky, Seneca, Van Wert, Williams, Wood and Wyandot.

Figure 207. Ohio's Northern Flatlands

Twenty-one counties make up the north central and northwestern sections of Ohio which have been combined under one heading here since so few wood truss bridges were built in this region compared to other parts of the state. In the north central part of Ohio, research has turned up only 82 wooden bridges, including those on the railroads, for a nine county area. Three covered bridges still stand in this region with a fourth in dire condition in use as a shed. There is no ready explanation for the paucity of covered bridges in this part of the state, but perhaps further research will add greatly to our list for north central Ohio.

ASHLAND COUNTY

The last covered bridge in Ashland County was the Rochester Bridge, Figure 208. This Smith truss was built in 1870 to span Jerome Fork southeast of Mohicanville on what is now SR 179. A 1937 road relocation ended the history of this old bridge. Another covered bridge spanned Jerome Fork at Jeromeville on what is now US Route 30. It was removed many years ago.

On SR 39, a Smith truss covered bridge spanned the Black Fork just south of Perrysville.

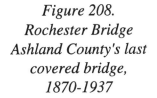

Figure 208. Rochester Bridge Ashland County's last covered bridge, 1870-1937

Our picture, Figure 209, shows the bridge and its replacement steel truss in 1928. There was yet another covered bridge over the Black Fork in Perrysville. It might be well to mention here that the Mohican River and its forks form the main drainage pattern for this area. There is the Black Fork, Lake Fork, Jerome Fork, Muddy Fork, and Clear Fork. In addition to the two covered bridges in and near Perrysville, there were others at Loudenville and Mifflin.

covered bridge was known as the Rome Bridge, a 114 foot Smith truss over the Black Fork, Figure 210. The Rome Bridge was built of Michigan pine by the Smith Bridge Company in 1874 to replace an earlier covered bridge. On August 10, 1971, the Rome Bridge was set on fire by vandals and completely destroyed. The first covered bridge on this site was built in 1857 and old county records describe it as "kingwork" on stone abutments.

Figure 209. Perrysville Bridges -- the old and new bridges together, 1928

Figure 210. Rome Bridge, 1874-1971

The only timber truss railroad bridges in Ashland County were two on the Erie Railroad, one over Jerome Fork at Ashland, and one over Black Fork near Five Points. The Railroad Reports simply said that these were both 145 foot Howe trusses.

CRAWFORD COUNTY

The only timber truss bridges known so far for Crawford County were three on the Toledo and Ohio Central Railroad built in 1881. A 100 foot through-Howe truss spanned Broken Sword Creek six miles northwest of the county seat of Bucyrus. Another through-Howe truss of 150 feet carried the railroad over the Sandusky River at Bucyrus, and the third railroad bridge, a 70 foot Howe pony-truss, spanned the Olentangy River near New Winchester.

RICHLAND COUNTY

The Mohican River and its tributaries also form the drainage pattern of Ashland County's neighbor, Richland County. The county's last

In 1867, a covered bridge was built to span Clear Fork on what is now SR 97 southeast of Bellville., Figure 211. In its later years, a sign on the side dubbed it "The Hero of the Clear Fork" because it had withstood all floods since it was built, including the great flood of March, 1913. What this bridge couldn't withstand was a truck loaded with pickles that attempted to cross it in September 1930. Both covered bridge and pickle truck came crashing down together and the bridge was never rebuilt. When some folks reminisce about this bridge, they call it the Pickle Bridge.

Old Richland County records on bridge building are frustrating to the researcher as they usually gave amounts of money paid to, for instance, the Smith Bridge Company, for "bridges built in the county". Thus, there is no doubt that the Smith Bridge Company was quite active in this area, building both wood and metal truss bridges, but detailed information is difficult to obtain. But we do know that Richland County had covered bridges at Bellville, in Butler at Rummel's Mill, Figure 212, at Newville and at Lexington, to name a

few. There were also seven Howe truss railroad bridges in Richland County of the through- and deck-Howe varieties.

Figure 212. Rummel's Mill Bridge

HURON COUNTY

Research has turned up two timber truss bridges for Huron County; one a highway bridge and one a railroad Howe truss bridge. The highway bridge was over the Huron River on South Main Street at Monroeville, Figure 213. This two-lane, three-span structure was built in 1836 by Benjamin Murphy, probably for a turnpike company. At some point in time, two of the three covered spans were replaced with

iron bowstring trusses. In 1909, one of the iron bowstring spans went down under a threshing rig and the entire bridge was removed the following year.

The Baltimore and Ohio Railroad had a fully covered deck-Howe truss over Slate Run. We know that this 12 panel, 102 foot bridge was built in 1875, but the date of its demise is unknown.

Figure 213. Monroeville Bridge on South Main Street over the Huron River 1836-1910

ERIE COUNTY

Erie County, which borders on Lake Erie, is another of our northern Ohio counties not known for its wealth of timber truss bridges.

127

*Figure 214.
Birmingham Bridge
once spanned the
Vermillion River in
Erie County*

Figure 214, shows the Birmingham Bridge over the Vermillion River on what is now SR 113. The date of this photo is unknown, but the men's clothing styles indicate the early 1900s. The removal date of this bridge, like so many others, is unknown.

Many years ago, a covered bridge known as the Harbortown Bridge was located in the town of Vermillion. Its history is unknown and it has been gone for many years now.

There were railroad Howe trusses in Erie County on the Baltimore and Ohio and Lake Shore and Michigan Southern Railroad. Unfortunately, little is known of their structural details or histories.

OTTAWA COUNTY

The recorded wooden truss bridges of Ottawa County were all railroad Howe trusses of various styles on the Lake Shore and Michigan Southern Railroad and the Wheeling and Lake Erie Railroads. Although we do not have any records listing highway timber truss bridges, there is no doubt that they existed.

SENECA COUNTY

The Kagy or Frazier Bridge over Honey Creek was the last covered bridge in Seneca County. A picture of this old structure can be found in Rosalie Wells' Covered Bridges of America, published in 1931. The first bridge in Seneca County was built in 1833/34 over the Sandusky River at the foot of Washington Street at Tiffin by Reuban Williams. This bridge was washed out in 1834 and was replaced by another wooden bridge. In 1847, the Seneca County Commissioners received an award for building a substantial bridge at this site, no doubt a covered bridge. There was another covered bridge over the Sandusky River on Market Street built in 1834 for $2200. The nearby Van Nest's Carriage Factory caught fire on January 26, 1854 and the fire quickly spread destroying many other structures, including the Market Street Bridge.[74]

The Sandusky River flows through Pleasant Township and the fact that there was no bridge over the river in this township until 1854 was an inconvenience to local residents. County Commissioner Calvin Clark used his influence to determine the site for the first bridge over the Sandusky about three quarters of a mile below Old Fort near the Pleasant-Union Cemetery. This site was not a unanimously popular choice and ended up costing Mr. Clark the next election.[75] Clark's Bridge as it was known, served until its destruction in the great 1913 flood.

In 1870, an uncovered timber truss known as the Watson Bridge was built a little over a mile south of Clark's Bridge. One source declared that the Watson Bridge was "more of an

128

experiment than a good job". It washed out in 1875 and area residents were quite irritated when they found out that the County Commissioners had decided not to rebuild at that site. The new covered bridge was built at Pool's Mill instead, just east of Fort Seneca.[76]

About this time, a civic-minded local gentleman went to the Commissioners and offered to build a substantial bridge on the abutments of the old Watson Bridge for a mere $2500, since wood and iron were cheap at the time. The Commissioners knew a good deal when they heard one and of course they accepted this most generous offer. A fine Howe truss was erected which actually cost $3,000., but the donor, D.V. Flummerfelt, was only too happy to make up the difference.[77]

The Baltimore and Ohio Railroad and the Northwest Ohio Railroad had several Howe truss bridges in Seneca County. The largest was the Baltimore and Ohio's two-span, 214 foot Howe truss over the Sandusky River at Tiffin. It was built in 1870 and covered the following year. In 1883, it was replaced by a steel truss.

SANDUSKY COUNTY

The venerable Mull Bridge, Figure 215, with its 99 foot two-span Town lattice truss over the east branch of Wolf Creek is the last covered bridge in the county. It was built as a one-span bridge in the early 1840s and served for 120 years before being bypassed in 1962. There are no records on when the concrete pier was added.

The Sandusky River is the main stream of Sandusky County and there were covered bridges over this river at Fremont, the county seat, in Ballville on the south edge of Fremont, and another bridge two miles southwest of town. The Ballville Bridge was built in 1858 and removed in 1924. The Fremont Bridge was built in 1841/42 by Cyrus Williams. The timber for the bridge came from the trestle of the Ohio Railroad Company at Fremont. This company failed in 1840 and the trestle timber was available for another bridge.[78]

The Lake Erie and Western Railroad had a gigantic bridge in Fremont over the Sandusky River. This bridge had eight through-Howe truss spans which totaled 1,088 feet in length, plus 4,800 feet of trestle approaches. The old Railroad Reports gave no information on either building or removal dates for this important structure.

WYANDOT COUNTY

Most of Wyandot County's roofed timber trusses spanned the Sandusky River and Tymochtee Creek. Today, there are still two fine Howe truss highway bridges carrying daily traffic over the Sandusky River, the Parker Bridge and the Swartz Bridge. The Parker Bridge, Figure 216, is a 101 foot Howe truss built in 1873 by J.C. Davis of Marion, Ohio.

The 93 foot Swartz Bridge, Figure 217, dates to 1878. In late 1992, work began on reroofing this bridge. Your author has never seen any bridge so covered with graffiti as is the Swartz Bridge.

Figure 215. Mull Bridge

Figure 216 a. Parker Bridge after the Fire

There is technically still a third covered bridge in Wyandot County, the Fox Farm Bridge, a 60 foot Howe truss that once spanned Tymochtee Creek southwest of Upper Sandusky. In 1964, it was moved to the nearby Fox Farm where is now serves as a shed. It is in very poor condition.

In May 1991, vandals set fire to the Parker Bridge, destroying about one third of the south end, causing that end to fall into the river. The county immediately set about raising the bridge out of the river and resting it on temporary steel piers and the county historical society began to raise money to rebuild the south end

Figure 217. Swartz Bridge -- lots of graffiti

Figure 216 b. Parker Bridge showing rebuilt south trusses in winter, 1991/92

of the bridge. The Cross Over the Bridge Again Committee was formed to handle the fund raising. Thanks to the hard work of many devoted people, enough money was raised to get the bridge off the temporary pier before ice dams on the river could cause more harm. The Howe trusses were rebuilt and the bridge was reopened to traffic in the fall of 1992. The Cross Over the Bridge Again Committee has decided to remain active to keep funds available for the repair work needed by both of the county's covered bridges. Lighting may be added at both covered bridges to provide some protection against vandalism.

At the old Indian Mill on the Sandusky River northeast of Upper Sandusky was a 140 foot two-span Howe truss covered bridge, Figure 218, built in 1860 for $595. by John Kennedy. Eyewitness accounts tell of the last persons to cross the bridge on March 24, 1913. A young girl was driving a horse and buggy on her way home from high school in Upper Sandusky. By the time she reached the bridge, the water was up to the horse's belly. The miller at Indian Mill came out and led the horse and buggy across to safety. He then turned around and walked back across the bridge to the mill. He was the last person to use the bridge.

Figure 218. Wyandot County's Indian Mill Bridge as it looked before the flood of March 1913

The next morning at 10 o'clock, a crowd of local people gathered on the banks of the river to watch the old bridge slowly lose its fight against the raging floodwaters and huge chunks of ice that were smashing into it. Then, a large tree uprooted by the flood, came tearing downstream and hit the bridge with great force. The bridge began to pivot on its center pier and then finally slid off into the swift current. It rode downstream in the middle of the river for less than a mile and then veered over and crashed into the bank, suffering great damage.[79]

The county decided to use some of the timbers from the Indian Mill Bridge to make repairs to the trusses of other county bridges damaged in the flood. The Parker Bridge was one of the covered bridges repaired with timbers taken from the wrecked Indian Mill Bridge. The remainder of the lumber was sold at auction in August of 1913. The old Indian Mill still stands today and is an historic site maintained by the Ohio Historical Society. An aging steel truss built in 1914 to replace the old covered structure now spans the river here.

As might be expected, there were a large number of covered bridges spanning the Sandusky River in Wyandot County. To name a few: Keller, Bowman, Herring, Kotterman, Hayman, Gier, Reile and Carter Bridges. The latter three bridges were destroyed by the 1913 flood.

A large number of covered bridges also carried traffic across Tymochtee Creek in Wyandot County: the Lortz, Michaels, Krebs, Frank, and Fox Bridges. The last covered bridge to be removed in Wyandot County was the Mutchler Bridge over Sycamore Creek on SR 231. The state removed this bridge in 1954. The Toledo and Ohio Railroad's 150 foot through-Howe truss over the Sandusky River was the largest of the county's railroad timber trusses. There were two 60 foot Howe pony trusses on the Toledo, Columbus and Hocking Valley Railroad.

The northwest section of the state of Ohio was the last region to be heavily settled. This is the Lake Plains Area and a large portion of it was covered by the Great Black Swamp. Transportation here was poor due to swampland drainage problems and it was not until after 1850 that the land was drained and good roads built. Another aid in opening up this part of the state was the construction of the Miami and Erie Canal and the railroads. The late permanent settlement of northwestern Ohio has been cited as one of the reasons that so few covered bridges were built here. So far, research has turned up only 16 timber trusses for the 12 counties included herein. Two of these counties, Van Wert and Fulton, have no wooden truss bridges recorded, but there is no doubt that they did have them, probably of the pony truss style. No timber truss bridges remain in this extreme northwestern section of Ohio today.

WILLIAMS COUNTY

Williams County occupies the extreme northwestern corner of the state and its principle streams are the Tiffin and St. Joseph Rivers. A 14 panel Smith truss bridge once spanned the Tiffin River near Stryker. It is believed that this bridge was lost in the 1913 flood (see Chapter XI). The Lockport Bridge, Figure 219, also crossed the Tiffin, just east of Lockport. Its fate is unknown.

Seven miles southwest of the county seat, Montpelier, the Denmark Bridge spanned the St. Joseph River. It was built in 1869 and stood into the 1940s.

*Figure 219.
Lockport Bridge
over the Tiffin River
in Williams County
removed 1919*

DEFIANCE COUNTY

The Auglaize, Maumee and St. Joseph Rivers flow through Defiance County and some large wooden bridges were built to carry traffic over these waterways. Perhaps the largest of these bridges was the Wabash Railroad's 677 foot fully covered through-Howe truss over the Maumee at Defiance. It was a short-lived structure however, built in 1867 and replaced by steel in 1870/71.

Brice Hilton built the Clinton Street Bridge over the Maumee at Defiance in 1859. It was described as a wooden superstructure on stone foundations and cost over $2,000.

Also in Defiance over the Maumee River was a covered bridge on Hopkins street built in 1875 by the Hamilton Brothers, probably the same men who built the Eldean Bridge in Miami County. If so, this bridge was quite likely a Long truss. The Hopkins Street Bridge cost $13.25 per linear foot and was 459 feet long and 18 feet wide. It had 5 foot wide sidewalks on each side.

From old county records we learned that Defiance County had another covered bridge somewhere in Mifflin Township over the St. Joseph River. It was built in 1864 for over $3,000.

D.H. and C.C. Morrison built a three-span wood and iron combination truss bridge with arches over the Auglaize River in 1875 for $10.96 per lineal foot. This bridge, known as the English Bridge, was probably quite similar to their Germantown Bridge. It was located about two miles south southwest of Defiance.

Except for the railroad bridge described at the beginning of the Defiance County section, we have no records on how long these other covered bridges served and exactly what happened to them.

PAULDING COUNTY

The only wooden truss bridge recorded so far for Paulding County was over the Miami and Erie Canal on the Wabash River at Canal Antwerp. It was a 111 foot through-Howe truss built in 1871. The terse Railroad Reports had nothing else to say about this bridge, so we do not know when it was removed.

HENRY COUNTY

The only known wooden truss bridges in Henry County were built to span the Maumee River on Monroe Street. The first bridge here was built in 1857 and had oak rafters, floor and sheeting for the roof. This bridge was replaced in 1873 by a five-span Howe truss built by the Smith Bridge Company. The fate of this second covered bridge on Monroe Street is unknown. The old Railroad Reports do not list any timber truss bridges on the rail lines of Henry County.

PUTNAM COUNTY

Putnam County had a large timber truss highway bridge over the Blanchard River just south of Gilboa. There was also a 130 foot railroad Howe truss over the Blanchard River on the Dayton and Michigan Railroad. The Norfolk and Western Railroad had a 350 foot three-span, through-Howe truss over the Auglaize River at Dupont. As might be suspected from this short description, nothing is known of the history of these bridges beyond the fact that they did exist.

ALLEN COUNTY

Howe's Historical Collections of Ohio has a sketch showing an early view of the town of Lima which shows a Town truss covered bridge over the Ottawa River. This is the only known fully covered bridge in Allen County. Sketches in the 1880 atlas of Allen County show several wood and iron pony trusses as well as the separately-covered wood pony truss over the Auglaize River near Westminster, Figure 220.

The Lake Erie and Western Railroad had an uncovered 80 foot through-Howe truss bridge over Riley Creek at Bluffton, built in 1873.

Figure 220. Westminster Bridge in Allen County -- a good example of the separately-covered pony truss

Figure 221. (Right) Scotch Ridge Bridge at Scotch Ridge in Wood County

LUCAS AND WOOD COUNTIES

The great Maumee River separates Wood and Lucas Counties along the entire length of their common border. Between Maumee and Perrysburg on the county line, there was a four-span, two-lane Town lattice truss bridge over the Maumee River on what is now SR 20. There was some type of bridge at this site (possibly not covered) that washed out in 1840 after only one year of service. That same year, an uncovered two-lane Town truss bridge was built on this site that served for the next nine years. In Howe's Historical Collections of Ohio, there is a picture of this bridge on page 147.

In 1849, the bridge was destroyed by high water and the tollbridge company that owned it hired Amos Campbell of Woodbury, New Jersey, to replace it with another two-lane Town truss bridge. Mr. Campbell did this in 46 days for the sum of $7200.[80] This third wooden bridge on the site was fully covered and had a tollgate and gate keeper's house on one end. The tollbridge company sold the bridge to the two counties in 1877 and the bridge continued to serve until it was replaced in 1880 by a metal truss bridge.

Less than six miles below the Maumee-Perrysburg Bridge, there was another large wooden bridge over the Maumee at Waterville. This was a six-span bridge, of 150 foot length each span, built in 1876 at a cost of $50,000. J.E. Strutton of Toledo was the engineer in charge of construction.[81]

Just south of the town of Scotch Ridge in Wood County was a little Smith truss bridge over the north branch of the Portage River on what is now SR 199, Figure 221. It is believed that this bridge was removed before 1930.

There were several timber Howe-truss bridges serving the railroads in both Lucas and Wood Counties on the Toledo and Ohio Central, the Cincinnati, Hamilton and Dayton, and the Lake Shore and Michigan Southern Railroads.

HANCOCK COUNTY

Hancock County had only a few timber truss bridges that served highways and railroads. The Main Street covered bridge in Findlay spanned the Blanchard River from 1850 to 1873. It was a two-lane, two-span structure, truss type unknown. There was another covered bridge over the Blanchard River near Mt. Blanchard that was believed to have stood into the 1940s.

In 1870, both the Main Street and Detroit Street bridges at Kenton were to be replaced by new metal bridges. One of these was the covered bridge mentioned above and the other may have been the wooden pony truss at Espy's Mill. The Hardin County Commissioners Journals were not very productive as far as bridge research goes and information on bridges was practically nil.

The Erie Railroad had a 160 foot through-Howe truss bridge over the Scioto River at Kenton built in 1871. Arches were added to strengthen this bridge in 1872. It was replaced by a steel bridge in 1882. The New York Central Railroad was carried over the Scioto River at Kenton on a 100 foot through-Howe truss bridge built in 1877.

Figure 222. Mt Corey Bridge over Ottawa Creek in Hancock County

Near the village of Mt. Corey, a one-span Smith truss covered bridge, Figure 222, crossed Ottawa Creek. Nothing more is known of this bridge, but according to the 1912 edition of the Automobile Blue Book, it was still in service at that time.

Three railroad Howe-truss bridges complete the meagre list for Hancock County.

HARDIN COUNTY

Most of the timber truss bridges of Hardin County were of the pony truss variety if the figures in old county records are to be believed. There was one fully covered highway bridge over the Scioto River at Kenton, the county seat.

EXISTING BRIDGE LOCATIONS

Sandusky County:

35-72-01 Mull Bridge, 99' Town, 1842, over Wolf Creek just off TR9, 3m NE Bettsville in Ballville Twp. sec 31. Bypassed

Wyandot County:

35-88-03 Parker Bridge, 100' Howe, 1873, over Sandusky River on CR 40, 5m NE Upper Sandusky in Crane Twp. sec 3.

35-88-05 Swartz Bridge, 93' Howe, 1878, over Sandusky River on CR 130, 2m N SR 294 in Antrim Twp. sec 19/20.

CHAPTER IX

THE WEST CORRIDOR ALONG THE NATIONAL ROAD

**Auglaize, Champaign, Clark, Darke.
Logan, Mercer, Miami, Montgomery,
Preble and Shelby Counties**

*Figure 223. The West Corridor along the
National Road*

The topography of west central Ohio is generally flat to gently rolling. Principle streams of this region are the Great Miami River, the Stillwater River, the Mad River and the Auglaize River, plus smaller creeks such as the Loramie and the Greenville. The Miami and Erie Canal traversed this region, too. Although there were many covered bridges in this area, there were perhaps more of the wooden pony trusses and the pony metal and wood combinations.

MERCER COUNTY

This is another rare instance of an Ohio county where there is no record of timber truss

bridges — even on the railroads. There is no doubt that there were wooden pony trusses in Mercer County and perhaps even a wooden truss bridge on the state line over the Wabash River (Jay County, Indiana), but documentation is poor.

DARKE COUNTY

Darke County lies along the western edge of Ohio between Mercer and Preble Counties, along the Indiana border. Our record of known timber truss bridges in Darke County is still somewhat skimpy, but ongoing research promises to add greatly to our list. So far, all of the former covered bridges identified in Darke County spanned Greenville Creek.

In the town of Greenville, the county seat, there were two covered bridges, one on North Broadway Street (SR49/118) and one on East Main Street (US 127). The latter was known as the Dutch Bridge and it was built in the late 1860s and removed in 1882. The covered bridge on North Broadway was torn down in 1881, but its building date is unknown. Not far from the North Broadway Street bridge was a 128 foot through-Howe truss bridge on the old Dayton and Union Railroad. It was built in 1878 and was still standing four years later according to the old Railroad Reports for 1882. Its history after that is unknown.

East of Greenville on the Gettysburg Pike (US 36), was a covered bridge known as the Old Red Bridge. It was probably built in the early 1800s by a turnpike company. The Old Red Bridge was destroyed by fire in 1895 and the local newspaper account of this event described the bridge as a "rattle trap to which the turnpike company paid no attention".[83] Obviously, no one mourned the passing of this covered bridge!

Figure 224 shows the covered bridge just south of the town of Gettysburg in Adams Township. As yet we have no building or removal dates but it is believed the old bridge

Figure 224. Gettysburg Bridge

Figure 225. Wellman Bridge

stood into the early 1900s, maybe as late as the 1920s.

On the Miami County line, on SR 721, was a covered bridge south of the town of Bradford. Darke and Miami County officials were negotiating the construction of this bridge in 1871. It was replaced by a steel truss in 1928.

AUGLAIZE COUNTY

In the late 1980s, there was discovered in Auglaize County a low wooden (pony) truss bridge over Muddy Creek on private property near New Knoxville. This is the Wellman Bridge, Figure 225, a 43 foot structure with separately covered trusses built in 1891 for only $2.90 per linear foot. After serving the public road for only 20 years, the Wellman Bridge was moved to the farm lane where it serves even today.

In its new location, it survived the 1913 flood, but its replacement bridge in the old location did not. The Wellman Bridge is an important relic of the many such pony truss bridges built in Auglaize County (and elsewhere in Ohio). They were economical to build and that recommended them for many situations where creeks were small and money was tight.

Thanks to the research of Dan Bennett, P.E., Auglaize County Bridge Engineer we have a list of at least 35 of these separately covered pony trusses. In addition, there were a few fully covered highway bridges in Auglaize County, plus four railroad Howe trusses on the Lake Erie and Western Railroad, all built in 1873.

In 1992, an authentic Howe truss covered bridge was built at St. Mary's to span the St. Mary's River in Memorial Park. The Memorial Bridge, Figure 226, is 110 feet long with a 14 foot roadway. Dan Bennett designed this bridge which was built by volunteer labor with donated materials. It was estimated that the new bridge would have cost over $90,000. if built with contract labor and commercially purchased materials.It is used for pedestrian and bicycle traffic.

Figure 226. St. Mary's Bridge

SHELBY COUNTY

In 1851, an important covered bridge was built to span the Great Miami River east of Lockington. The builder was Abraham Wilson and the truss type was Long's patent design. The two-span, 184 foot Lockington Bridge, Figure 227, cost $8.82 per lineal foot to build. In the late 1890s, a flood cut a new channel around the east end of the Lockington Bridge forming an island on which its east abutment rested. Two steel pony trusses were built to span the new channel and at some unknown date, a third steel pony truss was added to these two.

Figure 227. Lockington Bridge in Shelby County over Great Miami River

The bridge was closed in the mid-1980s and plans were made to bypass it. There was to be a hiking and bike path to the old bridge and a small park. Unfortunately, vandals set the bridge on fire on October 18, 1989 and it was completely destroyed. This act of vandalism ended the covered bridge era in Shelby County.

About 1850, the Baltimore and Ohio Railroad contracted with Thatcher, Burt and Company of Cleveland to build a Howe truss railroad bridge for them over the Great Miami River at Sidney. The Shelby County Commissioners were quite impressed with this railroad bridge and in 1852, they also hired Thatcher, Burt and Company to build a Howe truss covered bridge to carry Court Street over the Great Miami at Sidney.

The last covered highway bridge over Loramie Creek was located just west of Dawson. The Dawson Bridge was torn down in 1939 in a WPA project. This removal left the Lockington Bridge as the last covered bridge in Shelby County (see above).

There were several other railroad Howe truss bridges in Shelby County over Loramie Creek and the Miami and Erie Canal. All of these railroad bridges were replaced by steel structures many years ago.

MIAMI COUNTY

The principal streams of Miami County are the Great Miami and Stillwater Rivers and their tributaries. At least 14 covered bridges spanned the Great Miami in Miami County and the last covered bridge in the county crosses that river north of Troy. There were at least 15 covered bridges that spanned the Stillwater River in Miami County. None are still standing today.

The Eldean Bridge over the Great Miami River is a 224 foot, two-span Long truss, Figure 228, built in 1860 by James and William Hamilton. This last remaining covered bridge in Miami County cost a total of $4,044 to build: $2,632. for the superstructure (at $11.75 per lineal foot) plus $1412. for the abutments and

Figure 228. Eldean Bridge

pier. All of the lumber used in the bridge, except for the floor, was white pine from Michigan, shipped to the bridge site via the Miami and Erie Canal. Almost 500 perch of rock and cut stone was used in the stonework, priced at $2.73 per perch for the abutments and $2.95 per perch for the pier. Can you imagine what that amount of masonry work would cost today?

At the time of construction, the Eldean Bridge was known as the Allen's Mill Bridge. Origin of the name Eldean is a crossroads town to the west of the bridge site. The county bypassed the Eldean Bridge in 1964 with a new bridge and road relocation. They closed the covered bridge, intending to preserve it as an historic site. However, vandalism became such a problem on the old bridge at night that the county engineer decided to reopen it hoping that occasional traffic would deter the culprits. So far, this seems to be working. The Eldean Bridge is the second longest covered bridge in Ohio.

There were other large covered bridges over the Great Miami River in Miami County at Farrington, Troy, Piqua, Broad Ford, Ross Road and Tadmore Station. The Old Broad Ford Bridge, Figure 229, had a two-span multiple kingpost truss with arches that spanned the river just east of Troy. It was built in 1853 and major renovations were made in 1869 when the arches were added. One abutment had given way and the county specified that a new abutment was to be built of the best quality, second class stone (a frequent directive found in Miami County bridge contracts). The Old Broad Ford Bridge may have washed out in 1913. The Farrington Bridge, five miles north of Troy, fell into the Great Miami River on April 24, 1913, doubtless due to damages suffered the previous month in the great flood.

Both the Ross Road and Tadmore Station Bridges were on the Miami-Montgomery County line and building and repair costs were shared by the two counties. The Ross Road Bridge, also known as Long's Ford, was built in 1871/72 and was a 300 foot, two-span Smith truss. The Victory or Tadmore Station Bridge was built in 1867 (see Montgomery County for details). Removal dates of these two bridges are unknown, but they may have been destroyed in the 1913 flood.

Three covered bridges spanned the Great Miami River at Piqua. The Upper Bridge was located on Main Street at the northeast edge of town. The Middle Bridge was on what is now US Route 36 and the Lower Bridge was at south edge of town. The Upper Bridge was built in 1855 to replace an earlier wooden structure. The Middle Bridge was built in 1867/68 by Jacob Gray for $17.50 per linear foot. The Hamilton Brothers did the masonry. The Lower Bridge was a two-span Howe truss built in 1854 by Thatcher, Burt and Company. Removal dates of these three bridges is unknown, but is thought to have been before 1913.

The Howe truss was very popular with the Miami County Commissioners and in 1856 they asked the voters at the October elections to approve the use of the Howe patent truss for bridges over the Miami and Stillwater Rivers. In 1857, the Miami County Commissioners had to pay Thatcher, Burt and Company $250 in patent fees on the Upper Bridge at Piqua. Perhaps Thatcher, Burt and Company acted as agents in Ohio for William Howe? Miami County also used the Long truss for a few bridges. Then, in the late 1860s, they began specifying the Smith patent truss for most of their wooden bridges. The story of Robert Smith, a native of Miami County, is told in Chapter II.

Among the Stillwater River covered bridges in Miami County were the bridges in and around

Figure 229. Miami County's Old Broad Ford Bridge over Great Miami River

the towns of Covington, Pleasant Hill, Figure 230, and Ludlow Falls. It is almost certain that some of them were destroyed in the 1913 flood because steel truss replacement bridges on the sites today date from that era.

The last major wooden bridges in Miami County were built in the late 1860s. Many wooden pony trusses were still being built into the 1870s on the Smith and Howe truss plans. Bridge contracts after the mid-1870s were almost all for iron trusses.

We know of seven railroad Howe trusses built to serve the rail lines of Miami County. These Howe trusses utilized all forms of this design: pony, deck and through.

Figure 231. McColly Bridge over Great Miami River in Logan County built in 1876

Figure 230. Pleasant Hill Bridge spanned the Stillwater River

LOGAN COUNTY

The Great Miami River has its source in Logan County, fed by the waters of Indian Lake. Covered bridges spanned Logan County creeks with such colorful Indian names as Muchinippi and Buckongelas. Buckongelas Creek was named for a Delaware Indian Chief. The last two covered bridges in the county span the Great Miami River and the south fork of the Great Miami.

The McColly Bridge, Figure 231, is a 134 foot Howe truss built in 1876 by the Anderson Green Company of Sidney, Ohio for $13.25 per linear foot. Steel I-beams beneath the wooden trusses now reinforce the McColly Bridge. The Bickham Bridge, Figure 232, crosses the south

fork of the Miami River near Indian Lake. It is a 142 foot Howe truss built in 1877 by the Smith Bridge Company. Both of these Howe

Figure 232. Bickham Bridge

139

truss structures are in good condition, with the Bickham Bridge carrying heavy daily traffic.

There were also covered bridges over the Great Miami River at DeGraff and Quincey. Another Logan County covered bridge spanned the Waste Way at Indian Lake near Lakeview, Figure 233.

Big Darby Creek has its origin in Logan County and there was at least one covered bridge over this stream in Zane Township. Its history is unknown.

The old Railroad Reports mentioned only two railroad Howe trusses for Logan County, one at DeGraff and the other at West Liberty. Both of these bridges were removed many years ago.

CHAMPAIGN COUNTY

A turnpike company built a double-lane Town lattice truss bridge in Champaign County over the Mad River in the early 1800s. This bridge was at Steinberger's Mill, Figure 234, on the old Bobtail Pike, now SR 55. The Steinberger Mill Bridge was a one-span structure with horizontal siding, indicating a very old bridge. It served until 1910.

Another two-lane covered bridge carried the Urbana-Piqua Pike, now US 36, over the Mad River, Figure 235. It was a 75 foot one-span bridge with horizontal siding. A sign over the portal urged the traveler to visit Couffer's Dry Goods Store.

Black and Borneman (see Chapter II) were building Howe truss bridges in Champaign County in the 1870s, and later when that parnership was dissolved, William Black came home to Urbana and built bridges in Champaign County in the 1880s.

Figure 233. Old Covered Bridge over the Wasteway at Indian Lake Park

Figure 234. Steinberger's Mill Bridge on the old Bobtail Pike

140

Figure 235. Urbana Pike Bridge over the Mad River West of Urbana

Another builder, James Garber, built Smith truss bridges in Champaign County and was undoubtedly an agent for the Smith Bridge Company. Two of his Smith trusses were over Kings Creek near the village of Kings Creek.

The Erie Railroad also had a through Howe truss over Kings Creek east of the village. This same railroad had two other through Howe truss bridges in Champaign County over Spain Creek. The railroad reported that all three of these bridges were 100 foot in length. The fate of these railroad bridges is unknown.

No one knows today just when the last covered bridge was removed in Champaign County, but we do know that there was still a covered bridge over the Mad River in 1913 on the Wilson Baker Farm. Mr. Baker purchased the bridge from the county prior to 1913 and it is your author's opinion that he bought the old Steinberger Mill Bridge as this would have been the bridge closest to his farm in Mad River Township. In 1913, this bridge washed downstream but stayed intact and was brought back and secured in place again. The bridge was still on the Baker Farm in 1917 according to one county history.[84]

CLARK COUNTY

Clark County is bisected by the National Road and has as its major stream the Mad River. The county seat is the city of Springfield on the banks of the Mad River. Buck Creek, a principal tributary, joins the Mad River at Springfield. There were four covered bridges over Buck Creek in Springfield, including one on the National Road. The latter was a two-lane Town truss. Altogether, there were five covered bridges built to serve the National Road in Clark County and three of them were of the Town lattice design. The Buck Creek Bridge at Springfield and the Harmony Bridge were built in 1834 and the Mad River Bridge on the west edge of Springfield was built in 1839 by David Sniveley (see Chapter I). The Buck Creek Bridge, Figure 236, was replaced in 1925 and the Beaver Creek and Mad River Bridges served until 1932. On west of Springfield on the

Figure 236. Buck Creek Bridge on the National Road at Springfield 1834-1926

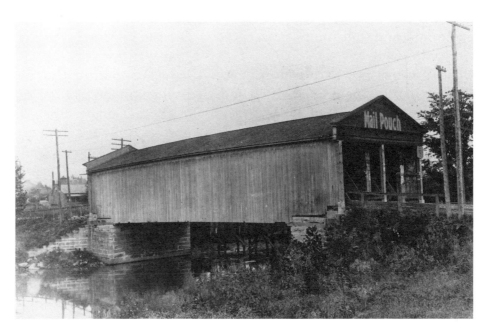

Old Pike there were covered bridges over Donnels Creek and over Jackson Creek at Tillie's Lane. Little is known of the structure or history of these last two bridges, but they were probably Town trusses.

North of Springfield and just east of Tremont City was a covered bridge over the Mad River near the Seitz and Bloses Mill, Figure 237. It was built in 1864 by J.B. Hartman, a well-known bridge builder in this area. The Bloses Mill Bridge was replaced in 1904. Other Mad River covered bridges in Clark County were at Eagle City, Hertzlers Mill and Enon. The Near and the Far Bridges spanned the Mad River on the Lower Valley Pike south-

Figure 238. Snyderville Bridge -- last in Clark County, 1869-1953

Figure 237. Seitz and Bloses Mill Bridge

west of Springfield and their names indicated their proximity to town.

Many wooden truss railroad bridges were built in Clark County including a 272 foot combination truss over the Mad River on the northwest edge of Springfield built to serve the Detroit, Toledo and Ironton Railroad in 1886. The Erie Railroad had three large Howe trusses over the Mad River in Clark County. All three were built in 1871 and replaced in 1881.

The county's last covered bridge was built by J.B. Hartman in the late 1860s to span the Mad River on Tecumseh Road southwest of Springfield. This was known as the Snyderville Bridge, Figure 238, and had 172 foot long Wernwag trusses. The old Snyderville Bridge

fell into disrepair and was closed to traffic, circa 1950. One day in 1953, two men and a dog strolled across the old bridge and it collapsed under them. The men managed to escape but the dog was killed. Thus, the covered bridge era in Clark County came to an abrupt end.

MONTGOMERY COUNTY

Three major streams flow through Montgomery County: the Great Miami, the Stillwater and the Mad Rivers. All three come together at Dayton, the county seat. A glimpse at a map of this area shows in an instant what happened at Dayton in March 1913. The great flood of that year was devastating to this region (see Chapter XI) and after the massive clean up effort, civil engineers set to work planning the series of Miami Conservancy District Dams that now protect this area from another such disastrous flood.

Fifteen covered bridges once spanned the Great Miami in Montgomery County, seven of them in the City of Dayton. There were also covered bridges in Dayton over the Mad River on Keowee, Findlay and Taylor Streets. Not far from Dayton there was a covered bridge over the Mad River at Harshmanville. Most of the wood truss bridges in the city were gone before the 1913 flood.

The old National Road, US 40, crossed the Stillwater River on a covered bridge near Englewood, Figure 239. This bridge survived the 1913 flood and served for many more years, even after one of the Miami Conservancy Dams

Figure 239. Englewood Bridge over the Stillwater River on the National Road

was built near Englewood in the early 1920s. At that time, US 40 was rerouted over the top of the dam, but the old covered bridge was left in place on the abandoned section of road. County officials anchored it to its abutments and pier with iron rods attached to the lower chords and bolted to the masonry about 12 feet below the lower chords. This was done to prevent the bridge from floating away when the water level rose behind the dam. How long the bridge remained in place after that is unknown.

Three covered bridges are in existance in Montgomery County in the early 1990s, two of them transplants from nearby Greene County (the Jasper Road and Feedwire Road Bridges). The third bridge is the well known Germantown Bridge built in 1865 by D.H.Morrison, one of Ohio's outstanding bridge builders and designers. (See Chapter II for details and pictures of the Germantown Bridge.)

In 1964, the owner of the Mud Lick Estates, Huston Brown, acquired the Jasper Road Bridge from Greene County for his property southwest of Germantown. The bridge, a 56 foot Warren truss, was dismantled and rebuilt over Mud Lick Creek. J.W. McLain built this bridge

for Greene County in 1869. The arch/brace was added sometime after 1930. The Jasper Road/Mud Lick Bridge is easily seen today just off Mud Lick Road.

Greene County's Feedwire Road Bridge is now a feature of Carillon Park in Dayton where it spans the bed of the old Miami and Erie Canal, Figure 240. The Smith Bridge Company built this 48 foot Warren truss in 1870. The arches and projected portals were added after the bridge was moved to the park in 1948. Today, hundreds of people visit this bridge with little thought as to its history, but nevertheless aware that it is a relic of the past and therefore to be greatly treasured.

A partial listing of some of Montgomery County's more important covered bridges of days gone by would include these Great Miami River bridges: at Sycamore Street and Linden Avenue in Miamisburg (south of Dayton), the Bridge Street Bridge at Dayton, the Waggoners Ford, Johnson Station, and Tadmore Station

Figure 240. Carillon Park Bridge

Bridges, and of course, the famed old Miami and Erie Canal Aquaduct, Figure 14, all north of Dayton. The Waggoners Ford Bridge is shown in Figure 241.

Montgomery County shared two Great Miami River covered bridges with neighboring Miami County: the Victory or Tadmore Station Bridge on the National Road and the Long's

Figure 241. Waggoner's Ford Bridge

Ford or Ross Road Bridge. The Victory/Tadmore Station Bridge was built in 1866 by C.C. Morrison for $18.50 per linear foot. This new bridge replaced an old timber structure built in the 1850s. R.W. Smith built the Ross Road Bridge for $15.95 per lineal foot. It too, replaced an earlier timber bridge.

In addition to the Englewood Bridge, mentioned earlier, other covered bridges spanned the Stillwater River at these crossings: Dog Leg Pike, Shoups Mill, Phillipsburg Pike and Eagle Ford. Nothing is known of the fate of the Eagle Ford or Shoup's Mill Bridge, but we know that the Phillipsburg Pike Bridge was removed circa 1917 and the Dog Leg Pike Bridge served into the late 1920s.

Many smaller wooden truss bridges crossed Big and Little Twin Creeks (two in the Germantown area), Wolf Creek and the Miami

and Erie Canal. Of course, there also were many wood truss railroad bridges in Montgomery County which was served by many major rail lines. One of these railroad bridges was a 620 foot, four-span through-Howe truss over the Great Miami river at the south edge of Dayton. It served from 1871 to 1882.

PREBLE COUNTY

Preble County lies along the western boundary of Ohio and the area is largely rural and is flat and open land. It is here that one finds Ohio's oldest and last two-lane covered bridge, the Roberts Bridge, a well-loved Preble County landmark built in 1829. (See Chapter I for details and pictures of the Roberts Bridge.)

The Roberts Bridge was just one of several two-lane covered bridges that were built to serve the early turnpikes in this western Ohio county. Among others was one at Stotler's Mill over Twin Creek near West Alexandria. This 166 foot Long truss with arches was built in 1858 for the Dayton-Western Turnpike Company to replace an earlier covered bridge that was destroyed when the nearby distillery burned in 1858. The second Stotler Mill Bridge, Figure 242, served until 1925. The Dayton-Western Pike became part of US Route 35.

On the Richmond-Hamilton Road (SR 177) over Four Mile Creek at Fairhaven there was another two-lane Burr truss structure known

Figure 242.
The crowd has gathered to see the wreckage of an interurban car that jumped the tracks beside the old Stotler Mill Bridge over Twin Creek

as the Old Red Bridge, Figure 243. The Old Red Bridge was built in 1847 by two men who immortalized themselves in the following poem which appeared over the portal of the bridge:

> The genius of man
> Is hard to discover
> This bridge was built
> by Wiley and Glover

The Old Red Bridge met its end in May of 1940 when a large truck loaded with potatoes, went out of control coming down the hill and smashed into the bridge.

Figure 243. Old Red Bridge

Still another two-lane covered bridge in Preble County was built by a turnpike company in 1848 to span Price Creek north of Lexington on what is now SR 503. When the company turned the bridge over to the county in 1892, county assessors termed the old bridge absolutely worthless. But, after $2,000. worth of repairs, it served well into the 1920s.

Many severe storms have swept over the open fields of Preble County and one such storm in May of 1886 tore a path of destruction across the county, destroying roads and bridges. Everett S. Sherman came to Preble County in the wake of this storm at the urging

of County Engineer Robert Eaton Lowery to assist in the reconstruction efforts. Sherman built 15 covered bridges in Preble County from 1886 to 1895, all on the Childs truss design. He also built a few combination truss bridges.

Seven of Sherman's Childs truss covered bridges are still standing in Preble County today: the 100 foot Geeting Bridge built in 1894 over Prices Creek; the 51 foot Warnke Bridge over Swamp Creek built in 1895; the 109 foot Harshman Bridge, Figure 244, over Four Mile Creek built in 1894; the 109 foot Christman Bridge over Seven Mile Creek built in 1895; the 88 foot open sided Brubaker Bridge built in 1887 to span Sams Run, Figure 245; and the Dixon's Branch Bridge, a 60 footer built in 1887 to span Dixons Run and moved in 1964 to Civitan Park at Lewisburg. The seventh bridge

Figure 244. Harshman Bridge

Figure 245. Brubaker Bridge

145

is the Sloane Bridge which was built in 1891 to span Bantas Fork on what is now SR 726. It now serves as a shed on a farm northwest of Eaton.

Much of the credit for the fine maintenance given to the Preble County covered bridges over the years must go to the late Seth S. Schlotterbeck of Lewisburg, deputy Preble County Engineer for many years. Seth Schlotterbeck was dean of Ohio bridgers and he knew his old bridge trusses well. Seth devised ways to make the bridge maintenance easier and looked after his covered spans with devotion. Seth was also an excellent historian who researched the history of each covered bridge in the county. Because of their fine condition, very few Preble County covered bridges have been removed in recent years.

The last covered bridge to be removed in Preble County was the Lycurgus Beam Bridge (Sherman-built), Figure 246, an 85 foot Childs truss built in 1887 to span Elkhorn Creek. For years, it bore advertising on its side for Cash and Beall of Richmond, Indiana. A fire, deliberately set in February, 1976, completely destroyed this old bridge.

Figure 246. Lycurgus Beam Bridge -- another lost to arson

At least 16 timber truss railroad bridges served the railways of Preble County. Seven of these were of the pony Howe design, while the others were deck- or through-truss structures. One of these bridges was a deck-Burr truss over Twin Creek near Winchester, a rare departure from the usual Howe truss found on the railroads of Ohio.

EXISTING BRIDGE LOCATIONS

Auglaize County:

35-06-05 Wellman Bridge, 55' timber pony truss, 1891, over Muddy Creek on the Bush Farm. 1.3 m N SR 219 just off Bay Road, NE of New Knoxville in Washington Twp. sec 16. Private

35-06-54 Memorial Bridge, 105' Howe, 1992, over St. Mary's River in Memorial Park off SR 66 in St.Mary's.

Logan County:

35-46-01 McColly Bridge, 125' Howe, 1876, over Great Miami River on CR 13, 2m SE Bloom Center off SR 235 in Bloomfield/ Washington Twps.

35-46-03 Bickham Bridge, 94' Howe, 1877, over s fk Great Miami River, on CR 38, 4m NW Huntsville in Richland Twp.

Miami County:

35-55-01 Eldean Bridge, 225' 2-span Long, 1860, over Great Miami River on bypassed section of CR 33, 1m N Troy in Concord/ Staunton Twps.

Montgomery County:

35-57-01 Germantown Bridge, 100' Suspension truss, 1865, over Little Twin Creek in Germantown in Germantown Twp.

35-57-03 Carillon Park Bridge, 42' Warren+arch, 1870, over Miami & Erie Canal in Carillon Park off Patterson Blvd in Dayton. Moved here 1948 from Greene County.

35-57-36 Jasper Road/Mud Lick Bridge, 50' Warren+arch, 1869, over Mud Lick Creek, SW of Germantown off Oxford Road in German Twp. sec 15. Moved here from Greene County 1964. Private.

Preble County:

35-68-03 Harshman Bridge, 104' Childs, 1894, over Four Mile Creek on TR 218, 4m N Fairhaven in Dixon Twp. sec 16.

Preble County (continued)

35-68-04 Dixon Branch Bridge, 50' Childs, 1887, in Civitan Park in Lewisburg. Moved here 1964.

35-68-05 Roberts Bridge, 80' 2-lane Burr, 1829, over Seven Mile Creek off S Beech St. in Eaton. Moved here 1990 and rebuilt. This is Ohio's oldest covered bridge.

35-68-06 Brubaker Bridge, 85' Childs, 1887, over Sams Run, on TR 328, 1m W Gratis in Gratis Twp. sec 4.

35-68-12 Christman Bridge, 92' Childs, 1895, over Seven Mile Creek on TR 142, 2m NW Eaton in Washington Twp. sec 28.

35-68-13 Geeting Bridge, 100' Childs, 1894, over Price Creek, on TR 436, 3m W Lewisburg in Harrison Twp. sec 25/36.

35-68-14 Warnke Bridge, 51' Childs, 1895, over Swamp Creek, on TR 403, 2m NE Lewisburg in Harrison Twp. sec 14/23.

Sloane Bridge over Bantas Fork (Page 146)

Greenville's Broadway Bridge over Greenville Creek in Darke County - removed 1881 (pg. 135)

Covington Bridge over the Stillwater River in Miami County (pg. 139)

CHAPTER X

NORTH AND EAST OUT OF THE QUEEN CITY

ADAMS, BROWN, BUTLER, CLERMONT, CLINTON, FAYETTE, GREENE, HAMILTON, HIGHLAND, and WARREN COUNTIES

Figure 247. North and East out of the Queen City

east from Cincinnati, known as the Queen City. Later, the Miami and Erie Canal flowed south through Dayton in Montgomery County and through Hamilton in Butler County to its terminus in Cincinnati.

The Cincinnati, Hamilton and Dayton area has been for many years the the location of many railway routes and these cities gave their name to one of the most prominent of these rail lines, the Cincinnati, Hamilton and Dayton Railroad, or C,H and D. This line became part of the old Baltimore and Ohio Railroad and had branches in many parts of the state. As time progressed, the counties to the northeast of Cincinnati were established (by the 1840s) and population had increased dramatically by the time of the great Civil War.

In keeping with the rapid development in this part of Ohio, transportation infrastructures, including bridges, were as advanced as in any part of the young Buckeye State. Throughout the last half of the 19th century, several notable bridge builders worked in this region. The production of covered bridges was prolific. In the early 1990s, 19 covered bridges, survivors of the earlier development, can still be found in this area.

Southwestern Ohio with its gently rolling green hills and rich farmland was one of the first areas in Ohio to be populated by the white man: first by military expeditions based along the river, and finally by settlers eager to establish new homes inland from the Ohio River. From the earliest days, the main roads in the area were Zane's Trace established through Adams and Brown County to Maysville (then Limestone), Kentucky, the Ohio River Road paralleling the river, and the military roads heading north out of Fort Washington (Cincinnati).

Populations centered around the major rivers, the Ohio, the Great Miami and the Little Miami. Roads fanned out into Ohio north and

ADAMS COUNTY

In July 1863, Confederate General John Hunt Morgan made his famous raid into Ohio, crossing the Ohio-Indiana border, heading east and keeping just north of Cincinnati. Morgan and his men stayed clear of the larger towns and cities to avoid direct confrontation with militia units. Many times, Morgan's Raiders would burn, or attempt to burn, the wooden bridges in their path to delay their pursuers. Sometimes, frightened citizens would decide to burn a bridge to prevent its use by the Raiders.

It is known that Morgan's Raiders galloped along Wheat Ridge Road, through two covered bridges and into the little community of

Harshaville. No doubt they paid a visit to the general store. This was a favorite trick of the Raiders as they liked to pillage these stores and take whatever struck their fancy at the time -- a hat, several yards of calico or a bird in a cage. They really liked to tie those bolts of calico onto their saddles and gallop away, dragging the fabric behind them![85]

The Harshaville Bridge, Figure 248, was only a few years old in 1863 and fortunate to survive the passage of the Raiders. This covered bridge is a fine, double-timber, multiple kingpost truss with sturdy laminated arches that were added as part of a 1930s renovation. Also added at that time were the concrete abutment reinforcements and the piers. The corrugated metal roof and siding were also put on at that time.

Figure 248. Harshaville Bridge over Cherry Fork in Adams County

The Raiders also left the Graces Run Bridge standing on Wheat Ridge Road, about a mile west of Harshaville. This single-span Burr truss went down under a tar truck in the 1930s, caught fire and was completely destroyed.

Adams County still has another covered bridge, the Governor Kirker Bridge, just off SR 136 over the east fork of Eagle Creek. Thomas Kirker was a pioneer settler in Liberty township, Adams County, as well as being an early legislator and interim governor of Ohio, 1807-1808. The old Kirker homestead and cemetery are a short distance south of the covered bridge on Rt.136. In 1950, the State Highway Department completely renovated this old multiple kingpost truss, heavily reinforcing it with steel. The bridge sets on steel beams and steel tension rods reinforce the old trusses. In 1974, a road relocation bypassed the Kirker Bridge and it is now locally maintained.

A strange combination of trusses was to be found in the old Fristoe Bridge, Figure 249,

(see photo next page)

which spanned Ohio Brush Creek near Jacksonville. It was basically a multiple kingpost truss bridge with arches, but the end panels had counterbraces, giving the bridge the appearance of a Long truss. The Fristoe Bridge was a single-span of 214 feet and was probably Ohio's longest single-span covered bridge. A flood in 1937 completely destroyed this old bridge.

Five miles east of West Union on SR 125, the Satterfield Bridge, a 221 foot, two-span Burr truss, Figure 250, crossed Ohio Brush Creek. This bridge had two other names: Forge Dam and Bloody. The latter name came about as the result of a fight on the bridge on its dedication day, July 4, 1876. The fight was between members of the feuding Osman and Easter families. Simon Osman was killed and his blood stained the floor of the new bridge.[86]

Figure 250. Satterfield Bridge

Figure 249. Fristoe Bridge over Ohio Brush Creek in Adams County on SR 41. Lost in the 1937 flood.

The Norfolk and Western Railroad (formerly known as the Cincinnati and Eastern) had a Warren combination truss, a deck-Howe truss and a through-Howe truss in Adams County. These timber railroad bridges were replaced by steel bridges many years ago.

Most of Adams County's covered bridges were on roads that became state routes and many stood into the 1940s and early 1950s. A court house fire in the early 1900s destroyed all county records, so we have few dates and no builders names for Adams County covered bridges.

BROWN COUNTY

More than 80 wooden truss bridges were built to serve the highways and railways of Brown County which lies along the Ohio River some 35 miles east of Cincinnati. The covered bridges of Brown county were generally very sturdy

and well maintained. Many different truss types were to be found in Brown County: the common multiple kingpost truss, the Burr, the Long, the Howe and Smith trusses. Two of the Long truss bridges had a feature found nowhere else in Ohio---double concentric arches.

The Marathon Bridge which spanned the Little Miami River on SR 286, also had these double concentric arches in conjunction with its double-timber, multiple kingpost trusses, Figure 251. The Marathon Bridge was built in 1861 for nearly $3,000. One evening in August 1949, two young men drove over it in a small truck and noticed that the old bridge was vibrating as they passed over it. They stopped at a nearby house to report this to authorities, but before help could arrive, a crash was heard as the old structure went down under a truckload of lime. Although bridge and truck dropped 20 feet, there were no injuries to the driver. The bridge, needless to say, was completely destroyed.

Figure 251. Interior of Marathon Bridge showing double concentric arches

Six covered bridges still stand in Brown County in the early 1990s. Two of these bridges span White Oak Creek near the village of New Hope. North of New Hope is the Brown Bridge, a 137 foot Smith truss built in 1878 by the Smith Bridge Company. Overloaded vehicles have caused damage to this bridge in recent years and there are plans to bypass it soon.

Just southwest of New Hope is the Bethel-New Hope Road Bridge, Figure 40, a 177 foot Howe truss with 11 ply laminated arches. This bridge was built in 1878 to replace an earlier covered structure. Cost of this second bridge was $13.95 per linear foot. The arches were added in 1902. Major renovation was again done on this bridge in 1932 by Louis S. Bower, Sr., of Flemingsburg, Kentucky (see Chapter II). In 1977, Louis S. "Stock" Bower, Jr. supervised another major renovation of this historic structure. A few years later, it was bypassed. At 170 foot clear span, the Bethel-New Hope Bridge is Ohio's longest single span covered bridge.

Over the west fork of Eagle Creek on SR 763, is another long, single-span, covered bridge, the 164 foot Bowman or Eagle Creek Bridge, Figure 252. This is the last covered bridge on a state route in Ohio and it is due to be bypassed soon. The Eagle Creek Bridge is an 1875 product of the Smith Bridge Company. The twin of the Eagle Creek Bridge can be found on North Pole Road over Eagle Creek. This is another Smith truss built in 1875 by the Smith Bridge Company.

John Griffith built the George Miller Road Bridge in 1879 to span the west fork of Eagle Creek near Russellville. This 154 foot Smith truss is still in daily service.

Just off US 50 in northern Brown County, the McCafferty Road Bridge, Figure 253, stretches its 165 foot Howe trusses across the Little Miami River southwest of Fayetteville. This handsome structure was erected in 1877 by the Smith Bridge Company.

Today's SR 32 was the route taken by part of Morgan's Raiders in their mad dash across Ohio in 1863. They burned two covered bridges over branches of White Oak Creek on this road

Figure 252. Eagle Creek Bridge in Brown County is the last on a state route in Ohio

Figure 253. McCafferty Road Bridge

Upstream, less than one quarter mile, the second covered bridge still stands today, the fine old Stonelick or Perintown Bridge, Figure 254. This bridge is a 140 foot Howe truss that has had its tangles with overloaded vehicles. It seems that every time Route 50 is closed, Williams Corner Road is used as a detour route by heavy trucks whose drivers should know better. Twice in recent years, it has been damaged so badly that it had to be closed for repairs. Traffic is normally heavy on Williams Corner Road and one can only wonder how long the covered bridge will last.

in Brown County, one just east of White Oak and the other a mile west of Sardinia. Both of these structures were replaced in 1864 by Burr truss bridges built by B.J. Wheeler and Sons of Clermont County. The bridge closest to Sardinia was replaced in 1944 and the other SR 32 covered bridge was removed ten years earlier.

The old Cincinnati and Eastern Railroad (Norfolk and Western) had through-Howe truss bridges over the east fork and north fork of White Oak Creek near SR 32 that were built in 1877. They also had a through-Howe truss bridge over Sterling Run near Mt. Orab. Removal dates for these railroad bridges are unknown.

Brown County has much to offer the tourist in addition to its well kept covered bridges. The fossiliferous limestone outcroppings of White Oak and Eagle Creeks are noted for their trilobite content and are a magnet for fossil hunters. The town of Ripley on the Ohio River is an important tobacco center.

CLERMONT COUNTY

In 1878, Clermont County officials decided to build two covered bridges to span Stonelick Creek north of US 50 on Williams Corner Road. The first crossing was at St. Philomena's Church, a double-timber Burr truss built by McChesney and Rich. The St.Philomena's Church Bridge was replaced in 1950 by an old steel Pratt truss moved here from another location.

Figure 254. Stonelick Bridge

Down on Route 50, another covered bridge carried the traffic of this important pike over Stonelick Creek. We do not know the building date, but it was probably built in the early 1800s by a turnpike company. The bridge burned in 1888.

Over the east fork of the Little Miami River on Jackson Pike, there was a covered bridge north of Williamsburg. B.F. Bower built this 170 foot Smith truss, Figure 255, in 1876. This was probably Benjamin Bower, member of the famed Bower bridge building family of nearby Brown County. In its later years, this old covered bridge became weak and signs were erected to warn travelers of an unsafe bridge with restricted load limits. Efforts were made to

Figure 255. Jackson Pike Bridge

have the bridge moved, but before anything could be done, the contractor in charge of building the new bridge demolished the old structure and burned it.

Several other Clermont County covered bridges were removed in the 1940s and 1950s, including the Red or Back Run Bridge on SR 222 over the east fork of the Little Miami River, the O'Banion Bridge over O'Bannion Creek near Goshen, and the Cedron Bridge near Utopia over Bullskin Creek.

Morgan's Raiders burned the covered bridge over the east fork of the Little Miami at Williamsburg, the county seat, in July, 1863. This was the second covered bridge on the site and it was immediately replaced by another roofed timber truss in 1863/64. The third Williamsburg Bridge, Figure 256, stood until 1935. According to ODOT records, it was a 164 foot Long truss with arches.

The Little Miami River is the boundary line between Clermont and Hamilton Counties and these two counties shared covered bridges at Loveland, Miamiville and Milford, as well as a large railroad bridge at Miamiville. There were many wooden Howe trusses of all types on the Norfolk and Western and the Baltimore and Ohio Railroads in Clermont County. These railroad timber truss bridges were all replaced many years ago. The same holds true for the covered bridges spanning the Little Miami River on the county line.

HAMILTON COUNTY

Hamilton County was once home to many large covered bridges over both the Great and Little Miami Rivers. Much of what we know about the early wooden bridges of Hamilton County has come from research in the records of the Board of Public Works and the early Acts of the Legislature. These records reveal that these early structures were built by private interests or by turnpike companies as a general rule.

In 1837, James Given, Engineer for the Cincinnati and Harrison Turnpike Company, wrote to the Board of Public Works on behalf of the President and Board of Directors of the

*Figure 256.
Williamsburg Bridge. Third
covered bridge to span the
Little Miami River on this
site, 1863-1935*

Figure 257. Daguerreotype view of the old Miamitown covered bridge in Hamilton County -- built by a turnpike company in the early 1800's

turnpike company, proposing that they be allowed to buy the Great Miami River bridge at Miamitown, Figure 257, from the Whitewater Bridge Company for $11,050. Mr. Given also asked the Board's permission to build a 120 foot Burr truss bridge over Dry Fork at $30 per linear foot --- a very hefty price for any bridge in that era. Mr. Given specified that the Dry Fork Bridge was to be built like the Schukyll River Bridge at Philadelphia.[87] These two important bridges were on what is now US 52 northwest of Cincinnati. They served the area well for many years.

Another major covered bridge spanned the Great Miami on the Colerain-Venice Pike just south of the Butler County line. The first covered bridge here was built in 1830 by the Colerain-Venice Tollbridge Company. In 1863, this bridge was burned by Morgan's Raiders and replaced in 1865/66 with a new covered

structure. This second Colerain-Venice Bridge served into the 1890s.

At Elizabethtown, a three-span covered bridge crossed the Great Miami River. It was built in 1867 and destroyed in a spectacular fire in 1903. We have always heard it referred to as the Lost Bridge but why it had this name is unknown. There was also a large covered bridge over the Great Miami at New Baltimore whose history is not known.

The Little Miami was spanned by covered bridges at Milford, Armstrong's Mill (Plainville), Loveland and Symmestown that served the public well for many years.

There were many bridges over Mill Creek and its branches in Hamilton County including covered bridges at Cumminsville on the Harrison Pike near Cincinnati, on Spring Grove Avenue in Cincinnati, Figure 258, and at McHenry's Ford on the Carthage, Springfield

Figure 258. Spring Grove Avenue Bridge over Mill Creek in Cincinnati -- one of many such bridges over Mill Creek in Hamilton County

and Hamilton Pike (now SR 4). The McHenry's Ford Bridge, built in 1823, was also an expensive structure at $3,600. All of these bridges were replaced by the early 1900s.

More than two dozen timber truss railroad bridges served nine rail lines in Cincinnati and Hamilton County. Most were through- or pony-Howe trusses. Probably the largest of these bridges was the 508 foot combination truss built in 1878 by the short-lived Cincinnati, Portsmouth and Georgetown Railroad to span the Little Miami River east of Cincinnati. This bridge had 2,000 feet of approach spans. It served only four years and the railroad itself never got further than Russellville in Brown County.

The lone survivor of all these covered bridges is the little Jediah Hill Bridge, Figure 259, over Mill Creek near Mt. Healthy, a suburb just north of Cincinnati. This is a 54 foot queenpost truss built in 1850 by Jediah Hill. Extensive repairs were made in the 1950s, but by the early 1980s, controversy arose over this bridge because it served as the only access to a small community on a dead end street. The old bridge could no longer carry emergency vehicles and this had the residents worried. Different plans were offered to preserve this bridge which included moving it a short distance downstream to preserve its historic integrity. Preservationists preferred this plan to the one which was finally adopted: a completely new steel and concrete substructure with the old wooden

Figure 259. Jediah Hill Bridge

bridge, widened and heightened, set on top of it.

BUTLER COUNTY

As in other Ohio counties that are bisected by major rivers, tollbridge companies authorized by Acts of the Legislature built massive timber truss bridges over the Great Miami River in the early days of Butler County. These companies built bridges at Poasttown (Manchester Bridge Company), at Middletown (Middletown Bridge Company), at Woodsdale (Miami Central Bridge Company), at Rossville (Miami Bridge Company), at the south edge of Hamilton (Columbia Free Bridge Company), and the Venice Bridge (Colerain-Venice Tollbridge Company --see Hamilton County).

The county's first tollbridge was the Rossville Bridge, built in 1819 to serve High Street in the town of Hamilton, Figure 260. The Rossville

Figure 260. The Rossville Bridge -- an early Ohio toll bridge

Bridge washed out in 1866 and was replaced by the county with a steel suspension truss structure.

The county found itself buying most of these private tollbridges (or their successors) in the 1860s. Most of the bridges either had to have major repairs or be completely replaced. Several of these bridges washed out in the 1913 flood.

It cost Butler County $7,000 to buy the Middletown Bridge in 1867. In addition to this expense, they had to build another bridge about 1,000 feet west of the old covered bridge to span the flood channel of the Great Miami. This new structure was a 150 foot, two-span covered bridge.

One Great Miami River covered bridge that was not built by a private bridge company was the Ball's Ferry Bridge at Trenton, built by the firm of Banden, Butin and Bowman for Butler County in 1866. The Ball's Ferry Bridge was destroyed in the 1913 flood.

This same bridge building firm was hired by the Butler County Commissioners in 1868 to build a one-span, 200 foot covered bridge over Four Mile Creek north of Oxford on what is now SR 732. The price was a whopping $30.25 per linear foot based on the lower chord measure. This covered bridge, known to us today as the Black or Pugh's Mill Bridge, Figure 261, is one of two covered bridges still standing in Butler County.

In June, 1869, the county commissioners hired Banden, Butin and Bowman to build a pier under the middle of this new bridge. Then, in November, 1869, the commissioners again contracted with this firm to "remodel" the Oxford Bridge (as they called it then) by putting in new braces so that the bridge had a proper bearing on the newly-built pier. When you examine the massive trusses of the Black Bridge, Figures 262 a and b, you see immediately that it appears to be a combination of both the Childs and Long trusses. This obviously, is

(see photos next page)

the result of the remodeling work done in late 1869 at a cost of $600.

When SR 732 was relocated in the early 1950s, the old Black Bridge was bypassed and is now maintained by the Oxford Museum Association.

Banden, Butin and Bowman built several other covered bridges for Butler County and Indiana builder, A.M. Kennedy, built a covered

Figure 261. Black Bridge near Oxford -- a winter scene in 1894

Figure 262 a. Childs truss, (left); b. Long truss, (right)

bridge for Butler County in 1871. Kennedy built the Taylor School Bridge to span Seven Mile Creek. Its removal date is unknown.

The second covered bridge still standing in Butler County is the Fairfield Pike/Bebb Park Bridge, a 120 foot Wernwag truss built to span Indian Creek west of Oxford close to the Indiana state line. Old county records failed to mention construction of this bridge, but we believe it was built prior to 1873. By the mid 1870s, steel truss bridges were becoming popular in Butler County and timber truss bridges were no longer being built. (Although old Butler County records do mention Wernwag truss bridges, it was not in relation to the Bebb Park Bridge). In 1966, it was dismantled and moved to Governor Bebb Park off SR 126 near Okeana. There it was rebuilt over a ravine in 1970. This is an excellent example of covered bridge preservation, Figure 263.

Butler County had other covered bridges over Indian Creek at Millville, at Reily (2 different locations there) and the Hogan's Bridge near Millville. Over Seven Mile Creek there were covered bridges near Collinsville and near Seven Mile. Floods took both of the Reily bridges, one in the 1890s and the other in

1917. The Collinsville Bridge was replaced in the 1930s and the fate of the bridge near Seven Mile is unknown.

Over a dozen wooden Howe truss railroad bridges were built in the 1870s to serve the many rail lines in Butler County. Most, if not all of these timber railroad bridges were gone before 1900.

Figure 263. Bebb Park Bridge in Butler County is Ohio's last Wernwag truss

Warren County

It has been many years since the last timber truss bridge disappeared from the Warren County scene. Although it is not certain, we believe that the last covered bridge in Warren County was the Springboro Bridge over Clear Creek. This oldtimer collapsed sometime in the 1930s.

Most of the major covered bridges in Warren County spanned the Little Miami River, but there was also a large, two-lane Town truss at Franklin over the Great Miami which flows through the extreme northwest corner of the county. The Town truss was built about 1845 to replace an old uncovered timber bridge. The covered bridge served until 1873 when it was replaced by a steel suspension-truss bridge. This was the only known covered bridge to span the Great Miami in Warren County.

Five wooden bridges were built to span the Little Miami River between Waynesville and Corwin, beginning in 1817 with an uncovered wood truss that stood for only a few years. About 1827, a fully-covered wooden bridge was built to replace the first Waynesville Bridge. This covered bridge was replaced in 1836 by an uncovered wood truss that served only six years. The bridge built here in 1842 was not described in the old County Journals, but was undoubtedly a wood structure. In 1861/62,

Henry E. Hebble built the fine Waynesville/Corwin Bridge that served these two towns until 1927. It was a Warren truss with arches, Figure 264.

There was a fine covered bridge at Foster's Crossing of the Little Miami that was lost in the great 1913 flood. It was the second covered bridge on this site. There also were early covered bridges over the Little Miami River at Kings Mills, Stubb's Mills, Fort Ancient and Oregonia (Freeport), Figure 265. All of these bridges were replaced by steel truss structures many years ago. The Oregonia Bridge was replaced in 1883 by a fine lenticular steel truss bridge which is still in use today.

Figure 265. Oregonia Bridge

Figure 264. Waynesville or Corwin Bridge over Little Miami River built 1861/62 by Hebble

Caesars Creek, which flows through the northeast section of Warren County to join the Little Miami below Waynesville, was spanned by covered bridges at Corwin Road and at Harveysburg. While the fate of the Corwin Road Bridge is unknown, we know that arsonists burned the Harveysburg Bridge in 1876.

Clear Creek, Muddy Creek, First Creek and Todds Fork all were crossed by significant timber truss highway bridges. All of these bridges have been gone for many years. The Cincinnati and Muskingum Valley Railroad had at least seven wooden Howe truss bridges in Warren County, all spanning Todds Fork. Most of these bridges were of the deck-Howe design. They were replaced by steel bridges years ago.

GREENE COUNTY

Greene County suggests lush and verdant fields and while indeed, this county is lovely, its name comes from Nathaniel Greene, Revolutionary War General. The county is drained by the waters of the Little Miami River, Caesars Creek and Massies Creek and their tributaries. Massies Creek was named for Nathaniel Massie, prominent early Ohio settler and surveyor who came here from Virginia in the 1790s to survey lands within the Virginia Military District.

Greene County had a great diversity of truss designs in its timber truss bridges: multiple kingpost, Burr, Wernwag, Long, Howe, Smith and Warren. Joseph J.Daniels (see Chapter II) built several Long truss bridges in this area before moving on to Indiana. None of Daniels bridges are standing today.

The Warren truss was the truss style most often built in Greene County, obviously favored by county officials. Two contractors were mainly responsible for the Warren truss bridges built in Greene County: Henry E. Hebble of Fairfield and The Smith Bridge Company of Toledo. Two of Greene County's Warren trusses are still in existence, but both have been moved to nearby Montgomery County. Greene County had Warren truss covered bridges on Waynesville Road, Dayton Road, and Feedwire Road over Sugar Creek and on Eleazor Road and New Hope Road over Painters Run. There were also Warren truss covered bridges over Caesars Creek on Jamestown Road, Paintersville Road, and two on Hoop Road.

Henry E.Hebble also built both the sturdy Howe and Wernwag trusses and two of his Howe truss structures are still standing today in Greene County: the Charlton Mill Road Bridge and the Cemetery/Glen Helen Bridge. The Charlton Mill Bridge, was built in 1882 to span Massies Creek and the Cemetery Road Bridge was built in 1886 to span Andersons Fork, a tributary of Caesars Creek.

The formation of the Caesars Creek Reservoir in the 1970s was going to cause the elimination of the Cemetery Road Bridge because the reservoir could back up that far in times of high water. The nearby village of New Burlington was engineered out of existance because of this possibility. Fortunately for the old covered bridge, a new site was found for it at Glen Helen, the nature preserve at Antioch College at Yellow Springs. In 1975, the 60 foot center section of the bridge was moved up to .Glen Helen where it now spans Yellow Springs Creek, Figure 266.

Figure 266. Cemetery Road Bridge

Greene County had two Wernwag truss covered bridges, both built by Hebble. The 137 foot Jacoby Road Bridge was built to span the Little Miami River in 1869 for $15.55 per linear foot. Arsonists destroyed this old landmark in 1970. In 1872, Hebble built the Henville Road Bridge,

Figure 267, to span Caesars Creek. The price for this Wernwag was only $12.50 per linear foot. Arsonists tried to destroy this bridge, too, but nearby residents were able to call for help in time. The county finally removed the bridge in 1965.

Figure 267. Henville Road Bridge over Caesars Creek, 1872-1965

Besides the Charlton Mill Road and Cemetery/Glen Helen Bridges, Greene County has three other covered bridges still standing in the early 1990s: the lovely old Ballard Road Bridge, Figure 268, over the north branch of Caesars Creek, an 80 foot Howe truss built in 1883 by J.C. Brown (Hebble was the mason on

Figure 268. Ballard Road Bridge

this contract); the Stevenson Road Bridge, a 95 foot Smith truss built in 1877 by the Smith Bridge Company to span Massies Creek; and the West Engle Mill Road Bridge, a 136 foot Smith truss moved to this site over Andersons Fork in the 1880s from Spring Valley. These bridges are "must see" features of historic bridge tours of this area.

Around the corner from the West Engle Mill Bridge on East Engle Mill Road was a 145 foot double-timber, multiple kingpost truss built in 1877 to span Andersons Fork. This old bridge developed a pronounced lean in its later years and finally collapsed under heavy snows about 1978.

There were at one time several grist mills and covered bridges on the Mad River in the northwest corner of Greene County, and one of them, the Harshman Mill Bridge, stood into the 1940s. Due to the construction of Wright-Patterson Air Force Base years ago, this entire area has been changed, including the course of the Mad River. It would be extremely difficult, if not impossible, to find the sites of those old mills and covered bridges today. Figure 269 is a view of one of the Mad River covered bridges in the Osborn area. While no one is quite certain, we believe it was the

(see photo next page)

Harshman Mill Bridge to the northwest of Osborn which stood until circa 1945.

Near the village of Bellbrook were three large covered bridges over the Little Miami River: the Bellbrook or Ducks Ford Bridge on SR 725, a 148 foot Howe truss built in 1880 to replace an earlier covered bridge; the Washington Mill Road Bridge, a 180 foot double Smith truss built in 1875 by the Smith Bridge Company; and the Lower Bellbrook Bridge, a 169 foot Long truss with arches built in 1855. Both the Bellbrook and Lower Bellbrook Bridges were torn down in the 1950s while the Washington Mill Bridge was destroyed by arson in 1968.

In the 1840s, the Greene County Commissioners ordered a covered Burr truss bridge to be built to span the Little Miami south of Alpha. When completed, they declared it to be

Figure 269.
Mad River Bridge near
Osborne in Greene
County -- possibly the
Harshman Mill Bridge

the finest bridge in the county. In 1877, they had it replaced by a Howe truss built by J.C.Brown. This was known as the Indian Ripple Road Bridge. Increasingly heavy traffic forced the removal of this bridge in 1957.

Greene County had its share of Howe truss railroad bridges including two over the Little Miami River just west of Trebeins, near the old highway covered bridge at Trebeins Mill on the Dayton-Xenia Pike (now US 35). Modernization of the rail lines saw the replacement of these bridges many years ago.

FAYETTE COUNTY

Fayette County is a largely rural area with rich, rolling farmland drained by Paint Creek and its tributaries. Very few of the 60 or more covered bridges of Fayette County stood into the 1900s and several of those that did were replaced in 1911. The last covered bridge in the county was the two-span Yankeetown Road Bridge over Deer Creek, a 246 foot Howe truss. For many years, the Yankeetown Road Bridge, Figure 270, was Ohio's longest timber truss bridge. It was destroyed in late October, 1965 by arsonists, perhaps as a Halloween "prank".

Figure 270
Yankeetown Road
Bridge over Deer Creek
was the last covered
bridge in Fayette County
burned as a Halloween
prank in 1965

*Figure 271.
New Holland Bridge was
built c 1840 by a turnpike
company - served for over
100 years*

One of the county's earliest and certainly the best known covered bridge, called the New Holland Bridge, was the 98 foot, two-lane Town truss, Figure 271, over the north fork of Paint Creek at New Holland. This bridge was built in 1840 for the Circleville-Washington Pike, which is now US 22. Towards the end of its long years of service, the New Holland Bridge was one of the covered bridges considered for moving to Henry Ford's Greenfield Village at Dearborn, Michigan. Village officials finally rejected the New Holland Bridge and it was torn down after serving for over a century.

One other Fayette County covered bridge was still standing in the 1940s; the Eber Bridge over Paint Creek, a 118 foot Howe truss built in 1874. It was torn down in 1948. Another of the very few Fayette County covered bridges that survived into the 1900s was the Grove Davis Bridge over Paint Creek on what is now US 35. It was removed in the late 1920s. Other Paint Creek covered bridges in Fayette County were: the Hidy Cemetery Bridge, the Lost Bridge in Washington C.H., the Wendall Ford, Ghormley Road and Carr's Mills Bridges to name a few.

Fayette County at one time had at least 66 wooden truss bridges spanning its streams: Paint Creek and its tributaries, as well as Deer, Sugar and Rattlesnake Creeks.

There was a number of wooden Howe truss bridges on the railways of Fayette County most of which were of the through -truss design. Like the other timber truss railroad bridges that once served Ohio's railroads, these Fayette County bridges have been gone for many years.

CLINTON COUNTY

The Long truss was one of the bridge designs favored by Clinton County officials and of the 21 known highway covered bridges in this area, at least seven were of this truss patent design. In addition to timber truss highway bridges, there were 19 wooden railroad bridges in Clinton County, the majority of which were of the pony Howe truss variety.

Clinton, Greene and Warren County officials got together in 1867 to decide on the site for a bridge over Caesars Creek in the extreme northwest section of Clinton County near the Warren and Greene County lines. The site chosen was just west of New Burlington, a small community on the Clinton-Greene County line (see Greene County section). The New Burlington Bridge, Figure 272, was a 167 foot Long truss with arches that served this area until 1957. Unfortunately for the researcher, nothing was recorded in any of the three county commissioners journals involved here about the builder or the price of this important structure.

Todds Fork is a major stream in Clinton County and many covered bridges were built to

Figure 272. New Burlington Bridge

span it including the large Clarksville Bridge, Figure 273. The Clarksville Bridge was a 165 foot Long truss with arches built circa 1870 and torn down in 1962. There were also covered bridges over Todds Fork and its tributaries on the old Bullskin Trail (SR 380) known as the Beech Grove Bridge; on the Xenia Pike (US 68) north of Wilmington; on Center Road; on SR 73; and on SR 730 at Pansy. Not far from Sligo was a covered bridge over Dutch Fork of Todds Fork that was the only Warren truss that we know of in Clinton County. None of these oldtimers survive today.

Figure 273. Clarksville Bridge

Clinton County's last covered bridge (not counting the Lynchburg Bridge on the Highland County line) is the 80 foot Martinsville Road Bridge, Figure 274, over Todds Fork west of Martinsville. This multiple kingpost truss was built in 1871 by Zimri Wall who founded the Champion Bridge Company the following year. This company considers the Martinsville Road Bridge to be their oldest existing bridge. Major repairs were made here in the 1970s which included the installation of steel I-beams, channels, gussets and new concrete abutments. Should anything happen to the old wooden superstructure, the concrete and steel substructure will serve as the base for a new bridge.

As mentioned earlier in this section, Clinton County had at least 19 wooden truss railroad bridges on the old Cincinnati and Muskingum Valley Railroad. Most of these were pony-Howe trusses, but four were of the through-Howe design. The old Railroad Reports made no mention of roof or siding on any of these bridges, but some of them may have been covered as the Cincinnati and Muskingum Valley did cover many of their Howe truss bridges. These timber railroad bridges were replaced by steel bridges at an early date.

Figure 274. Martinsville Road Bridge

HIGHLAND COUNTY

Scenic Paint Creek forms the northeastern boundary of Highland County and its tributaries, Rattlesnake and Rocky Fork Creeks, drain much of the county.

The best known of the Rocky Fork bridges was the Barrett Mill Bridge, Figure 275, southeast of Rainsboro and US 50. The bridge, a 156 foot Long truss, was built circa 1870 and most

likely by John C. Gregg. Historic Barrett Mill and the old Barrett home were nearby. All were destroyed by arson in the fall of 1980, a tragic loss of an important part of the history of Highland County.

Nearly a dozen covered bridges spanned Rocky Fork Creek in Highland County. Near Carmel, the Beaver Mill Bridge, a 122 foot Long truss, crossed Rocky Fork from 1872 to 1955 when both the mill and the covered bridge were demolished to make way for a road relocation project. Three major roads heading south out of Hillsboro all crossed Rocky Fork on covered bridges. These bridges, on Routes 73, 138 and 247, all stood until the 1950s.

Highland County also had multiple kingpost truss bridges as well as Howe truss railroad bridges. Large highway and railroad bridges spanned Paint Creek on the Highland/Ross County line. A sampling of the other Highland County covered bridges include the Belfast Bridge, Figure 276, which spanned Ohio Brush Creek near Belfast; and the Buford, Pricetown and Pulse Bridges over Whiteoak Creek. All but the Buford Bridge were on state routes and all were removed in the 1950s.

The county's last covered bridge spans the east fork of the Little Miami River at Lynchburg on the Clinton County line. John C. Gregg built the Lynchburg Bridge, Figure 277, in 1870 for $3,138. It is a 120 foot Long truss. In 1969, the old bridge was bypassed and Clinton County withdrew all interest in it. It is now maintained privately by a local group with no county assistance.

Figure 276. Belfast Bridge

Figure 277. Lynchburg Bridge

John C. Gregg (see Chapter II) was one of this area's most outstanding bridge builders in the 1860s and 1870s. He specialized in building the Long truss and he built at least eight Long trusses in Highland County. A study of the old Highland County records shows that the county commissioners specified Long's Improved Patent Truss in most of their bridge contracts from this era.

Highland County had just a few railroad Howe truss bridges, including an 800 foot deck-Howe truss over Paint Creek on the Highland/Ross County line at Greenfield. The Marietta and Cincinnati Railroad had a two-span, deck-Howe truss bridge over the falls of Rattlesnake Creek at East Monroe Falls. Both of these important railroad bridges were removed many years ago, probably before the turn of the century.

EXISTING BRIDGE LOCATIONS

Adams County:
35-01-02 Harshaville Bridge, 110' MKP+arch, 1855, over Cherry Fork on CR 1 at Harshaville in Oliver Twp.

35-01-10 Governor Kirker Bridge, 63' MKP, over E Fork of Eagle Creek just off SR 136, 5m SW West Union in Liberty Twp.

Brown County:
35-08-04, Brown Bridge, 129' Smith, 1878, over White Oak Creek on CR 5, 2m N New Hope in Scott Twp.

35-08-05 New Hope Bridge, 170' Howe+arch, 1878, over White Oak Creek just off CR 5, 1m SW New Hope in Scott Twp. Bypassed.

35-08-08 McCafferty Road Bridge, 157' Howe, 1877, over E Fork Little Miami River on CR 105, 2m SW Vera Cruz in Perry Twp.

35-08-18 Bowman/Eagle Creek Bridge, 172' Smith, 1875, over Eagle Creek on SR 763, 3m S Decatur.

35-08-23 North Pole Road Bridge, 157' Smith, 1875, over Eagle Creek on CR 13, 3.5m NE Ripley in Union Twp.

35-08-34 George Miller Road Bridge, 154' Smith, 1878, over W Fork Eagle Creek on CR 15, 3m SE Russellville in Byrd Twp.

Butler County:
35-09-02 Fairfield Pike/Bebb Park Bridge, 120' Burr, over ravine in Bebb Park off SR 126, 3.5m NW Okeana in Morgan Twp. Moved here in 1966.

35-09-03 Black/Pugh's Mill Bridge, 209' 2-span Long, 1868, over Four Mile Creek off SR 732, 1m N Oxford in Oxford Twp. sec 14. Bypassed.

Clermont County:
35-13-02 Stonelick Bridge, 140' Howe, 1878, over Stonelick Creek on CR 116, 3m E Perintown, 1.25m N US 50 in Stonelick Twp.

Clinton County:
35-14-09 Martinsville Bridge, 72' MKP, 1871, over Todd's Fork on CR 14, 1m W Martinsville in Clark Twp.

Greene County:
35-29-01 Cemetery Road/Glen Helen Bridge, 60' Howe, 1886, over Yellow Springs Creek off CR 27, 1m S Yellow Springs in Miami Twp. Moved here in 1975.

35-29-03 West Engle Mill Road Bridge, 136' Smith, rebuilt here c.1887, over Andersons Fork off TR 46, 5m ESE Spring Valley in Caesar Creek Twp.

35-29-15 Stevenson Road Bridge, 95' Smith, 1877, over Massies Creek on CR 76, 6m N Xenia in Xenia Twp.

35-29-16 Charlton Mill Bridge, 119' Howe, 1883, over Massies Creek on TR 29, 1.5m N Wilberforce in Xenia Twp.

35-29-18 Ballard Road Bridge, 80' Howe, 1883, over N Branch Caesar Creek on TR 6, 5m E Xenia, .5m S US 35, in Jasper Twp.

Hamilton County
35-31-01 Jediah Hill Bridge, 44' QP, 1850, over Mill Creek on Covered Bridge Road off US 127, N of Mt. Healthy in Springfield Twp. sec.28

Highland County
35-36-06 Lynchburg Bridge, 120' Long, 1870, over E Fork of Little Miami River on Covered Bridge Lane E of SR 134 on W edge Lynchburg in Clark Twp. Bypassed.

THE END OF AN ERA—A NEW BEGINNING

The covered bridge was the sturdy, reliable, often shabby workhorse of the Ohio transportation system for many years. In the heyday of the covered bridge in Ohio (and here we count ALL wooden truss and combination wood and metal truss bridges under the heading of covered bridges), there were well over 3,700 of these sturdy structures in service on the highways, canals and railroads in Ohio. These wooden bridges were taken for granted by the people who used them everyday, just as people today take little notice of modern highway bridges. Relatively few pictures were taken of the covered bridges unless they were on a major, well-traveled route. Many of the bridges on back roads were never photographed. Pictorial records are scanty on Ohio's railroad and canal bridges, too. We must make our mental pictures using what we know of their truss types, builders and the surviving wooden bridges. Less than 140 wooden truss bridges still stand in Ohio and only 61 carry traffic. When did it all begin to end? How and why?

Covered bridges were built routinely in Ohio for nearly 80 years, and then rebuilt and rebuilt again. It is not uncommon to find that more than one covered bridge had been built on the same site, in some cases, three or four times. The early covered bridges in Ohio were built on the multiple kingpost, Burr and Town truss designs and as these bridges were destroyed by flood or fire, or simply became out-of-date, they were replaced by more "modern" wood truss designs such as the Howe and Smith trusses.

But nothing remains static forever and the winds of change began to blow through the bridge building industry during the second half of the 19th century. There was a rise in the technology of the iron and steel industry which had a great influence on bridge design. Engineers and county officials opted to replace aging wooden truss bridges with the modern metal truss structures. Some counties, such as Fairfield and Washington, remained loyal to

the wood truss bridge until 1900 and beyond, but many counties started building the iron truss bridges as early as the 1860s. The decision on bridge type was up to the county officials and these men were being bombarded constantly with literature from the various bridge building companies extolling the virtues of their metal truss bridges. In those days, metal truss bridges were almost always referred to as iron bridges.

Several great floods in the late 1800s and early 1900s washed out many covered bridges and for the most part, after 1884, those bridges were replaced by metal truss designs. As was discussed in Chapter II, the failure of Ohio's canal system was responsible for the disappearance of many of the old wooden truss bridges. Some of these bridges were sold at auction--the price was usually quite low, but often the buyer had to agree not only to remove the old bridge, but to fill in the canal where the bridge had stood. Two of Fairfield County's covered canal bridges were moved to farms in 1912 and one of them, the Jackson/Ety Bridge, Figure 278, served a private farm road in Liberty Township until its collapse in April, 1993.

Figure 278. Jackson/Ety Bridge - 1874-1993

The story of Fairfield County's old Basil Canal Bridge is told in Chapter I and Figure 12 shows the little bridge as it looked while spanning the canal about 1900. Many of Ohio's canal bridges, like that on the Barger Farm in Pike County, Figure 11, were privately-owned and the fate of the majority of them is unknown. However, we do know the fate of the Circleville aquaduct covered bridge over the Scioto River. It was abandoned in 1911 and became a dance hall. In 1915 it was destroyed by fire, a fate it had narrowly missed on two other occasions.[88]

Constant updating of railroad equipment with heavier and heavier rolling stock caused replacement of the earlier wooden truss railroad bridges with newer and stronger Howe trusses. Arches were added to some of these bridges to further strengthen them. The railroads continued to build Howe trusses into the 1880s, but most of them had been replaced by steel bridges by the turn of the century. The interurban lines, which enjoyed a brief popularity in Ohio, also built a few Howe trusses, but the majority of their bridges were steel or concrete. Few wooden truss railroad bridges were still standing at the time of the great 1913 flood.

The flood that devastated the Midwest in March 1913 began over California on March 20th and gathered in intensity as it swept eastward over the Rockies. It spawned a tornado in Oklahoma that killed 94 persons. On March 23rd, it was stormy from the Rockies to the Atlantic coast. A steady rain fell over Ohio on Easter Sunday March 23, 1913. The rain continued on the 24th and 25th. The greatest flood in Ohio history was in the making.[89]

Most signs pointed to a spring flood along the river valleys of Ohio that year, but few people were prepared for the enormity of the waters and the swiftness with which they rose and tore through towns and farmland. The velocity of the water was so great in some areas that it literally peeled the asphalt off the streets and left great trenches. Houses, barns and bridges were tossed about like balsawood.[90] Human suffering was great and many people disappeared, never to be seen again. Figure 279 shows the Maple Street Bridge at Marysville in Union County, at the height of the floodwaters. Needless to say, this bridge was completely destroyed.

Figure 279. Maple Street Bridge at Marysville at height of 1913 flood

There was great devastation all along the valley of the Great Miami River from Piqua south to Cincinnati. Miami County lost many bridges, at least seven of which were covered wooden trusses. Perhaps the worst damages were inflicted on the City of Dayton where the Stillwater and Mad Rivers flow into the Great Miami River. Some historians believe that at least two covered bridges were still in existance in the city in 1913 and both were lost in the flood along with most of Dayton's steel and concrete bridges. Butler County lost covered bridges over the Great Miami at Poasttown, Trenton and Deardorff's Mill. Hamilton County suffered great damage as the flooded Great Miami River roared south from Butler County bearing a huge load of debris from upstream.

Another area hard-hit by the great flood was Delaware County in central Ohio. This county is drained by the Scioto and Olentangy River and Alum and Walnut Creeks. Delaware County lost 41 highway bridges with many more badly damaged. Eight Scioto River covered bridges plus at least 10 others in the county were lost. Included among those covered bridges that washed out were: the Shiveley Bridge, the Marysville Pike Bridge, Figure 280, the White Sulphur Springs Bridge and the Bellepoint Bridge, Figure 66, all over the Scioto River. Only the Lavender Bridge, Figure 107, was left standing. Low lying pasture land

Figure 280. Marysville Pike Bridge

Figure 281. Casparis Quarry Bridge

around this bridge allowed the floodwaters to spread out and spare the old structure. Five Olentangy River covered bridges were destroyed as well as several more on the smaller streams.

Flood losses were also high in Franklin County as the Delaware County floodwaters surged southward and gathered volume. Two large Scioto River covered bridges were lost, one at Casparis Quarry, Figure 281, on Trabue Road and the other at Shadeville. Both of the covered bridges at Georgesville, one over Big Darby Creek and the other over Little Darby Creek, washed out. Figure 282 shows the extent of the flooding at the confluence of the Big

Darby (right) and the Little Darby (left). Farther south on the Scioto River covered bridges were destroyed in Pickaway County at South Bloomfield and Lindsey's Ford. The only remnants left of the Lindsey Ford Bridge were the cut-stone piers and abutments, Figure 283. Pike County lost the large Jasper Bridge, Figure 120, to the floodwaters.

The Muskingum and Licking River valleys were hard-hit in 1913, too. On the Muskingum River in Coshocton County, both the Randles Bridge over the river and the Randles Canal Bridge were lost. Figure 179 in Chapter VI shows these bridges. Below the

Figure 282. The scene at Georgesville, March 1913 at the confluence of Big and Little Darby Creeks

169

Figure 283. Lindsay Ford Abutments and Piers all that was left after the flood

its confluence with the Ohio River. The 1913 flood waters reached almost to the eaves of the bridge. Smaller streams all over Ohio, such as Wolf Creek in Morgan County, also overflowed with disastrous results. Figure 285 shows a Wolf Creek covered bridge near Pennsville at the height of the flood.

Ohio suffered over $8,000,000 just in bridge losses or damages.[91] The entire state was faced with a monumental rebuilding job. Counties cleared up the debris, patched up what bridges they could to await the time when they could

Randles Bridge, the old Conesville Bridge, Figure 178, held fast despite being battered by flood debris from upstream. Zanesville in Muskingum County lost the old Third Street or Putnam Bridge over the Muskingum River and there was some damage to the new concrete Y Bridge. Below Zanesville, the Philo/ Duncan Falls Bridge was swept away and down further on the Muskingum, Washington County lost both the Beverly and Lowell Bridges.

Flooding was greatest where streams entered the larger rivers and Figure 284 illustrates this with a view of the Coolville Bridge over the Hocking River in Athens County near

Figure 285. A Wolf Creek covered bridge in Morgan County during the 1913 flood

Figure 284. Coolville Bridge at height of 1913 flood -- it survived to serve into the 1920's

Figure 286.
Remains of the
Indian Mill Bridge
in Wyandot
County after the
1913 flood

afford to replace them. In Wyandot County, timbers from the Indian Mill Bridge were salvaged to repair the Parker Bridge which is still in service today. Figure 286 shows what was left of the Indian Mill Bridge after the flood waters receded. No one is certain just how many of our covered bridges were lost in the great 1913 flood, but the dates on many of our older steel truss bridges are from 1913 to 1915, giving a clue to the great devastation that struck the Buckeye State that year. The heyday of the covered bridge was over in Ohio. Of course, it had been over for some years, but it took a giant disaster like the March 1913 flood to really end that chapter in Ohio's transportation history.

As stated earlier, the building of covered bridges in Ohio dwindled after the 1880s, but there were counties that continued building the wooden truss bridges into the 20th Century. The decision on what type of bridge to build always rested with the county engineer and commissioners. In Preble County, these officials favored the well built Childs truss bridges of Everett S.Sherman who continued to win wooden bridge contracts in that county until 1895. In that year, Sherman lost out on a bridge contract to a company that built steel bridges. Muskingum and Washington Counties were building covered bridges into the 1890s, mostly on back roads, while building the metal bridges on the more heavily traveled main routes.

The county that was committed to the covered or "house" bridge as they termed them, was Fairfield. Their county commissioners journals have revealed that many of their covered bridges were built after 1900. The well known Rock Mill Bridge, Figure 94, was built in 1901 by Blue Jeans Brandt. James W. Buchanan was busy building house bridges until 1916. His last covered bridge was the Macklin House Bridge, Figure 287.

Figure 287. Macklin House Bridge

Two flat-roofed Town trusses were built in Ohio in the 1910s, the Larrimer Bridge in Fairfield County over Rush Creek, and the Creola Bridge, Figure 288, over Brushy Fork in Vinton County. Both were built under the supervision of the Ohio Highway Department.

171

Figure 288. Creola Bridge a state-built Town truss
with a flat roof, 1919-1955

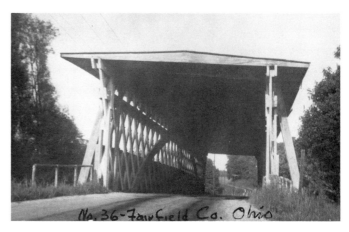

Figure 289. Fairfield County's Larrimer Bridge

The Fairfield County Commissioners Journals tell of the firm of Creager and Kober building the Larrimer Bridge for over $6,000 in 1917 on what is now SR 312. There was definitely some state involvement here, but we do not know the full extent of it. The Larrimer Bridge, Figure 289, was built with arches, but this feature was left out of the Creola Bridge which was built in 1919 on what is now SR 93 near the village of Creola. Both of these flat-top Town trusses were removed in the mid-1950s.

Despite the fact that some counties were building timber truss bridges in the 1900s, a general trend was toward building the newer style metal bridges in most of the counties of Ohio. From 1913 to the 1950s, there was a

steady decline in the number of covered bridges surviving in the state. By 1953, only 353 1/2 covered bridges were still standing in Ohio. Increasingly heavy traffic necessitated the removal of many of the old timber bridges. Overloaded vehicles with drivers who disregard load limit warning signs have abruptly terminated the service of many a fine old timber truss bridge. Figure 290 shows the wreckage of the Blacklick Bridge over Blacklick Creek in Fairfield County in September 1977 after a truck carrying 17 tons of gravel attempted to cross it.

One method of eliminating an unwanted covered bridge was to simply bypass it with a new road location and bridge. This usually

Figure 290.
Wreckage of the
Blacklick Bridge,
another victim of an
overloaded truck

meant that ownership of the old bridge reverted to the nearby landowner who would often use it for storage. This was the case with Perry County's Kendall Farm/Chalfont Bridge, Figure 291, bypassed in a 1929 relocation of SR 204. For many years the old bridge housed a Model T Ford truck and was a landmark for travelers along Route 204. There was little or no maintenance and the old bridge finally collapsed in 1978, its 100th year. Noble County's Wood/Huffman Bridge, Figure 292, has fared much better since it was bypassed by a road relocation in the late 1920s. It is still in fairly good shape today and is easily seen from SR 564 south of Middleburg.

In 1953, Morgan County Engineer Edward Ervin was planning to replace the little covered bridge near Rosseau in Union Township when he got the idea of moving it to the county fairgrounds at McConnelsville. County officials approved and the bridge was dismantled and moved to the fairgrounds at a cost of $1,642 which included materials and labor. This was the first time in Ohio where a covered bridge was moved to a new site purely for the purpose of historic preservation.

Construction of flood control reservoirs has also had its impact on Ohio's covered bridge census, taking out at least 20 timber truss bridges since the 1940s. Noble County lost six bridges when Seneca Lake was formed and Morgan County lost six to the formation of Burr Oak Lake. Tappan and Clendenning Lakes claimed several of Harrison County's small covered bridges. Rocky Fork lake in Highland County took out one of that county's Long trusses, Figure 293 and Clinton County lost the Villars Chapel Bridge, Figure 294, also a Long truss, when Cowan Lake was built.

Another enemy of the covered bridge in Ohio has been strip mining and both Morgan and Noble Counties have lost covered bridges because of this industry. There were a number of covered bridges in Manchester Township in Morgan County where the Ohio Power Company was mining, but none of them were saved. One such covered bridge, threatened by strip

Figure 291. Kendall Farm Bridge

Fihure 292. Wood or Huffman Bridge

Figure 293. Rocky Fork Creek, 1948

Figure 294. Villars Chapel Bridge removed for formation of Cowan Lake c.1950

mining in the early 1960s, was the Milton Dye Bridge, Figure 295.

In the early 1920s, farmer Milton Dye of Brookfield Township near Renrock in Noble County, decided that he was tired of trying to ford Dyes Fork on his farm, especially in times of high water. Mr.Dye bought a set of plans for a multiple kingpost bridge and then proceeded to build a 48 foot bridge with the help of his employees. In the early 1960s, the Ohio Power Company bought the Dye Farm to strip mine it. They moved the little covered bridge, intact, to their recreational area in Morgan County to Campsite D where it now spans Brannons Fork. At first, the bridge was open to traffic, but as might be expected, heavy campers put too great a strain on it and it is now open to pedestrian use only.

One item that appeared regularly under expenditures in the Muskingum County Commissioners Journals was brooms --for the Y Bridge and the Third Street Bridge in Zanesville. The bridge keepers were expected to keep these valuable timber bridges swept clean of all debris because the bridges were lighted at night by oil lamps and it was essential that they be clean of all combustables in case of an accident with one of those lamps. Fire, the greatest enemy of all wooden structures, has taken an untold number of wooden bridges historically and 28 Ohio covered bridges since 1945 and remains a problem today. Fairfield County has been hit the hardest with seven losses since 1965. Licking County lost the Mercer/Thumwood Bridge (Johnny Little) in April 1985.

Figure 295. Milton Dye Bridge

Figure 296. Mercer/Thumwood Bridge (Johnny Little Bridge) -- lost to arson

Most devastating to Ohio bridge historians was the arson attempt on the Roberts Bridge in Preble County in August 1986. The arsonists poured gasoline or some other accelerent on the bridge and set it on fire. The roof and siding were destroyed and the trusses were badly scorched to a depth of an inch and a half. The sturdy Burr arches kept the bridge from collapsing, Figure 297. Expert evaluation was made of its remaining strength and the verdict was that there was still life left in those old trusses. The char was gently sandblasted from the old timbers which were then waterproofed and wrapped in plastic to await the decision on the future of the bridge. It took four years of hard work and dedication on the part of many people on the Roberts Bridge Restoration Committee to finally get the money raised so that the bridge could be moved into Eaton in November 1990. (see Chapter I).

Figure 297. Burned trusses of the Roberts Bridge, 1986

Recently, there were arson attempts on the Jacks Hollow Bridge in Perry County, Figure 31, and the Lynchburg Bridge in Highland County, Figure 276. Damage to the Lynchburg Bridge was confined mainly to the roof trusses and roofing, but the Jacks Hollow Bridge was more seriously damaged and had to be closed until repairs could be made.

In 1941, a young engineer named John A.Diehl of Cincinnati, founded the Ohio Covered Bridge Committee under the auspices of the Ohio Historical Society. Mr.Diehl, a graduate of the University of Cincinnati in Civil Engineering, wanted to get a group of interested people together once a year to discuss Ohio's wooden truss bridges and ways to preserve them for posterity. He also wanted to enumerate Ohio's covered bridges, past and present, and he instituted an ongoing research program that is still active today despite the inactivity of the Ohio Covered Bridge Committee itself. Mr.Diehl developed the numbering system for Ohio's covered bridges that has been adopted nationwide by every state.

There was a reawakening of interest in covered bridges in Ohio in the 1950s. The Ohio Historical Society had published the first Ohio Covered Bridge Map in 1953 in cooperation with the Ohio Covered Bridge Committee. In 1958, the Northern Ohio Covered Bridge Society was formed and just two years later, the Southern Ohio Covered Bridge Association, now known as the Ohio Historic Bridge Association (OHBA) was founded. The latter group owns and maintains the last covered bridge in Muskingum County, Figure 68. OHBA has been quite active in promoting the preservation of Ohio's covered bridges by sending out resolutions urging the preservation of threatened covered bridges and commending those county officials who have preserved old timber bridges. This organization puts out a quarterly journal with news and stories of Ohio's covered bridges. Many covered bridges that would have been lost are still in existance, thanks to the Ohio Historic Bridge Association.

Another factor which has raised public awareness of covered bridge preservation has been the program of the United States Department of the Interior to nominate as many of the old timber truss bridges as possible to the National Register of Historic Places. This program began in the 1970s and Ohio now has over 50 of its covered bridges on the National Register. With very few exceptions, local people and county officials have accepted these nominations with pride, considering it an honor to have national recognition for a local treasure.

Several Ohio covered bridges have been completely rehabilitated since 1980. These include

Delaware County's Chambers Road Bridge, Summit County's Everett Road Bridge, two in Union County, the Spain Creek Bridge, Figure 298 and the Axe Handle Road Bridge, Figure 299, the Roberts Bridge in Preble County, Wyandot County's Parker Bridge, and the Benetka, Harpersfield and Doyle Bridges of Ashtabula County. Rehab work began on Ashtabula County's Dewey Road Bridge in late 1992.

Figure 298. Spain Creek Bridge

Nowhere in Ohio is the resurgance of interest in covered bridges more apparent than in Ashtabula County in the northeastern corner of the state. Two authentic wooden truss cov-

ered bridges have been built there for public highway use in 1983 and 1986 and a third bridge is in the planning stages. In addition to this impressive record, there is a systematic program underway to rehabilitate all the historic covered bridges in the county. It is to be hoped that other Ohio counties will follow the lead of Ashtabula County, not only in bridge maintenance, but in the construction of new wooden truss bridges to carry on an Ohio tradition dating back to 1809.

Indeed, two Ohio counties dedicated new, authentic covered bridges 1992. The Canal Greenway Bridge, in Licking County, Figure 300, was built by the Civilian Conservation Corps from plans drawn up by Ashtabula County Engineer John Smolen. It is a 75 foot Town truss, eight feet wide and eight feet high. This small bridge was designed specifically for the biking/hiking trail that follows the old railroad right-of-way along the old Ohio and Erie Canal near Hebron. In Auglaize County, the Memorial Bridge at St.Marys was dedicated in October, 1992 (see Chapter IX and Figure 225).

To illustrate the renewed interest in covered bridges and the old ways of doing things, replica covered bridges have sprung up all over the Ohio countryside. Some of them are well built although they do not follow authentic timber truss designs and are often supported

Figure 299. Axe Handle Road Bridge, massive arches were part of 1989 renovation

176

by steel beams. While many purists scorn these replicas, they do serve a purpose in directing attention to covered bridges and rousing an awareness and appreciation of the authentic structures.

Ohio's covered bridges---whether unique, ordinary, picturesque or plain, shabby or well-maintained, all played their role in the transportation history of this great state. Most of them are gone now, but enough remain to remind us all of the type of bridge that everyone once used to get to the other side.

Figure 300. Canal Greenway Bridge

Vinton County's Ray Bridge shortly before removal, 1956 (pg. 79)

Village of Vales Mill in Vinton County and its covered bridge (pg. 78)

BRIDGE
LEGAL LOADS
REDUCED 85%
FOR
TOTAL WEIGHT
AND AKLE LOADS
DIRECTOR OF HIGHWAYS

Gallia County's Harrisburg Bridge over Raccoon Creek, 1883-1954 (pg. 75)

Appendix

Hogan's Bridge over Indian Creek in Butler County (pg. 158)

Table A-1 Builders

The Builders and Where They Worked

* = worked in more than one county
** = not an Ohioan
+ = prolific builder

Builder	County
Abbott	Union
Ackley & Crowell	Ashtabula
J S Albert	Butler
S & Wm Alexander	Pike
Wm Alkire	Pickaway
A Allen	Coshocton
Allen & Gale	Muskingum
B C Allen	Trumbull
G W Ambrose	Pickaway
A Armstrong	Guernsey
B & P Armstrong	Columbiana
J Arney	Greene
Jas Arnold	Fairfield
B Asbrook	Trumbull
J Asire	Coshocton
Atherton & Price	Ross
G Augustine	Tuscarawas
T Ayres	Tuscarawas
A V Babcock	Licking
S W & Wm A Badger	Columbiana
E B Bailey	Muskingum
Chas Bailey	Delaware
G W Baird	Allen
Jas Baker	Ross
J Balthaser	Fairfield
T J Banden	Miami
Banden, Butin & Bowman +	Butler
J H Banks	Tuscarawas
D S Barber	Greene
C L Barlow	Union
Jas Barnes	Vinton
——Barrett	Fayette
Barrick & Brown	Licking
P C Barton	Scioto
R Bates	Noble
H Baumgardner	Pike
G R Bell	Vinton
Bennett, Hodges & Beltknopf	Tuscarawas
——Bentley	Ashtabula
M Bishop	Muskingum
Bivens & Snowhill	Brown
Wm Black +	Fairfield *
S Blake	Pickaway
Blakely & Hartley	Vinton
H H Blakesly	Richland
A Blessing	Fayette
M Blessing	Greene
J Blickensderfer	Tuscarawas
Boggs & Davis	Gallia
L M Bogle	Perry
A Booth	Greene
A Borneman +	Fairfield *
F Born	Fairfield
J S Boulby	Perry
Thos Bowen	Vinton
B. Bower	Brown *
D C Bower	Miami *
L S Bower, Sr.+	Brown **
C H Bowers	Fairfield
P Bowers	Hocking
Bowman & Graham	Perry
——Boyce	Washington
J & E Boyle	Brown
J Brady	Tuscarawas
E Brainard	Tuscarawas
J R Brandt +	Fairfield *
Branson & Stone	Miami
H Breslin	Highland
F Brewer	Auglaize
Brock & Magee	Tuscarawas
Jas Brook	Fairfield
S Brophy	Ross
E Brown	Jefferson
J E Brown	Greene
J R Brown	Muskingum *
J T Brown +	Licking *
Brown & Hott	Pickaway
Brown & Savers	Guernsey
J Bryant	Brown
J W Buchanan +	Fairfield
C Buckingham	Muskingum *
G & J Bunz +	Hocking *
——Buxton	Coshocton
Calvin & Cottrill	Vinton
A Campbell	Lucas/Wood **
S Campbell	Pickaway
J Carey	Jefferson
——Carfney	Pickaway
J W Carpenter	Noble
Carper & Goodrich	Pickaway
J Carr	Perry
D Carrel	Coshocton
B Cave	Hocking
S L Chamberlain	Columbiana
S Cheff	Tuscarawas
A Chesnut	Scioto
Church & Akers	Fairfield

J Clark	Guernsey
J S Clark	Cuyahoga
L Claypool	Muskingum
Cochran & DeLong	Perry
R Coe	Vinton
T Coffman	Fairfield
A Cole	Scioto
S R Collier	Pickaway
Collins & Bell	Licking
M Collins	Clermont
Collins & Mullen	Greene
J M Compton	Vinton
I W Conan	Fayette
I Coons	Muskingum
J Coulson	Belmont
Jno Coulson +	Fairfield *
John Coulson	Athens (RR Bridges)
Coultas & Lovell	Fairfield *
J R Cowgill	Vinton
A N Cozad	Vinton
J Craig	Fairfield
Creager & Kober	Fairfield
W Croft +	Columbiana
E Crook	Hocking
H H Crouse	Columbiana
W J Crow	Guernsey
Cutter & Suers	Jackson
A Culpe	Jefferson
G Damar	Tuscarawas
J J Daniels +	Greene *
S Daniels +	Lawrence *
A Davis	Gallia
J C Davis +	Marion *
Jos Davis	Pickaway
T Davis	Washington
W Dawley	Hocking
——Day	Pickaway
Wm Dean +	Perry
Deardorf & Slinghoff	Tuscarawas
T J Dency +	Jackson
H Dennison	Perry
S Denton	Fairfield *
M Derringer	Tuscarawas
Jos Diber	Pike
A R Dickon	Hocking
Diltz & Steele	Vinton
D & J Dodge	Scioto
C Dodson	Highland
T Dollarhide +	Highland
——Dornrife	Pickaway
D Douglas	Richland
M Downey	Jackson
Drennen & Woltz	Hocking
Dresback & lindsey	Hocking
J Dufor	Gallia
B F & H C Dum +	Fairfield
J P Dunkle	Vinton
R Dunn	Muskingum
W Dutro +	Muskingum
M Dye	Noble
J Earles	Lawrence
T B Edwards	Columbiana
R D Edwards +	Vinton *
Edwards & Austin	Scioto
J P Elderkin	Sandusky
H Emfield	Coshocton
J Emmit	Pike
W E Ervin	Highland
J Evans	Madison
W Ewing	Fairfield
N Fagan	Vinton
V B Farney +	Scioto
W Ferguson	Columbiana
R F Fields	Madison
Fife & Graves	Gallia
G & T Fisher +	Muskingum
W Fledderjohn +	Auglaize
Flegele & Company +	Fairfield
J Fleck	Union
J L Fleming	Pickaway
M Forgrier	Perry
J W Fouts +	Washington *
E S Fowler	Washington
E Fox	Ross
D Fulton	Athens
W Funk	Fairfield
J Garber +	Champaign
R Garber	Belmont
——Garringer	Fayette
S L Gerard	Greene
P Giles	Gallia
M Gilham	Greene
A B Gillette +	Fairfield *
Gilligan & McBride	Muskingum
O Gilman +	Vinton
Ginn & Henry	Greene
J Graham	Fairfield
Graves & Scott +	Vinton *
J Gray	Miami
H Grayum	Gallia
G H Greene	Jackson
Greeno & McCrady +	Franklin *
J C Gregg +	Highland *
J Griffith	Brown
C M Grubb +	Washington *
T A Hacock	Pike
A A Haensel	Fairfield
G J & J B Haggerty +	Licking *
T Hague	Noble
W & J Hale	Jefferson
J & D Hall	Jefferson
J & W Hamilton +	Miami *
J & E Harmon +	Greene
Harmon & Crowell	Tuscarawas

J Hartman + ...Clark *
J M Hatfield ....Perry
A Hathaway ....Miami
J C Hayes ....Ross
H E Hebble + ...Greene*
W Hempreville + ...Miami
C Henahan ....Perry
E B Henderson + ...Washington *
J Hendricks ....Hocking
J G Henshaw + ...Gallia
G Heoredh ....Scioto
H R Hepburn ....Vinton
Joseph Herrold..Athens
Heskett & Hesley ....Coshocton
Hess Brothers ....Franklin
——Hiles ....Hocking
J Hill ....Hamilton
O Z Hilleary + ...Licking
R S Hine ....Fairfield
D H Hinton ....Greene
Hoadley & Flood ....Ross
L Hogle ....Coshocton
G Holdren ....Vinton
W B Hollister + ...Washington
D Horne, Jr. ....Muskingum
W Hosey ....Lawrence
J Houck ....Tuscarawas
J Hough + ...Ross *
Householder & Deford ....Fairfield
G Howell ....Morrow
H D Howell ....Coshocton
N Howell ....Brown
G M & L M Hubbard + ...Scioto
W H Hubbard..Jackson
A Hughes ....Highland
D & J Hunt ....Guernsey
N Hunt ....Miami
E Irey ....Columbiana
Isaac Jackson + ...Athens
W Jackson ....Tuscarawas
S G James ....Licking
H Jeffords ....Scioto
T Jones ....Gallia
W S Jones ....Muskingum
A Johnson ....Miami
M & T Johnson ....Coshocton
W Johnson ....Gallia
R Johnston...Jefferson
S S & W N Julian +.....................................Pickaway
S D & H Karns ....Muskingum
Karshner & Hanninger ....Pickaway
P H Kelly ....Pickaway
A M Kennedy ....Butler **
J W Kennedy ....Wyandot
Kidnocker & Chilcoate ....Hocking
C King ....Fairfield
J Kneisley ....Greene

——Knoop...Miami
W Knowlton ....Lawrence
S Krieg ....Hocking
H Laflin ....Washington
J Lamb ....Fairfield
S Lambert ....Gallia
J R Lancaster ....Washington
J Landon + ...Franklin *
G Langley ....Muskingum
M Lapp ....Coshocton
——Larrimer ....Fairfield
A Lawless ....Gallia
E Lefever ....Miami
Lehman & Robinson ....Hocking
Jacob Lentner ....Vinton
T B Lewis ....Coshocton
Lewis & Whitcraft ....Hocking
A Lind ....Stark
J Lindsey ....Hocking
A Little ....Greene
A Livisay ....Pike
W Long ....Tuscarawas
Longwith & Wilson ....Franklin
C C Lymon ....Washington
Manfull & Black ....Jefferson
J Markel ....Pickaway
J F Martin ....Gallia
A R Martindale ....Vinton
F Mayer + ...Coshocton
J McCall ....Brown
——McCarthy ....Hocking
McChesney & Rich + ...Clermont *
R McClellan + ...Columbiana
D McCollough ....Guernsey
W McCollum ....Tuscarawas
J McConnell ....Highland *
J & W McCoy ....Jefferson
McCoy & Skinner ....Pickaway
R H McCracken + ...Columbiana
McCreary & Hayes ....Tuscarawas
W H McCurdy + ...Lawrence *
S McDowell ....Richland
J McElroy ....Tuscarawas
S McFarland...Ross
——McFarland ....Tuscarawas
H McGath ....Gallia
J W McLain ....Greene
McGrath & Wells + ...Vinton
W D McQueen + ...Licking
C Melony ....Perry
Mentzer, Dimes & Co ....Tuscarawas
R Merydith + ...Washington *
J Miller ....Coshocton
S Miller + ...Licking
W Miller...Hocking
W Miller...Noble
Miller & Smith ....Morrow

183

Milligan Bros +	Guernsey
J Mirise	Coshocton
J Morgan	Trumbull
J Morris	Marion
D H & C C Morrison +	Montgomery *
J Morrow	Muskingum
J C Mountz +	Columbiana
J Moutz	Muskingum
J Mumma	Preble
G W Murphy	Tuscarawas
Myers, Hale & Co	Delaware
T Nesmith & Co	Pike
I Neuse	Scioto
Nixon, Dixon & Ervins	Tuscarawas
J & I Noland	Miami
R H Nugen	Tuscarawas
J E Nye +	Fayette *
H O'Blenness	Washington
J Odaffer	Pickaway
Oliver & McCan	Scioto
T E Osborn	Licking
B Osbrook	Trumbull
R Patten	Belmont
D Parker	Pike
R L Partridge +	Union *
R Patterson	Jefferson
J Pedley	Belmont
W Penniston	Pike
——Persinger	Fayette
J Pettit	Miami
G W Pilcher +	Vinton
F Phillips	Licking
Phillips & Stevenson	Ross
D Pollack	Scioto
D Pope	Fairfield
——Potter	Ashtabula
S Price	Washington
Pritchard, Bailey & Laffer	Tuscarawas
J Raab	Fairfield
A C Ramsey	Columbiana
A Rarick +	Fayette *
J Rarick +	Franklin *
M Ratcliff	Vinton
L Raymond	Trumbull
Ream & Westenberger	Fairfield
Reed & Dobbins	Muskingum
M Reeve	Muskingum
W H Richardson	Morrow
J Richmond	Coshocton
Rich & Thompson	Noble
E N Ridgeway	Gallia
J Rieser	Miami
Ritter & Rough	Tuscarawas
O Roberts	Preble
Rockwell & Showers	Perry
R Roney +	Pike *
Roswell & Hunter	Miami
S Rothgeb	Gallia
Rucker & House	Noble
D Rudolph	Fairfield
S Russell	Gallia
W Russell	Perry
W Salkeld	Champaign
J L Samson	Pike
Sarber & Myers +	Franklin *
R W Saunders	Perry
Shannon & Kincaid	Guernsey
J Schutz	Trumbull
M Scott +	Gallia *
W Scott	Miami
J Seitz	Fairfield
P Shaffer	Perry
H Sharp	Richland
J Shell	Columbiana
E S Sherman +	Delaware *
D T Sherman +	Delaware
J & A Sherritts	Tuscarawas
——Shoemaker	Pickaway
John Shrake +	Licking *
Simon Shrake +	Licking *
F T & P Q Shrake	Licking *
Sikes & Graham	Fairfield
J M Skinner	Miami
J W Slee	Ross
J N Slife	Fairfield
J Sluthower	Tuscarawas
Smith & Cook	Coshocton
Smith & McCready	Fairfield
J Smith	Guernsey
J D Smith	Scioto
I Smith	Scioto
R W Smith +	Miami *
R Smith	Licking
R Smith	Fayette
J Smock	Muskingum
J Smolen	Ashtabula
J G Smutz & Co	Fairfield
J W Sniff	Muskingum
D Sniveley	Clark
T J Snyder	Pike
J Sotes	Hocking
G Speice	Pickaway
Sprague & Co	Coshocton
Sprague & Winters	Pickaway
J G Stengall	Jackson
G Sterling	Tuscarawas
T B Stevenson	Greene
N Stewart	Gallia
R Stewart	Trumbull
J Stigall	Pike
Stineman & Chapman	Brown
E Stinson	Madison
B Stone	Pike
P Stonebarger +	Montgomery *

J F Stotler	Guernsey
J Strickler	Fairfield
J E Strutton	Lucas
Stultz & Townsend	Washington *
R D Sutphen	Fairfield
Swick & Kent	Gallia
R Thomas +	Muskingum *
A Thompson	Gallia
W Thompson	Lawrence
R Toops	Pike
C Trupp	Miami
S Tubbs	Coshocton
J J Tuttle	Clark
R Tweed	Ross
S G Tyley	Scioto
J Tysinger	Muskingum
E Uhrich	Tuscarawas
——Von Chester	Highland
D & J Vroom +	Muskingum
H Waggoner	Coshocton
C H Waldron +	Scioto
W Walker	Trumbull
Z Wall +	Clinton
J Wallace	Tuscarawas
N Walp	Gallia
P M Walston	Pickaway
A Ward +	Vinton
E P Warne +	Muskingum
E Watkins	Hocking
J Watt	Jefferson
Weaver & Sewell	Tuscarawas
Weeks & White	Trumbull
J E Welty	Tuscarawas
——Wertz	Fairfield
M Weymouth	Washington
——Wharton	Guernsey
B J Wheeler & Son +	Clermont *
I H Wheeler	Scioto *
White & Evans	Licking *
Wickham & Thomas	Tuscarawas
W B Wiley	Noble
Wiley & Glover	Preble
Williams & Ensley	Pike
Williams & Smith	Pickaway
D Williams	Gallia
J W Wiliams	Gallia
Wilson & McDowell	Vinton
A Wilson	Shelby
J Wilson	Hocking
W Wilson	Ross
W Willis	Coshocton
S S Winget	Clark
——Winkles	Scioto
R & T Wisever	Vinton
J N Withim	Washington
——Wolford	Union
W Wood	Gallia

G Woods	Jefferson
E Woodward	Morrow
Workman & Williams	Coshocton
M Worstall	Muskingum
R I Wynn	Pike
J Youart	Miami
Young & Hull	Lucas
Young & Rettig	Miami
N Zane	Belmont
J Zimmerman	Columbiana

Incorporated Bridge Companies

E Anderson & Co +	Shelby *
Columbia Bridge Works +	Montgomery *
Columbus Bridge Co +	Franklin *
Smith Bridge Co (R W Smith) +	Lucas *
B L Pugh & Co (Oregonia) +	Warren *
Hocking Valley Bridge Works (A Borneman) +	Fairfield *
Dodge, Case & Co +	Franklin *
Dresden Manufacturing Co	Muskingum
Thatcher, Burt & Co +	Cuyahoga *

Bridge Truss Inventors Whose Designs were used in Ohio

William Black
Theodore Burr **
Horace Childs **
William Howe **
Stephan H Long **
T W Morzani **
Reuban L Partridge
Caleb Pratt **
Robert W Smith (Smith Bridge Co)
Ithiel Town **
James Warren **
Lewis Wernwag **
Isaac H Wheeler

Table A-2 Bridge Distribution

Distribution of Ohio Timber Truss Bridges by County

Key: MKP = multiple kingpost; MKP/A = multiple kingpost with arch; KP = single kingpost; QP = queenpost

County	Documented Total	Remaining Total	Present Truss Types
Adams	24	2	MKP,MKP/A
(Once had longest single span covered bridge in Ohio)			
Allen	6	0	
Ashland	13	0	
Ashtabula	61	14	Town,Howe,Pratt
(Longest covered bridge in Ohio located in Ashtabula Co)			
Athens	64	3	MKP, Howe
(Has only bridge in Ohio boarded on inside and out)			
Auglaize	54	2	Howe, pony
(Has last covered pony truss and a new covered bridge)			
Belmont	38	1	MKP
(Only a transplant from Fairfield County remains)			
Brown	88	6	Howe,Smith
(Has last covered bridge on a state highway)			
Butler	41	2	Long, Wernwag
Carroll	13	0	
Champaign	23	0	
Clark	34	0	
(Two men and a dog caused collapse of last covered bridge)			
Clermont	32	1	Howe
Clinton	40	1	MKP
Columbiana	240	5	KP, MKP
(Home of Ohio's shortest covered bridge—19 feet; also county with second largest timber truss bridge count in Ohio)			
Coshocton	90	1	MKP
Crawford	3	0	
Cuyahoga	24	0	
(Once had covered bridge with center draw span)			
Darke	7	0	
Defiance	5	0	
Delaware	64	1	Childs
Erie	6	0	
Fairfield	279	16	MKP,Smith,QP, Howe, Bowstring
(Once had most timber truss bridges of any Ohio county)			
Fayette	66	0	

Franklin   146   2   MKP, Partridge
(Bergstresser Bridge is a model of bridge preservation)
Fulton   0   0
Gallia   85   0
(Bridges were reinforced with inverted wood arches)
Geauga   6   0
Greene   107   5   Howe, Smith
Guernsey   115   2   MKP
(Home of fourth oldest covered bridge in Ohio —1849)
Hamilton   45   1   QP
Hancock   7   0
Hardin   12   0
Harrison   53   1   MKP
Henry   2   0
Highland   46   1   Long
Hocking   112   0
(County started building steel bridges in 1870s)
Holmes   3   0
Huron   2   0
Jackson   32   3   Smith
(This county favored the Smith truss)
Jefferson   36   0
(Also built steel bridges early)
Knox   34   0
(Another county that went early to steel bridges)
Lake   11   0
Lawrence   80   1   MKP
(Last covered bridge heavily reinforced with steel)
Licking   160   8   MKP
(Home of one of Ohio's newest covered bridges—1992)
Logan   11   2   Howe
Lorain   6   0
Lucas   12   0
(Shared some Maumee River bridges with Wood County)
Madison   22   0
(Removed last covered bridge in 1957)
Mahoning   21   0
Marion   20   0
(Parts of a covered bridge survive as a barn)
Medina   10   0
Meigs   8   0
Mercer   0   0
(So far, not even one timber truss bridge recorded!)
Miami   102   1   Long
(Has second longest covered bridge in Ohio—224 feet)
Monroe   31   2   MKP
Montgomery   63   3   Bowstring, Warren

(Home of the famed Germantown Bridge)

Morgan	58	5	MKP
Muskingum	167	1	Warren

(Had third highest bridge count—reduced drastically 1950s)

Noble	112	4	MKP
Ottawa	3	0	
Paulding	1	0	
Perry	85	5	MKP,Smith

(Excellent example of MKP construction)

Pickaway	111	1	

(Only covered bridge a transplant from Fairfield County)

Pike	56	0	
Portage	6	0	
Preble	50	8	Burr, Childs

(Has Ohio's oldest covered bridge, 1829)

Putnam	3	0	
Richland	18	0	

(Lost one of last covered bridges to a pickle truck)

Ross	92	1	Smith

(Had famous 1817 tied arch bridge over Scioto River)

Sandusky	7	1	

(Once had longest timber truss bridge in Ohio—1088 feet)

Scioto	84	1	Smith

(At one time home to the Wheeler truss bridges)

Seneca	11	0	
Shelby	10	0	

(Lost last covered bridge to arson, 1989)

Stark	18	0	
Summit	18	1	Smith

(Bridge part of Cuyahoga Valley National Park)

Trumbull	33	1	Town
Tuscarawas	107	0	

(Lost last covered bridge in 1948)

Union	58	5	Partridge

(Remaining bridges all built on Partridge truss design)

Van Wert	0	0	
Vinton	70	5	MKP,MKP/A,QP

(Home of Ohio's lovely Humpback Bridge)

Warren	36	0	
Washington	108	10	MKP,MKP/A Long, Howe, Smith

(Historic and scenic county — many truss designs remaining)

Wayne	10	0	
Williams	5	0	
Wood	9	0	
Wyandot	21	2	Howe

(Home of the recently-rebuilt Parker Bridge)

TOTALS	**3850**	**135**	

References

1. Cramer, Zadok. The Navigator, Pittsburg, 1814. Page 72. Courtesy of the Ohio Historical Society Archives/ Library.

2. Cumings, Fortescue. Sketches of a Tour to the Western Country, Pittsburg, 1810. Page 84. Courtesy of the Ohio Historical Society Archives/Library.

3. Atwater, Caleb. History of Ohio. 1838. Page 178. Courtesy of the Ohioana Library.

4. Benson, Myron C. "Along the College Township Road". Part I. Vinton County Courier.
    29 April, 1981, Page 16.

5. McKee, Harley J. "Original Bridges on the National Road in Eastern Ohio". Ohio History, Spring 1972, Pages 131-134

6. "The Cumberland Road in Ohio". Copied from original script in files of the National Contractors Association, Washington, D.C. Courtesy of The Ohio Department of Transportation.

7. Ogan, Lew. History of Vinton County, Ohio: Wonderland of Ohio. McArthur, Ohio, 1954. Pages 63-66.

8. Roseboom, Eugene and Weisenberger, F.P. A History of Ohio. The Ohio State Archeological and Historical Society, 1953. Pages 225-226.

9. History of Franklin and Pickaway Counties, Ohio.   Williams Brothers, Publishers, 1880. Page 51.

10. A History of Ohio. Pages 225 and 226.

11. Annual Report of the Commissioner of Railroads and Telegraphs of Ohio, 1881. Pages 123-135. Courtesy of the State Library of Ohio.

12. Annual Report of the Commissioner of Railroads and Telegraphs of Ohio, 1880. Page 293. Courtesy of the State Library of Ohio.

13. Tyrell, Henry G. History of Bridge Engineering. Chicago, 1911. Pages 121 and 122.

14. James, J.G. "The Evolution of Wooden Truss Bridges to 1850." The Journal of the Institute of Wood Science. June 1982, Volume 9, Number 3.

15. Schneider, Norris F. The Famous Y Bridge at Zanesville, Ohio. Published by the author, Zanesville, Ohio, 1958. Pages 7-13.

16. Miller, Terry E. The Covered Bridges of Tuscarawas County, Ohio. Published by the author, 1975. Pages 2 and 3.

17. Henry, William Brandt. Letters to the author. 23 July 1985 and 11 August 1985.

18. Henry, William Brandt. Personal Interview. October 1985.

19. "Little Future for Bridges with a Past." Lancaster, Ohio Eagle Gazette. 7 April 1955. Page 2.

20. Pilcher, Mary Will. Letter to the author. 21 July 1984.

21. Allen, Richard S. Covered Bridges of the Northeast. The Stephan Greene Press, Brattleboro, Vermont, 1974. Pages 13 and 14.

22. American Wooden Bridges. American Society of Civil Engineers Historical Publication Number 4, 1976. Page 43.

23. Allen, Richard S. Covered Bridges of the Middle West. The Stephan Greene Press, 1970. Pages 7 and 8.

24. Bower, Louis S. Personal Interview. 29 April, 1987.

25. Ibid.

26. American Wooden Bridges. Page 132.

27. CHE-LO-CO-THE: Glimpses of Yesterday. Published by the Committee on the 100th Anniversary of Chillicothe, 1896. Page 121. Courtesy of the Ohioana Library.

28. Covered Bridges of the Northeast. Pages 15 and 16.

29. Covered Bridges of the Middle West. Pages 18 and 19.

30. Covered Bridges of the Northeast. Pages 18 and 19.

31. Ibid. Page 18.

32. Annual Report of the Commissioner of Railroads and Telegraphs of Ohio, 1882. Pages 187 and 188.

33. Files of the Ohio Historic Bridge Association, Volume VII, Preble County.

34. History of Bridge Engineering. Page 142.

35. Neff, Eldon M. "Highlights in the Life of Robert W. Smith." Paper written circa 1960. Files of the Ohio Historic Bridge Association Volume VIII.

36. Wilson, Raymond E. "The Story of the Smith Truss." Covered Bridge Topics. Volume XXV Number 1. April 1967, Pages 3, 4 and 5. Courtesy of the National Society for the Preservation of Covered Bridges.

37. Marysville, Ohio Journal Tribune. Article on Reuban L. Partridge. Willela S. Kennedy. 22 March 1962.

38. United States Patent Office Records, RG 241. National Archives Center, Suitland, Maryland.

39. Files of the Ohio Historic Bridge Association. Volume VIII.

40. American Wooden Bridges. Page 136.

41. Allen, Richard S. Covered Bridges of the South. The Stephan Greene Press, 1970. Pages 11 and 12.

42. Wood, Miriam F. "History of the Wooden Truss Bridge in Ohio." First Historic Bridges Conference, Columbus, Ohio. 1 November, 1985.

43. Simmons, David A. "D.H. Morrison, Bridge Builder and Civil Engineer." Annual Conference of the Society for Industrial Archeology, Detroit. 31 May 1980.

44. Ibid.

45. Ibid.

46. Ibid.

47. Wood, Miriam F. "History of the Wooden Truss Bridge in Ohio."

48. Engineering News Record. 29 July 1877. Page 246.

49. Ibid. 9 August 1879. Page 255.

50. Jones, Frances A. "John Bright #1 Iron Bridge." Historic American Building Record, OH-44. 1986.

51. Goulder, Grace, This is Ohio. The World Publishing Company, Cleveland and New York, 1953. Pages 209 and 212.

52. Evans, Lyle S. Ross County History. Lewis Publishing Company, Cleveland and New York, 1917. Page 195.

53. Portsmouth Tribune. Article on the collapse of the Sciotoville Bridge. 21 January 1874.

54. Collins, H.R. and Webb, D.K., Jr. The Hanging Rock Iron Region of Ohio. Published by The Ohio Historical Society, 1966.

55. Ibid.

56. The Herald-Advertiser. Article on the covered bridge at Getaway. 7 July 1938.

57. A History of Ohio. Page 58.

58. This is Ohio. Page 223.

59. Dunlap, Roberta. Historic Bridges Preserved in Vinton and Clinton Counties. Ohio County Engineer, Number 4, Winter, 1992, Page 17.

60. Robertson, Charles, M.D. History of Morgan County, Ohio. L.H. Watkins and Company, Chicago, 1886. Page 142.

61. Annual Report of the Commissioner of Railroads and Telegraphs in Ohio, 1882. Page 435.

62. Maienknecht, Stanley E. and Theresa A. Monroe County, A History. Windmill Publications, Mt. Vernon, Indiana, 1989. Page 191.

63. This is Ohio. Pages 19 and 20.

64. Files of The Ohio Historic Bridge Association. Volume 8, Washington County.

65. Ibid.

66. Walker, Charles M. History of Athens County, Ohio. Cincinnati, 1869. Page 456.

67. Sketches of a Tour to the Western Country, Page 205.

68. Schneider, Norris, Muskingum River Covered Bridges. 1971, Page 13.

69. A History of Ohio, page 59.

70. Allison, Grace C. Covered Bridges of Niles and Trumbull County, Ohio. Published by The Niles Historical Society and The Fine Arts Council of Trumbull County, c.1986. Page 52.

71. Ibid. Page 42 - 45.

72. Files of the Ohio Historic Bridge Association, Volume 7, Stark County.

73. Coats, William R. History of Cleveland and Cuyahoga County. Published by the American Historical Society, Cleveland and New York, 1924. Pages 71 and 72.

74. History of Seneca County, Ohio. Warner, Beers and Company, Chicago, 1886. Pages 480 and 481.

75. Lang, W. History of Seneca County, Ohio. 1880. Page 573.

76. Ibid. Pages 574 and 575.

77. Ibid. Page 575.

78. History of Sandusky County, Ohio. H.Z. Williams and Brothers, 1882. Pages 202 and 203.

79. Lowery, Annette. Paper given at the Eden Center School Reunion. 20 July 1969. From the Files of the Ohio Historic Bridge Association.

80. Howes History of Ohio. Page 147.

81. Maumee Times. 17 November 1849. Courtesy of Richard S. Allen.

82. Engineering News. 22 July 1876. Page 239.

83. Seiler, Toni T. Our Old Bridges, Darke County, Ohio. Published by the author, 1992. Page 26.

84. Middleton, Evan P. History of Champaign County, Ohio. B.F.Bowen Company, Indianapolis, Indiana, 1917. Volume I, page 66.

85. Evans, Nelson W. and Stivers, Emmons B. A History of Adams County, Ohio. Published by E.B.Stivers, West Union, Ohio, 1900. Pages 362-364.

86. Ibid. Page 481.

87. Letter from the Directors of the Cincinnati and Harrison Turnpike Company to the Board of Public Works, 25 August 1837. From the Collection of the Ohio Historical Society. 1211 GRVF

88. Gieck, Jack. A Pictorial History of Ohio's Canal Era, 1825-1913. Kent State University Press, 1988. Page 114.

89. Morgan Arthur E. The Miami Valley and the 1913 Flood. The Miami Conservancy District Technical Reports, Part I. Dayton, Ohio 1917.

90. Conner, Charlotte E. Dayton, Ohio - An Intimate History. Landfall Press, Dayton, Ohio, 1970. Page 268.

91. Records of the Ohio Department of Transportation, courtesy of Mrs. Karen Young, Bureau of Environmental Services.

Bibliography

Lafferty, Michael B. <u>Ohio's Natural Heritage</u>. The Ohio Academy of Science and the Ohio Department of Natural Resources. Columbus, 1979.

Searight, Thomas B. <u>The Old Pike: An Illustrated Narrative of The National Road</u>. Green Tree Press, Orange, VA. 1971 Ohio. 1835.

<u>Centennial History of Belmont County</u>, 1903.

Evans, Nelson W. <u>Pioneer Record of Scioto County and Southern Ohio</u>.
Volumes I and II.

<u>1883 History of the Hocking Valley</u>. Interstate Publishing Company, Chicago. 1883.

Van Tassel,C.F. <u>The Book of Ohio</u>. Volumes I & II. 1903.

Schlotterbeck, Seth S. Personal Correspondance, 1962 to 1983.

Files of the Ohio Historic Bridge Association.

Files of the Ohio Department of Transportation.

Files of the Ohio Covered Bridge Committee.

County Commissioners Journals of: Athens, Belmont, Brown, Butler, Clinton, Columbiana, Coshocton, Delaware, Fayette, Fairfield, Franklin, Gallia, Greene, Guernsey, Hardin, Harrison, Highland, Hocking, Jackson, Jefferson, Lawrence, Licking, Madison, Miami, Muskingum, Perry, Pickaway, Pike, Preble, Richland, Ross, Scioto, Trumbull, Tuscarawas, Union, Vinton, Warren, and Washington Counties.

INDEX